GROWING OLD ISN'T FOR SISSIES

by
Dr. Marshall L. Cook

Order this book online at www.trafford.com
or email orders@trafford.com

Most Trafford titles are also available at major online book retailers.

Printed in Victoria, BC, Canada.

ISBN: 978-1-4269-2487-3 (sc)
ISBN: 978-1-4269-2488-0 (eb)

Library of Congress Control Number: 2010900410

Our mission is to efficiently provide the world's finest, most comprehensive book publishing service, enabling every author to experience success. To find out how to publish your book, your way, and have it available worldwide, visit us online at www.trafford.com

Trafford rev. 3/29/10

 www.trafford.com

North America & international
toll-free: 1 888 232 4444 (USA & Canada)
phone: 250 383 6864 ♦ fax: 812 355 4082

Table of Contents

ACKNOWLEDGEMENTS

I want to thank the congregations of the churches I have served for their inspiration for this book. Thank you to the members of Trinity United Church of Christ, Lewisville, Ohio; St. Paul's United Church of Christ, Trail Run, Ohio; Emmanuel United Church of Christ, Valley City, Ohio, Paramus Congregational Church, Paramus, New Jersey; Boynton Beach Congregational Church, Boynton Beach, Florida; and First Congregational United Church of Christ, Ft. Pierce, Florida.

A special thanks to Earl Hawkins of Boynton Beach, Florida, whose ideas formed the basis for this book.

CHAPTER ONE

"Old age ain't no place for sissies." Bette Davis

On October 29, 1998, Sen. John Glenn Jr. became the oldest American at age 77 to orbit Earth. He already had the record of becoming the first American to orbit Earth when he launched into space in 1962. This was not a new journey for him, but what was new was his age. He hoped to study the effects of weightlessness on his 77-year-old body.

Many thought he was too old to travel into space. Yet, age has never been a factor in the lives of many men and women. Take Abraham, for example. The Bible tells us that Abraham was seventy-five when God came to him and said to him, "Leave your country, your people and your father's household and go to the land I will show you."

Abram (as he was first called) came originally from "Ur of the Chaldeans" (Gen. 11:28), a Sumerian city in the Euphrates valley, near the head of the Persian Gulf. With his father Terah, his wife Sarai (later Sarah) and his nephew Lot, he moved up the river until they came to Haran, a trading center in northern Aram (Syria, and now Iran). They settled in this area, and here Terah died.

After the Lord appeared to him, Abraham traveled with Sarah and Lot several hundred miles to the land of Canaan

(Palestine). Such travel would have been slow and difficult in the ancient world of the early or mid-second millenium B.C., but perhaps especially so due to their ages. Abraham was seventy-five and Sarah was sixty-five years-old. Like John Glenn, Abraham and Sarah were willing to travel to a new land and a new life.

But is that so strange? Thousands of people retire each year and move to other parts of the United States, sometimes hundreds of miles from where they have lived for many years to begin a new life in retirement. Sometimes the move is to be closer to children and grandchildren. But often the move is to a warmer climate. And this at age 65 or older!

Travel today is much easier than it was in the time of Abraham and Sarah. Back then there were no Holiday Inns or McDonald's at each major intersection. They could not call ahead for reservations. There were no weather reports to help them plan their trip. In a desert climate, food and water could be scarce. Roads were dirty and dusty. Travel would be by foot or on the back of a donkey. There were dangers. Robbers would station themselves in isolated locations. It would not have been an easy trip.They knew that they might never see their loved ones or their home again. In our minds, too, is the thought of someone of Abraham and Sarah at their ages making such a trip. Many wonder if the ages of people as reported in the Bible are accurate. Methuselah, for example, is reported to have lived to the age of nine hundred and sixty-nine years (Gen. 5:27)! Probably the author is trying to say that someone like Methusaleh lived a long time. We should not be concerned about the literal age of many of the Biblical men and women. What is important is that they were still active as they grew older.

Age doesn't matter. Oh, sometimes we think that it matters. Yet, I can think of others who began new lives at a time in which many might be ready to sit back and take it easy for the rest of their lives.

Paul Harvey tells the story of Harlan. At age fourteen he dropped out of school. He tried odd jobs as a farm hand, but hated it. He tried being a streetcar conductor and hated that. At age sixteen he lied about his age and joined the Army. He hated that, too. When his one year enlistment was up he headed for Alabama, tried to be a blacksmith, but gave up. He became a railroad locomotive fireman with the Southern Railroad. He liked that job. At eighteen he got married. His wife announced she was pregnant the day he was fired. Then, one day, while he was out job hunting, his young wife gave away all their possessions and went home to her parents.

Then came the Depression. Harlan just couldn't seem to make a go of his life. It wasn't because he didn't try. Once, while working at a succession of railroad jobs, he tried studying law by correspondence. But he dropped out of that. He tried to be a salesman. He sold insurance, then tires, but no luck. He tried running a ferry-boat, running a service station, but no use.

Late in life he became chief cook and bottle washer at a restaurant in Corbin, Kentucky. He did all right until a new highway bypassed the restaurant.

By now the years had slipped by and he didn't have much to show for his life. He had not really felt old until that day he received his first Social Security check in the mail. That day, something within Harlan resisted. The government was telling him, more or less, it's time to give up and retire. His restaurant customers in Corbin said they'd miss him, but the government had sent him a "pension" check saying he was "old."

Harlan got so angry he took that $105 check and started a new business.

Today that business has mushroomed beyond his expectations. For the man who seemingly failed at everything save his last venture, the man who never got started until past the age of sixty-five, was Harland Sanders. The new business he started with his first Social Security check was Kentucky Fried Chicken![1]

As we age that time of life can be our best! Ask Othmar Ammann. During his "retirement" he designed such structures as the Connecticut and New Jersey turnpikes, the Pittsburgh

Civic Arena, Dulles Airport, the Throgs Neck and Verrazano bridges in New York.

Winston Churchill would agree. At the age of seventy-nine he won the Nobel prize in literature. And there are others.

When Clara Barton was sixty-one, she founded the American Red Cross and remained its president for twenty-two more years. When she was eighty-four, she established the National First Aid Association and actively led it until she was ninety-one.

Verdi, at age seventy-four, produced his famous opera, "Othello;" at age eighty, he composed "Falstaff;" and at age eighty-five, he wrote his famous hymn, "Ave Maria."

Titian painted his memorable picture, "Battle of Lepanto," when he was ninety-eight.

Gladstone was prime minister of Great Britain at eighty-three and fought the greatest battle of his political career for the Home Rule Bill.

At age seventy-four the philosopher Emmanuel Kant wrote some of his finest philosophical work.

Alfred Lord Tennyson, at age eighty, penned his unforgettable poem, "Crossing the Bar."

George Bernard Shaw retained his superb wit until past ninety. Justice Oliver Wendell Holmes at age ninety was still writing brilliant judicial opinions.

Those of you who are waiting to make your first million might take hope in the fact that between the ages of seventy and eighty-three, Commodore Vanderbilt added one hundred million dollars to his fortune.

Jack Lalanne, the well-known T.V. exercise coach, celebrated his seventieth birthday sometime back by towing seventy boats containing seventy people for a mile across Long Beach Harbor in California. That may seem amazing in itself, but he did it by holding the rope in his teeth while handcuffed and wearing leg shackles!

Those are some of the more famous men and women who have attained success later in life. Of course there are many others who accomplish great things later in life who go unnoticed, except for an occasional mention in the news because of their age. Joe Dean, for example, has a special place in bowling records. As of this writing, he is the oldest person, at age eighty-seven, to bowl a sanctioned 300 game. He broke a record previously held by Joe Norris, who rolled a 300 game in 1994 at age eighty-six.

Or, there is Lin Lawrence of Palm City, Florida, who at age 88 flies his homemade airplane. He's a member of the United Flying Octogenarians, an international organization of about 450 aviators older than 80.

Fifteen years ago, Lawrence began his first home-built airplane, as his late wife, Emilie, suffered from the initial stages of Alzheimer's disease.

When he finished the RV-6A in 1992, he dubbed the plane "Miss Emilie."

But one airplane wasn't enough. In 2000, he started construction on his second plane.

Or, there's Lucille Borgen, who survived polio, cancer and the loss of vision in one eye, and at age 90 competed in the 62nd annual Water Ski National Championships in 2004.

Trick skiing is also in her repertoire. Her two 20-second trick runs, performed on a single ski, include 360-degree turns and turning backward while crossing the wake, and holding the tow rope with one foot.

Borgen used to jump over a ramp for distance. Her best jump was 64 feet, but she stopped jumping at age 77 when the doctor told her the impact of landing could require her to get an artificial hip.

Then there are the men and women of the Bible. Whether we accept their given ages literally, or not, they must have been up in years. We have mentioned Abraham and Sarah. There was also Noah, who was reported to have been over five hundred years old at the time he built the ark. Moses was one hundred twenty when he died, which would have put him in his seventies when he led the Hebrews out of Egypt. Joshua was one hundred when he died, after spending forty years in the desert helping Moses lead the people. Joshua then helped the people to settle the land of Canaan. Anna was an eighty-five year-old widow who prayed for the coming of the Messiah and then recognized him when he came in the form of the baby Jesus. The apostle John was elderly, according to tradition, when he wrote the last book of the Bible from an island home. There are others, as we shall see, but perhaps, the words of Caleb, as found in the Old Testament book of Joshua best express how age need not be a factor. In the fourteenth chapter of Joshua , having crossed the River Jordan into Canaan, the Israelites now await their inheritance. Joshua, their great leader, stands before them and gives to each respective tribe its inheritance, according to the Lord's command to Moses.

Then an individual breaks from the group and meets Joshua. Caleb had a claim to make. He reminds Joshua of the time when they both were much younger. They and ten other men had been chosen as representatives of each of their tribes to spy out the land of Canaan. Upon their return only Joshua and Caleb believed it was possible for their people to possess the land. Because of the way they exercised their faith, the two men were greatly blessed by God. Joshua became Moses' successor and Caleb became a trusted and courageous soldier and leader.

But Caleb kept remembering a beautiful place he had seen while spying out the land. The place was called Hebron and he hoped to one day own it.

The day had come and Caleb says to Joshua:"So here I am today, eighty-five years old! I am still as strong today as the day Moses sent me out; I'm just as vigorous to go out to battle now as I was then. Now give me the hill country that the Lord promised me that day…" Joshua 14:10-12

One of the facts of life is that we are all aging. There is nothing we can do about it except, perhaps, to laugh. The *Reader's Digest* has carried some delightful humor about aging. For example, one woman was quoted as saying that her 81-year-old mother is proud of the fact that she doesn't look her age. One summer day, however, her mother went into a drugstore and, talking about the heat, said to the clerk, "Going to be ninety-seven today." The man reached across the counter, shook her hand and said, "Happy birthday." The woman went to bed for a week over that comment, her daughter said.

Then there was a 96-year-old man, who, on admission to a nursing home, was interviewed by a social worker. She asked, "Did you have a happy childhood?" With a twinkle in his eye he replied: "So far, so good!"

Some people live in a make believe world where no one ages, or where everyone ages but you. There is a story of two classmates who were returning for their fiftieth reunion at their alma mater. They hadn't seen each other since graduation, and one of them said to the other, "Well, John, you haven't changed a bit." John thought a moment and said, "Bill, you look exactly like you did fifty years ago." Finally, one of their wives chimed in with the truth. "It sounds to me that what has happened here is that both of your eyesights have gotten considerably worse."

Many people dread growing old. I think many people worry what they will be like as they age. Will I still know who I am, or like President Ronald Reagan and so many others, develop alzheimer's or other forms of dementia and not know anyone, including myself? If I have my mind, what will my body be like? Will I be able to walk, to drive, to see, to hear? What will death be like? Is there an afterlife? As Bette Davis said, "Old age ain't no place for sissies."

And yet I feel there is a lot of truth to the cliché, "You're only as old as you feel." The purpose of this book is to verify that cliché.

I have been an ordained minister in the United Church of Christ for over thirty-five years. I have served several congregations with a wide variety of ages. The congregations I have been serving in Florida are comprised mostly of men and women from the early sixties to 100 years young. From ministering to them and other elderly, and from my own personal observations, I do believe that what really matters as we age is not the condition of the body, but that of the spirit.

This was also verified by a 2004 article in *Time* magazine. The authors told of a study by Swedish scientists in 1998, who compared the role that genes and heredity play in longevity. The scientists looked at the only set of people who share genes but not lifestyle: identical twins who were separated at birth and reared apart. If genes were most important, you would expect the twins to die at about the same age. In fact, the study showed, they didn't, and the average difference convinced the scientists that only about 20% to 30% of how long we live is genetically determined. They concluded that the dominant factor is lifestyle.[2]

We encounter problems in life no matter what our age. Each age in life also has its own unique problems. This book is an attempt to help those who are growing older to understand some of the changes and problems associated with growing older, whether you are twenty, forty, sixty or eighty. It is also an attempt to help you understand the spiritual resources that are important in coping with growing older. And it is an attempt to show how important faith in God is in helping us in our journey through life and beyond.

Perhaps the poet John Browning said it best:
Grow old along with me
The best is yet to be
The last of life,
For which the first was made.

CHAPTER TWO
THE AGING BODY

"The length of our days is seventy years—or eighty, if we have the strength; yet their span is but trouble and sorrow, for they quickly pass, and we fly away." Psalm 90:10

The Biblical life span of seventy or eighty years has not changed a whole lot in over two thousand years since these words were written. Advances in medicine and health care, diet and technology have made it possible for many, at least in western society, to live longer. Those who can take advantage of health care that is available, such as in western societies, are able to receive treatment and medicines that can help to prolong their lives.

Aging seems to have a fixed end. Even though there are reports of long-lived people, there is little substantial evidence to suggest that hardly anyone lives past 110.

Our society's concept of when old age begins has tended to be fixed at age 65. This has been the age when most Americans retire and begin to receive Social Security checks. In recent years, however, many people have elected to work longer, unless pushed out by their company. There has been talk in Congress about changing the age for Social Security full benefits to age 67 or higher.

There are other ways to know when you're getting old. For example, as an anonymous observer suggested in the bulletin of St.Olaf Roman Catholic Church in Minneapolis, you are getting old when...

Everything hurts and what doesn't hurt, doesn't work.

You feel like the night after when you haven't been anywhere.

You get winded playing chess.

Your children begin to look middle-aged.

You know all the answers, but nobody asks you the questions.

You turn out the light for economic rather than romantic reasons.

You sit in a rocking chair and can't get it going.

Your knees buckle and your belt won't.

You're 17 around the neck, 42 around the waist, and 96 around the golf course.

You burn the midnight oil until 9 p.m.

Your back goes out more often than you do.

Your pacemaker raises the garage door when you see a pretty girl go by.

The little gray-haired lady you help across the street is your wife.

You have too much room in the house and not enough in the medicine cabinet.

Most biological signs that we equate with aging, though, can set in before age 65. There is great variability among individuals in the rate of physical aging. Some 70 year-olds seem physically more like 40; others appear much older.

In spite of individual variation, however, there are certain specific changes that characterize normal physical aging. One might think such signs are obvious, especially if you know a relative or friend, but some changes might not be quite so obvious, and it can be helpful to know what to expect, in general, especially if you are young or in middle age and not certain what to expect.

Graying of hair. This is an obvious sign of aging, though not necessarily. I have known people whose hair turned gray when they were in their twenties. Hair begins to turn gray because cells at the base of the hair follicle that produce the pigment for one hair either die or just produce less pigment. As more and more of these pigment cells malfunction and die, a person gets gradually grayer.[3]

Skin Changes. Skin usually begins to wrinkle about the same time as hair begins to get gray. Wrinkling begins in the areas used the most, so people who are used to laughing may find their personality indelibly fixed in little lines around their eyes and mouth. Those used to frowning suffer the same fate. Their mood may be permanently imprinted on their face. As we get older, our face, then, can be a visible reflection of who we are inside.

In the very old, wrinkles may appear over a person's total skin surface. This type of wrinkling occurs because subcutaneous fat tissue is lost as a person ages, causing the skin to hang slackly. In addition, protein collagen, part of intercellular connective tissue, contributes to wrinkling by causing skin to lose its elasticity.[4]

A little girl was sitting on her grandfather's lap as he read her a bedtime story. From time to time, she would take her eyes off the book and reach up to touch his wrinkled cheek. She was alternately stroking her own cheek, then his again. Finally she spoke up, "Grandpa, did God make you?"

"Yes, sweetheart," he answered, "God made me a long time ago."

"Oh," she paused. "Grandpa, did God make me, too?"

"Yes, indeed, honey," he said. "God made you just a little while ago."

Feeling their respective faces again, she observed, "God's getting better at it, isn't He?"

Changes in Joints and Bones. In mid life the density of a person's bones begins to decrease gradually. This condition is called osteoporosis. The name means 'porous bones.' Bones are weakened by loss of minerals, especially calcium. Their insides become full of holes, like a dry, hard sponge. When bone loss reaches 30 percent, bones may break under the slightest pressure. The degree to which osteoporosis affects a person can depend upon other variables, such as exercise and by calcium and vitamin intake during adulthood.

Women who are slight, who have small bone structure and have reached menopause, when estrogen leads to bone loss, are especially at risk.

Osteoporosis is not life-threatening, in itself, but it can indirectly cause disability and hasten death because the bones, being so fragile, are liable to be broken at the slightest fall. My great grand-mother, for example, was sleeping on her sofa, rolled over onto the floor and broke her hip. This happened when she was in her late eighties. She never fully recovered from the fall and break, as so happens with many elderly when they break a bone. Fractures tend to heal much less easily and completely in the elderly. This can have serious consequences for them. It often means a loss of their independence. My great grandmother had difficulty taking care of herself after her hip was broken and had to move to a nursing home for care.

According to the National Osteoporosis Foundation (www.nof.org), osteoporosis will cause half the women over 50 to experience a fracture in their lifetime, and one in eight men over 50, as well.

Bone loss begins in the 40s for women and in the 50s for men. Increased calcium is recommended to help prevent osteoporosis. Take at least 1,200 mg of calcium daily. Good sources include low-fat dairy products, broccoli and other leafy greens, tofu, calcium fortified foods and supplements. It is also recommended to exercise regularly.

Osteoporosis is a silent disease that rarely alerts those who have it, but today it is both treatable and preventable.

The other most prevalent age-related change in the skeletal system, osteoarthritis, involves a gradual wearing away of the joint cartilage that cushions the bones. In severe cases the resulting exposure of bone on bone without a protective cushion causes pain and stiffness. Although all older people have this deterioration to some degree, only a minority have painful osteoarthritis, and today many people, at least in my congregation, have had replacement surgery, especially for hips or knees.

Basic to living is our ability to receive information about our environment and to respond to the data we receive. Limitations in either or both of these abilities can have far-ranging effects on the elderly. They can make the person less independent, impair self-confidence and make relationships with others more difficult. However, individuals vary greatly in the extent of sensory and motor limitations. The typical older person, in fact, does not have impairing problems. Some elderly show no losses at all.[5]

Vision. The most basic seeing difficulty that may befall us as we grow older is poor visual acuity. A person with limited acuity has problems seeing things distinctly. Acuity is what is being measured when we are asked to identify the letters and numbers on an eye chart.

A second major impairment is the inability to see near objects clearly. Its technical name, presbyopia ("old eyes") reflects its prevalence in later life.

As we age we may also have other visual difficulties. We may not see as well in dim light. The ability to distinguish colors may be difficult, especially those in the blue-green range. We may be more bothered by glare. The field of vision is likely to be narrower.

Changes can occur in the various parts of the eye that cause some of these problems. For example, the iris is a pigmented, circular structure with a hole, the pupil, in its center. In bright light the iris expands in width, causing the pupil to become smaller. This enables less light to enter and so protects the sensitive retinal receptors from damage. In dim light the iris narrows so that the pupil dilates, allowing more light to enter. As a person ages, the iris becomes less able to change its width. In both dim and bright light, older adults, on the average, have smaller pupils than the young. This means that when the pupil needs to be as large as possible to permit optimal vision in conditions of darkness, having a smaller pupil means older adults have more difficulty.

Deterioration in the lens is important in a variety of other late-life vision problems. As we get older the lens gradually gets cloudy. Such clouding impairs general visual acuity and also makes the person more sensitive to glare because rays of light are scattered when they hit the partly opaque lens. The process can result in a severely clouded or completely blocked lens, a cataract, which can often be surgically corrected.

A second change in the lens's transparency affects color vision. The lens becomes yellowish as a person ages. This yellowing causes a decrease in color sensitivity across the whole visual spectrum. However, in particular it impairs the ability to see hues in the blue-green range and causes difficulty in distinguishing these colors.

The main purpose of the lens is to bring objects at different distances into clear focus on the retina. It does this by changing shape. When we view near objects, the lens curves outward. When we view distant objects, it flattens out and becomes elongated.

The lens's image focusing job becomes more difficult with age. Both it and the ciliary muscle, which control changes in its shape become less functional. An overall loss in lens elasticity occurs, limiting the ability to shift focus quickly from near to far objects and vice versa.

Glaucoma is a visual disorder that seems to be related to growing older. Glaucoma is excessive fluid buildup in the aqueous humor causing pressure within the eye to gradually increase. Often without warning sight is lost as a result of retinal or optic nerve damage. Glaucoma can often be corrected.

Macular degeneration is the result of a decreased blood supply to the center of the retina. It may cause a loss in vision. It is the leading cause of blindness in persons over age 65. Unfortunately, it is an irreversible illness.

According to Dr. Steve Pratt, a senior ophthalmologist at Scripps Memorial Hospital, La Jolla, California, the nutrient lutein may help to reduce the risk of age-related macular degeneration, if started at an early age.

Lutein is most highly concentrated in dark leafy green vegetables like spinach or kale. There are also supplements containing lutein.

Lutein deposits in the macula, the part of the eye that controls 20/20 vision, and helps filter out blue light or harmful rays from the sun.[6]

Hearing. Like vision, problems in hearing seem to accelerate in the elderly, though hearing and visual problems that severely limit one's abilities to function are not a general aspect of growing old. Many people have severe problems, most do not.

My father-in law had a hearing aid, but he wouldn't wear it because he wouldn't admit he had a problem.

Hearing problems due to aging have some specific characteristics. There may be difficulty distinguishing high-pitched tones. As a result, they may have more difficulty hearing certain categories of speakers, such as women. They may have problems hearing certain sounds (such as consonants) or certain phrases (such as warnings) that may be fairly loud but are usually delivered in a higher-pitched voice. They may have difficulty with background noise. A general difficulty in being able to filter out irrelevant stimuli as well as one did when young may add to a person's problems of hearing in a noisy place.

They are also likely to hear less when someone speaks rapidly or when they cannot see the speaker. This is because, to compensate for their loss, many people with hearing problems read lips.[7]

Believing his wife's hearing was failing, a husband slipped up behind her and said softly, "Can you hear me?" Not hearing an answer, he repeated the question two more times in a normal tone. Still not receiving a reply, he moved closer, raised his voice, and announced, "I asked you three times if you could hear me!"

This time he clearly heard her agitated answer, "Yes, and three times I told you I could hear you! Now what do you want?"

Taste and Smell. As with vision and hearing, most studies show that the elderly taste and smell less well than the young. In one study, for example, blindfolded college students and elderly adults were asked to identify and rate for pleasantness a variety of blended foods after smelling and tasting them. The older people could not distinguish the vast majority of the foods as well as the students, and the elderly were more likely to rate the foods as weak-tasting. Impairments in these areas can create problems. Poor nutrition can result because food becomes less appetizing. A loss in sensitivity to smell can also be dangerous because smell alerts us to such dangers as fire.

Many people have special dietary requirements. Diabetics need to watch their sugar intake. Those with high blood pressure or heart disease need to watch their salt intake.

Other factors may influence the choice of diet and nutrition. Unfortunately, many people trying to survive on social security alone may choose between food and medications. Economics may influence the choice of diet, thus resulting in poor nutrition. Being alone may take away the incentive to eat. A poor mouth condition may make for painful chewing and influence the choice of diet. Many elderly have problems with constipation, also influencing one's choice of diet.[8]

One's environment and living space can be somewhat modified to help those living in their homes with physical limitations to continue to live as independently as he or she is capable of doing for as long as possible.

Imagine a robot alerting an elderly woman that she needs to take her medication. Sensors in her kitchen and her bedroom have already noted she has not eaten yet and has been lying in bed all morning.

Her caregiver, although not in the house, is en route because this information and the woman's vital statistics have been relayed to the caregiver through a computer program that inferred the potential health problems.

This technology is not science fiction. It is being developed today. Until it is fully developed, there are other ways to help seniors live more safely and comfortably.

Continuing to live in one's own home has a great advantage. It is a familiar setting. However, some of the design features can be changed to meet the changing physical conditions and needs of the aging person.

Vision problems can be mitigated by a well-lit environment. Some builders will install chic-looking, low-intensity lighting under bathroom counters that glow onto the floor and serve as a night light for failing eyesight. Bright, contrasting colors and different textures and shapes of spaces and furniture can be used to help accentuate differences. To prevent accidents caused by poor vision or motor problems, there should not be too much furniture, nor poorly designed furniture, pieces that one might have difficulty seeing and trip over. Ideally, there should be no raised floor areas. Large numerals can be placed on appliances like ovens and telephones. Varying the heights of kitchen cabinets and counters adds visual appeal to a room and provides easy-to-reach work spaces for someone who has trouble reaching for items.

For hearing difficulties devices can be bought that amplify the sound of doorbells or telephones.

For the person who has difficulty with speed, strength and agility, doors should open automatically or be light to the touch or doorways should be made wider for wheelchair access, shelves and storage places should be easy to reach and such devices as grab bars should be installed in places like the bathroom where falls are more likely. Faucets should be easy to turn on and off, controls should be at the front of the stove, and knobs on all appliances should not be too small or too smooth to be easily grasped by stiff fingers.

In the bathroom, for those who prefer to shower, the curb can be lowered or eliminated so that the person can roll right into the shower with a wheelchair. It isn't necessary to use a shower chair, which requires the assistance of a caregiver to lift the person from chair to chair. A sliding handset is a way for everyone in the household to use the shower and is easy for those in a wheelchair or shower chair. For those who prefer tub bathing, a lift system can be installed to assist the caregiver in transferring the person in and out of the tub. Showers should also have an anti-scald device to protect aging skin that might lose its sensitivity.

A floor drain in the bathroom is the ideal. This enables an individual in a wheelchair to roll out of the shower to the drain area, where they can dry off and the water can drain off the floor. Ideally, the shower floor and the bathroom floor should be seamless and of the same material. Mosaic tiles are more slip resistant because the water collects in the naturally occurring indentations rather than on the tile surface. A heat lamp installed in the ceiling is also an inexpensive way to increase the room temperature while bathing or drying off.

The differences in toilet design to meet Americans With Disabilities Act guidelines are slight. Where a standard toilet seat is 14 inches high, an accessible toilet is 17 inches high to reduce the need for lowering and lifting oneself on and off the seat.

Install thermostats at eye level, with large, easy-to-read digital numbers.

Make electrical outlets and light switches easier to reach by placing outlets higher up on walls, and switches lower. Switches should be 36-42 inches off the floor. Outlets should be 28-30 inches from the floor.[9]

Motor Performance. Older adults seem to move or respond more slowly than the young. Generally this is true, but can vary. Movement speed can be affected by health problems such as arthritis, making it more difficult to raise one's arm or to move one's leg.; or by hearing loss, which makes it more difficult for the person to know what is being asked of them to do. Often, though, it is one's reaction time that shows the most evidence of slowing. Studies have shown that where decision making is involved, the older person often takes longer. Slowing occurs somewhere in the sequence between the time a signal to respond occurs and the time action is actually carried out. In other words, age-related motor deficits are due to a problem in deciding on the appropriate action and then deciding how it is to be carried out, an impairment in the speed with which the central nervous system can process the information to respond. Thus, the older person tends to exhibit a slowing in all aspects of life. Again, slowness varies greatly among older individuals. [10]

Intelligence. There is some controversy regarding changes in intelligence as one ages. Verbal and performance scores on intelligence tests have shown a decline as one ages, leading to what has been called as "the classic aging pattern." A person's store of knowledge, the facts a person has accumulated through the years, tends to remain relatively stable throughout life. However, intelligence requiring problem-solving and reasoning abilities not dependent on learning, is directly related to physiology. It requires a brain at its neurological peak. As neurons are lost and other changes occur in brain functioning, this type of intelligence shows a decline as one grows older.

Much of the controversy surrounding IQ tests comes from such tests not taking into account problems the elderly might have in taking such tests stemming from such problems as health and anxiety. Many IQ tests measure skills important specifically to doing well in school. Some psychologists have attempted to devise tests more appropriate for the elderly that tap knowledge appropriate to their age such as finances, diseases, and death and dying. In such tests those in their fifties and sixties fared much better than those in their twenties. Others have attempted to improve older adults' performance on the skills involved in intelligence as currently defined. Many such efforts have been successful, demonstrating that IQ in the elderly is capable of being enhanced.[11]

An elderly man in Florida had owned a large farm for several years. He had a large pond in the back, with picnic tables, horseshoe courts, and some apple and peach trees.

The pond was properly shaped and fixed up for swimming when it was built. One evening the old farmer decided to go down to the pond, as he hadn't been there for a while, and look it over. He grabbed a five-gallon bucket to bring back some fruit. As he neared the pond, he heard voices shouting and laughing with glee. As he came closer he saw it was a bunch of young women skinny-dipping in his pond.

He made the women aware of his presence and they all went to the deep end. One of the women shouted to him, "We're not coming out until you leave!" The old man frowned, "I didn't come down here to watch you ladies swim naked or make you get out of the pond naked."

Holding the bucket up he said, "I'm here to feed the alligator."

Moral: Old men can still think fast.

Sexuality. For a long time the idea of older men and women having sex seemed repugnant to many. Older people are thought to be asexual. People still seem to hold ideas that sexuality in late life is abnormal. The "dirty old man" comes to mind as a topic in jokes and entertainment. Years ago the comedian Artie Johnson portrayed a "dirty old man" on the TV show, "Laugh In." Jokes about older people may also reveal attitudes about sexuality.

The truth is, older people are very much interested in and enjoy sexuality. The hit movie "Cocoon," back in the '80's depicted older adults as being very much interested in a sexual relationship.

A recent study by the American Association of Retired Persons also reflects an interest in sexuality among older Americans. In 1999, AARP and Modern Maturity magazine commissioned a study of the sexual attitudes and practices of Americans ages 45 and older, the first such nationwide inquiry to span midlife to old age. The final number of respondents selected for the survey was 1, 384.

Among the findings:

About half of 45 through 59 year-olds have sex at least once a week, but among 60 through 74 year-olds, the proportion drops to 30 percent for men and 24 percent for women.

While frequency drops with age, more than 70 percent of surveyed men and women who have regular partners have intercourse at least once or twice a month.

About two thirds of those polled were extremely or very satisfied with their physical relationships.

With advancing age partners make a difference. More than 50 percent of men and women with partners, but less than half of 1 percent of women and only 6 percent of men without a regular partner have intercourse at least once a week." A 75 year-old widow who says she has no interest in sex may really be saying she has no opportunity for sex," says Shirley Zussman, Ed.D., a couples therapist in New York City and past president of the American Association of Sex Educators, Counselors and Therapists.

At every age, though, sex does seem to hold greater importance for men than women. Nearly 60 percent of men, but only about 35 percent of women say sexual activity is important to their overall quality of life.

However, men and women 45 and older cited close ties with friends and family, financial security, good spirits, spiritual well-being and a good relationship with a partner as very important to their quality of life, more important than "a satisfying sexual relationship."

"Less stress" and "more free time" are the top things 45-59 year-olds say would most improve their sex life; "better health" heads the list for men 60 and older, "better health for partner" for women 60-74, and "finding a partner" for women 75-plus.

Men think about sex more than women do: 58 percent of men say they have sexual thoughts at least two or three times per week, but less than 20 percent of women say they do.

Men and women who are free of illness and are not taking medication report feelings of sexual desire more than those who are being treated for illness or are taking medication. Many medications are known to have as side effects a decrease in sexual desire as well as impotence in men.

Nearly 36 percent of women ages 45-59 (but only 10 percent of women 75 and older) say they take hormone replacement therapy.

Only 5.6 percent of men are currently trying new treatments for impotence, but half of those taking some form of medication are taking Viagra. The majority of the men and their partners said that the drug had increased their enjoyment of sex.

Americans 60 and older believe that better health would do more to enhance their sexual pleasure than any other life change. Nevertheless, more than half of men and 85 percent of women say that their sex lives are unimpaired by illness, even those age 75 and older.

In another finding, women 75 and older are much more likely than women under age 60 to describe their husbands as romantic.

Ratings of physical attractiveness are even more interesting. Among 45 through 59 year-old men, approximately 59 percent gave their partners the highest possible rating for physical attractiveness; for those 75 and older, that figure was 63 percent.

Among women, the proportion who described their partners as highly attractive was 57 percent at age 75 and older; compared that with the 52 percent rating from their younger counterparts, who are in their mid to late 40s and 50s.

As author Susan Jacoby states in her article,"At an age when physical beauty, as measured by the standard of youth, is declining, these older lovers are holding up a different mirror to one another. They are seeing what no statistical portrait can truly capture- what John Donne described in the 17th century in his 'Autumnal' elegy:

No spring nor summer beauty hath such grace,
As I have seen in one autumnal face…
If we love things long sought, age is a thing

Which we are 50 years in composing."[12]

According to Dr. Janet Belsky," in all older women there are general changes in the vagina that occur after menopause and may affect the sexual response. As a result of decreased hormone levels at menopause, the walls of the late-middle-aged woman's vagina become thinner, pinkish rather than reddish, and generally more fragile. The vagina also becomes shorter and narrower and loses some of its expansive ability."[13]

The well-known study by Masters and Johnson in 1966 revealed that the rate and amount of vaginal lubrication during sexual arousal was less as women aged. These changes made intercourse more painful for some older women resulting in a lessening of sexual enjoyment and even cause some women to avoid sex.

Masters and Johnson also found the clitoral response to sexual stimulation was virtually unchanged. Also, the older women were just as capable of orgasm as the younger group.

The males Masters and Johnson studied showed pronounced physiological changes. The older men took longer to have erections. Once attained, their erections could be maintained for a longer time without ejaculating.[14]

Master's and Johnson's research also showed that ejaculation in the older male was different. The older men had much less intense ejaculations. If a man had maintained an erection over a long period, ejaculation sometimes resulted in a seepage of seminal fluid rather than an expulsion.[15]

These changes do not suggest that the sexual response is absent in older men. Since erections can be maintained longer before ejaculation need occur, the older man may even, from the woman's point of view, be a superior sexual partner.

Memory. Poor memory is the complaint that seems to epitomize old age. This seems to be a perception about old age and older adults share this perception. Most, if asked, would probably say they are more forgetful than they used to be. Many jokes have been made about memory and the elderly.

For example. There once was a bishop in England who was very forgetful. Following a marriage of a young couple, he was present at the wedding reception. When the bridegroom responded to the toast made to the bride and groom, the groom said: "I have a confession to make to my bride in front of all of you. I confess, dear, that before I married you, I spent many happy hours in the arms of another woman…my mother."

All present enjoyed it. The bishop made a mental note to use it on the occasion of his 50th wedding anniversary which he was to celebrate that week.

The bishop's house was full of guests to honor the bishop and his wife. The bishop rose to speak. "After fifty years of married life, my Dear, I have a confession to make to you in front of all our friends," he said. "Before I married you I spent many happy hours in the arms of another woman…and for the life of me, I can't remember who she was."

Our memory can get us into trouble at times.

There's also the story of a senior couple sitting in their front room, when the husband said, "I'm going to get some ice cream." His wife said, "You'd better write it down." He said, "I don't need to do that." He went into the kitchen, but just before he got the ice cream, the phone rang. He hung up after talking and tried to remember what he'd come after. He saw a pot of soup on the stove, so he dished up two bowls of soup. When he took the soup to his wife, she said, "I told you, you should have written it down." He said, "Why, what did I forget?" She said, "The crackers."

According to studies, memory problems seem to occur when a person attempts to retrieve information. However, some of the problem may be attributed to environmental reasons. Research has shown that practice and mental exercise helped to facilitate one's memory.

Dr. Amir Soas of Case Western Reserve University Medical School in Cleveland, Ohio, says: "Read, read, read. Do crossword puzzles. Pull out the chessboard or Scrabble. Learn a foreign language or a new hobby. Anything that stimulates the brain to think. And cut back on TV. When you watch television, your brain goes into neutral."[16]

Scientists used to believe that the brain was wired before age five, and that over time a person lost neurons and crucial brain circuitry until eventually mental decline became noticeable.

Scientists now believe the brain continually rewires and adapts itself, even in old age, so cognitive decline doesn't have to be inevitable.

But physical health is important, too. A healthy brain needs lots of oxygen pumped through healthy arteries. That means exercising and eating right, the very things that prevent heart disease and diabetes, helps the brain, too.

Studies appearing in the *Journal of the American Medical Association* confirm the importance of exercise on brain function.

One study, involving 2,257 retired men ages 71 to 93, found that those who walked less than a quarter-mile a day were almost twice as likely to develop Alzheimer's or other forms of dementia as men who walked more than 2 miles daily.

A study of 16,466 female nurses ages 70 to 81 found that women who walked a leisurely 1 ½ hours a week did better on tests of mental function than less active women.[17]

Mental Disorders. Because old age tends to be viewed negatively, older people are thought to be more prone to have psychological problems. Many are thought to be senile. The fear of alzheimer's is prevalent.

Surveys in the past have shown that some psychological problems are less prevalent in those over age 65, namely schizophrenia and manic-depressive psychosis. One reason is that these conditions less frequently develop for the first time in old age. Likewise, anxiety disorders in their various forms are very common in children and young adults and less common in old age. It may be that as we age we develop a kind of wisdom or less-stressed outlook on things.[18]

Older people do have their share of emotional problems, especially depression and the dementias.

The term dementia refers to a group of chronic diseases that have basically similar symptoms. There is a progressive decline in intellectual functions. Problems are usually first seen in a person's memory for relatively recent events. The individual is able to remember past events from years ago, but has difficulty remembering things that occurred within the last few days, hours, or even minutes. A person may forget, for example, that he or she has just made a phone call or turned on the stove.

Over time these problems get worse, and every aspect of the person's thinking becomes involved. Abstract reasoning becomes impossible. The person can no longer think through options when making decisions. Judgment becomes faulty. Individuals may act inappropriately, perhaps undressing in public or in other ways embarrassing themselves and others. They may behave recklessly and be unable to understand that they are endangering their life or health. Language becomes limited. They may not be able to communicate their own thoughts.

Later, if the condition progresses to its final stage before death occurs, victims become disoriented to time, place and person; that is, they have no idea of the date, where they are, or whom they are speaking to. Individuals may forget basic facts about themselves, such as their name, date of birth, or birthplace. At this point, they may need full-time nursing care, as they are often unable to dress, feed themselves, or go to the toilet independently.[19]

Alzheimer's disease and senile dementia are now used to refer to one disease having the same symptoms and physical basis. Even though dementia may be exacerbated by environmental change, such as entering a nursing home or moving to a new city because the anxiety can impact our thoughts, it does have a primarily organic basis. The brains of people with dementia and normal older people do reveal observable differences.

The second most common dementia of old age, multi infarct dementia, is caused by the death of a significant amount of brain tissue due to many small infarcts, or strokes. Because these strokes are generally caused by high blood pressure, they may be lessened by lowering blood pressure through diet and medication. Normally, however, multi infarct dementia gets progressively worse because these strokes tend to accumulate and affect progressively larger segments of the person's brain.

Everybody is forgetful now and then; everybody has emotional highs and lows. But anyone with several of the following symptoms, or with frequently recurring symptoms, needs a thorough medical exam. The warning signs of Alzheimer's and other forms of dementia include:

1. Memory loss that affects job performance.
2. Difficulty performing familiar tasks.
3. Forgetting simple words or using inappropriate ones.
4. Getting lost in time and space.
5. Poor judgment.
6. Problems with abstract thinking, such as adding numbers.
7. Misplacing things and putting them in odd places, like a hat in the microwave.
8. Rapid mood changes, often for no obvious reason.
9. Dramatic changes in personality, either suddenly or gradually.
10. Loss of initiative or interest in one's usual pursuits.

Even though changes in thinking are characteristic of the dementias, there are also emotional symptoms. Emotional responses may be unpredictable. The person may become verbally or physically abusive or overly passive and compliant. There may even be no change in the person other than a cognitive one.

Many dementias in their less severe stages are also accompanied by depression, an understandably common response to the knowledge that one has memory problems.

There is no cure for dementia, but with medications and behavior modification, it's possible, at least early on, to delay and ease its effects.

Depression is not a normal part of aging, but unfortunately because many older adults and their caregivers believe it is, depression in the elderly may be overlooked and go untreated. Although older adults may experience losses in later life such as changes in health, loss of loved ones and friends or relocation, the majority of people cope with these losses without becoming clinically depressed. If the sadness that accompanies these life changes lingers for a long time, it may be a sign of clinical depression, which should be treated.

Many things can contribute to clinical depression, such as life changes, but it can be triggered by chronic illnesses common in later life such as diabetes, stroke, heart disease, cancer, chronic lung disease, Alzheimer's disease, Parkinson's disease, and arthritis.

Depression is a medical illness caused by a chemical imbalance in the brain and not a weakness as many people may still think.

The warning signs of depression are often masked by another disease or medications, missed, or explained away. While clinical depression is a common medical illness, it is never a normal reaction to another illness.

No two people experience clinical depression in the same manner. Symptoms will vary in severity and duration among people. See your doctor if you experience five or more of the following symptoms for more than two weeks:

1. Persistent sad, anxious, or "empty" mood.
2. Sleeping too little, especially early morning awakening, or sleeping too much.
3. Reduced appetite and/or weight loss, or increased appetite and weight gain.
4. Loss of interest in activities once enjoyed, including sex.
5. Restlessness, irritability.

6. Persistent physical symptoms that do not respond to treatment (such as headaches, chronic pain, or digestive disorders).
7. Difficulty concentrating, remembering, or making decisions.
8. Fatigue or loss of energy.
9. Feeling guilty, hopeless, or worthless.
10. Thoughts of suicide or death.[20]

Some symptoms are common to both depression and other medical disorders. For example, weight loss, sleep disturbances, and low energy may also occur in diabetes, thyroid disorders, some neurologic disorders, heart disease, cancer, and stroke.

Depression is very treatable using antidepressant medication, psychotherapy, or a combination of the two.

The taking of medications can sometimes be a problem. If a memory problem is present, one can either forget to take their medication or take too much. If one's spouse or partner is alert they can help the other with a medication routine. The issue becomes more serious if one is alone. Hopefully, a family member, caretaker, or friend would be alert enough to monitor the situation.

Alcoholism can also be a problem in the elderly. People may begin to take alcohol as a means to relieve boredom, worries, pain, or other problems, but end up isolated, depressed and addicted. This can lead to physical problems, such as confusion and nutritional deficiency.

Perhaps one day science will be able to solve the genetics of aging and even reverse the process. Would we want to live indefinitely is another question. Until then everyone must learn to accept and cope with the physical and mental changes that accompany growing older. How we can cope is the subject matter for subsequent chapters.

There's nothing the matter with me.
I'm just as healthy as can be.
I have arthritis in both knees.
And when I talk, I talk with a wheeze.

My pulse is weak, my blood is thin,
But I'm awfully well, for the shape I'm in.
All my teeth have had to come out,
And my diet, I hate to think about.

I'm overweight, and I can't get thin,
But I'm awfully well, for the shape I'm in.
Arch supports I need for my feet,
Or I wouldn't be able to go out in the street.

Sleep is denied me night after night,
But every morning, I find I'm all right.
My memory's failing, my head's in a spin,
But I'm awfully well, for the shape I'm in.

Old age is golden- I've heard it said,
But sometimes I wonder, as I go to bed.
With my ears in a drawer, my teeth in a cup,
And my glasses on a shelf, until I get up.

And when sleep dims my eyes, I say to myself,
Is there anything else, I should lay on the shelf?
The reason I know, my youth has been spent,
Is my get-up and go, has got-up and went.

But really I don't mind, when I think with a grin,
Of all the places my get-up has been.
I get up each morning, and dust off my wits.
Pick up the paper and read the obits.

If my name is missing, I'm therefore not dead,
So I eat a good breakfast, and jump back into bed.
The moral of this, as the tale unfolds,
Is that for you and me, who are growing old.
It is better to say, "I'm fine," with a grin,
Than to let people know the shape we are in.

CHAPTER THREE
LET GRATITUDE BE YOUR ATTITUDE

"If we fill our hours with regrets of yesterday and with worries of tomorrow, we have no today in which to be thankful."

There are perhaps three ways of looking at life and at the world. We can see reality as indifferent. It's out there and whatever happens is what we've got to make of it.

Perhaps such a view was expressed by a little boy on his return from a birthday party. He was asked by his mother, "Bobby, did you thank the lady for the party?"

"Well, I was going to," he replied," but a girl ahead of me said, 'Thank you,' and the lady told her not to mention it. So I didn't."

In such a world view God isn't against us, but God isn't for us, and we're basically on our own. It's a view in which God may be out there somewhere, but doesn't really make much difference in my life.

There is another world view which says that the universe is hostile, destructive or judgmental.

Perhaps such a view was expressed by a boy who was asked by his teacher to write a composition on the things for which he was thankful. He said," I am thankful for my glasses. They keep the boys from hitting me and the girls from kissing me."

I have a feeling he may change his mind about the kissing part in a few years, but at this point in his life he saw the world as hostile, as against him. Likewise, some people view God as somehow out to get them. A loved one dies and someone will say, "It was God's will."

Even if we don't think it, we may feel that God is against us. The death of a loved one, an illness, financial difficulties, the loss of a job, personal problems, all can lead us to feel bitter towards life and towards God. We may wonder why God allows such problems and losses to occur.

The third world view is that we do live in a benevolent universe. God is viewed as neither indifferent, nor against me, but on my side. The foundation of all of life is a God of love, and that love, no matter how tragic the world events, can be trusted.

In 1636, amid the darkness of the Thirty Years' War, a German pastor, Martin Rinkart, is said to have buried five thousand of his parishioners in one year. His city was ravaged by war, death, and economic disaster. The other pastors had died, leaving him all alone to minister to the residents of the city. It is said that he sometimes preached burial services for forty to fifty persons in one day. His wife was among the victims. Yet, in the midst of that darkness, he sat down and wrote this table grace for his children:

Now thank we all our God
With heart and hands and voices;
Who wondrous things hath done,
In whom his world rejoices.
Who, from our mother's arms,
Hath led us on our way
With countless gifts of love
And still is ours today.

What a difference our lives can be when we let gratitude be our attitude towards life. It is a gratitude that is aware that

God loves us and will help us, but it is also an outlook towards all of life no matter what our circumstances.

Many people, however, seem to be stuck in the second world view. They aren't happy with life, nor with themselves. How easy it is to complain about life, and allow a complaining attitude to dominate our outlook. A bakery customer was complaining about the pastry. "I was making pastry before you were born," replied the indignant baker. "Maybe so," answered the customer, "but why sell it now?"

Many of us complain from time to time. How often do we complain about being stuck in traffic, waiting in line or complaining about the weather is always in vogue. Some people like to complain all the time. Nothing is ever right. They can find fault with everyone and everything. It's as if it's their way of looking at life. With such a view of life it is difficult to be thankful.

There is a portion in the Old Testament Book of Exodus when the people of Israel are wandering in the wilderness. They had recently witnessed the saving acts of God. The Passover experience had freed them from slavery in Egypt. Pharaoh had allowed them to go free. Pharaoh changed his mind and caught up with them at the Red Sea, but God enabled them to cross the Red Sea safely and then caused the Red Sea to cover the Egyptian army. One would think they would be grateful. They were, for the moment, until the next crisis occurred. They were hungry and thirsty and complained to Moses that God didn't care.

There are times when complaining is justified. If we go to a restaurant, for example, and the food we received is cold, when it should be hot, then we are justified in complaining to the waiter. If we receive a bill and find items listed we did not purchase, then we have a right to complain. If we are treated unfairly and we suspect its because of our race or gender, then we have a right to complain.

There are those, however, who complain all the time about everything. They have a negative or pessimistic attitude about life in general and everything in specific. A man saved his money for years so he could go to Italy to see the Pope. He stopped by to get a haircut the day he left and his barber found fault with everything he said.

"How are you getting to Italy?" the barber asked. "I'm taking an Italian airline," the man responded. "Forget it," said the barber," they have awful service, you'll hate it."

"Where are you staying?" asked the barber. And the man replied, "At the Hilton in Rome." And the barber replied, "Forget it; it's a terrible hotel. Don't stay there."

Then the barber asked the man, "What are you going to do while you're in Rome?" "See the Pope," the man said. And the barber had a complaint for this answer, too. "You'll never get in. You're a nobody."

Six weeks later, the man returned from his trip and went to see the barber. "I had a fabulous trip," he told the barber. "I flew on an Italian airline and the service was perfect. I stayed at the Hilton and had the best room in the hotel. It was wonderful. I went to see the Pope and had a private audience with him and got to kiss his ring."

"Wow!" the barber replied. "You actually kissed his ring! What did he say?"

"Well, he looked down at me and said, 'Gee, where did you get that terrible haircut?'"

Some people like to complain, and often complaining can lead to bitterness. The death of a loved one, an illness, financial difficulties, all can lead us to feel bitter towards life and towards God. That's why it can be helpful for us to develop the habit of focusing on what we have going for us and not concentrate on what we have lost.

A woman wrote into newspaper columnist Ann Landers saying, "A few days ago my mother, who lives several thousand miles away, phoned me and for twenty minutes I listened to her complain about her various aches and pains. I wish I could help her, but of course there is nothing I can do. After we hung up, I sat down and composed the enclosed prayer."

Her prayer reads: "My children are grown now, and I have wonderful grandchildren. I love them all, but please God, let me remember that I have lived, loved and enjoyed this life. Do not let me take away from their enjoyment by complaining about every ache and pain. I have earned them all. Please keep me from mentioning my swollen joints, stiff knees, poor eyesight, and anything else that isn't as good as it once was. Let me remember that I have enjoyed a full and wonderful life and have been blessed in so many ways. Now is not the time for me to begin complaining. Please let my mouth be closed, while my ears are open to hear the fun they are having. Let me remember that I am still setting an example for them and that if I keep quiet, they will forever think that I never had a single ache or pain in my life, and that I miraculously escaped the ills of old age. They will, in later years, remember me with pleasure and say, 'I wish I had her genes. She never had anything wrong with her!' That, dear Lord, will be the best legacy I can leave them."[2]

So often we look at only what we don't like, what's wrong in our lives and with the world, but thinking about what we do have going for us can enable us to feel better about ourselves and about life. This is gratitude as a way of thinking. I remember delivering food baskets at Thanksgiving to families in our community who were experiencing financial difficulties. Our church would have a Thanksgiving eve service and people were asked to bring in staple food items to bring to the altar during the service. Our women's fellowship would purchase turkeys. The food would then be divided among several families and I and other church members would distribute the food to families from church or in the community. One family, I remember in particular, had said they had been bitter because things just weren't going their way. The father had been laid off from work and was having difficulty finding another job. Receiving the gift of food from people they didn't even know enabled them to realize that there is goodness in the world.

If we could practice thinking about what we have going for us, what we like about our lives or the world today, and do this routinely each and every day, what a difference it can make on our happiness. The real difficulties may still be there, but they won't seem as overwhelming or as problematic. They will be put into perspective with the realization that there are some things, some persons, some blessings we do have. Surely we can find something to be thankful for. It's like a Peanuts cartoon in which Lucy is staring rather gloomily out a window. Her brother Linus is behind her. Lucy says: "My life is a drag. I'm completely fed up. I've never felt so low in my life." Linus says: "When you're in a mood like this you should try to think of the things you have to be thankful for. In other words, count your blessings." Lucy says: "Ha. That's a good one. I could count my blessings on one finger. I've never had anything, and I never will have anything. I don't get half the breaks that other people do. Nothing ever goes right for me. And you talk about counting blessings. You talk about being thankful. What do I have to be thankful for?" Linus says: "Well, for one thing you have a brother who loves you."

Lucy puts her arms around her brother and as she is letting out all her frustrations in tears, Linus says, "Every now and then I say the right thing."

As we grow older, some of the physical problems we encounter might result more in feelings of bitterness than feelings of gratitude. It can be difficult to feel grateful or to think of reasons to be thankful when you're experiencing the pain of arthritis, and other health problems. Yet, the Apostle Paul writes: "Rejoice always, pray constantly, give thanks in all circumstances; for this is the will of God in Christ Jesus for you." 1 Thess. 5:16-18.

How can we be grateful in all circumstances? Its not that we're grateful necessarily for the circumstance, but rather in each circumstance, no matter what it is, we can be grateful that God is with us.

The first Thanksgiving in America is a good example. It had taken the Pilgrims sixty-six days to cross the Atlantic Ocean in their boat the Mayflower. Captain Christopher Jones had brought over 102 passengers, among them eighteen married couples. It had been a grueling voyage. There had been disease, childbirth and death aboard. The Mayflower was blown off course. Instead of reaching Virginia, where Englishmen had settled thirteen years earlier, the Pilgrims first landed near Provincetown, Massachusetts in December. It was a dreadfully cold winter in New England, which claimed half of their number. At one point only six persons were strong enough to attend the ill. Graves were camouflaged so the Native Americans could not keep track of the dead. Food was scarce and severely rationed. The Mayflower had sailed back to England for supplies but no one knew when it would return.

Come the Spring the colonists had befriended the Native Americans, who showed them how to plant corn. They planted twenty acres of corn. Then came a drought and hopes of a harvest almost vanished. But some crops came in. As a result, Governor William Bradford set aside a "solemn day" for public thanksgiving. The pilgrims and the Native Americans celebrated together for several days with food, games and fellowship.

Think, too, of Abraham Lincoln. It was President Lincoln who made Thanksgiving an ongoing national holiday. He did so not at the height of our nation's peace and prosperity, but during our country's darkest hour, in the midst of the Civil War. In his proclamation of the holiday, Lincoln spoke of something besides mayhem and death. He spoke of "the blessings of fruitful fields and healthful skies" and of other bounties that could not "fail to penetrate and soften even the heart which is habitually insensible to the ever watchful providence of Almighty God."[22]

Thanksgiving is not just a feeling. The Pilgrims, Martin Rinkart, Abraham Lincoln, and countless others, including the Apostle Paul, certainly didn't feel thankful. They were giving thanks in the midst of the deaths of friends and loved ones.

In each and every circumstance of life, no matter what the circumstance, no matter what problems we are having in life, we can be grateful because God is with us, seeking to help us, seeking to empower us with His love to help us meet our problems. That is why the Pilgrims gave thanks. That is why Martin Rinkart could sing, "Now Thank We All Our God." That is why President Lincoln could issue a proclamation of thanksgiving. That is why the Apostle Paul could "give thanks in all circumstances." And that is why we can give thanks today in the midst of world terrorism or our individual problems and concerns.

Another way to help us go from bitter to better is to take the "I" out of bitter and focus on how God has helped us, and how God can help us.

When we feel bitter, we are separated from God and God's help. When we are bitter we tend to focus on what we feel is unfair, what we didn't deserve, or didn't receive, or had taken from us. Rather than continuing to focus on what we feel is unfair, we need to focus on what God can do to help us. God didn't cause what we feel is unfair. God didn't cause a loved one to die. God didn't cause us to be ill. God didn't cause us to have economic difficulties or hardships. But God can help us to find strength, peace, and solutions to our problems.

We need to look back in our lives and recall or recognize those times when God has touched us or saved us; those times when God has brought healing to our bodies or our relationships; those times when we have experienced God's forgiveness; those times when God has answered our prayers; those times when God has given us strength and courage; those times when God has guided us safely through a problem. God is with us all the time, but sometimes we don't realize when or how God has been helping us.

Life should not be judged on the basis of our immediate situation. Many a man and woman has gone through a terrible and terrifying situation only to discover later, even years later, upon looking back at the situation, that good has come out of it, that God had led them through that time or that God was reaching out to them to help.

If we can develop the habit of looking for the good of each day and being grateful, we will find that we are much happier.

The happy persons are those who are able to perceive that they have been greatly blessed. They are not necessarily the world's successes or the people who have it easy. They are the people who know that there is One greater than ourselves who is present to help us and guide us. They are happy because they are grateful for the love and strength of One who can help them make it through life.

It helps explain why the Judeo-Christian tradition places such emphasis on thanking God. "It is good to give thanks to the Lord," begins the 92nd Psalm. We do so not because God needs our gratitude, but because we need it.

Learning to be thankful on a daily basis is a key to happiness. If you develop the habit of looking at your blessings and being grateful for them, as opposed to complaining about your problems, you will fill your life with happiness.

In Hebrew, the word for gratitude, *hoda'ah*, is the same as the word for confession. To offer thanks is to confess dependence, to acknowledge that others have the power to help or benefit you, especially God.

To be thankful requires a certain amount of humility. We have to come to the realization that we are all indebted beings. We are all recipients of a grace operating through nature and history. We did not create ourselves. We have our parents to thank and their parents, and so on. We did not create the universe that supports our life and provides us with countless opportunities for work and play. If we live in America, we are indebted to those who established our democracy and those who fought in our wars to maintain our freedom. We are living longer, in part, due to those who developed vaccines to prevent such problems as polio or measles that years ago used to result in death at an early age.

In a society filled with abundance it is so easy to put ourselves first. We can come to think that we don't need God. If we are fortunate to have a good pension, a nice home, and good health, we may become self-satisfied and not bother with any thoughts about God or the importance of having a relationship with God.

In the Old Testament, Moses warned the people about such a danger. When the Hebrews were about to enter the promised land, Moses said to them: "When you have eaten and are satisfied, praise the Lord your God for the good land he has given you. Be careful that you do not forget the Lord your God, failing to observe his commands, his laws and his decrees that I am giving you this day. Otherwise, when you eat and are satisfied, when you build fine houses and settle down, and when your herds and flocks grow large and your silver and gold increase and all you have is multiplied, then your heart will become proud and you will forget the Lord your God, who brought you out of Egypt, out of the land of slavery. He led you through the vast and dreadful desert, that thirsty and waterless land, with its venomous snakes and scorpions. He brought you water out of hard rock. He gave you manna to eat in the desert, something your fathers had never known, to humble and to test you so that in the end it might go well with you. You may say to yourself, 'My power and the strength of my hands have produced this wealth for me.' But remember the Lord your God, for it is he who gives you the ability to produce wealth, and so confirms his covenant, which he swore to your forefathers, as it is today." (Deut. 8:10-18 NIV).

Pride can be dangerous at any age. By pride I don't mean self-esteem. I mean the attitude that puts "I" at the center of the universe and may see no need for God. For example, a woman walks in a store to return a pair of eyeglasses that she had purchased for her husband a week before.

"What seems to be the problem, madam?"

"I'm returning these glasses I bought for my husband. He's still not seeing things my way."

At any age it is not always easy to be humble and admit our limitations, but especially as we grow older. On the one hand it's healthy to keep going and doing as much as we are able. A woman in my congregation was so proud of herself. I had come over for a visit and she told me how she had just finished washing all the walls and carpeting in her condo. At age 98! She was happy she was still able to keep up her house. On the other hand, another woman in my congregation, in her late 70's, was proud she was able to renew her driver's license. And yet her memory was not good, she often got confused and lost while driving. She recently had an accident. It was her fault the police had said. To make matters worse, she had forgotten to renew her automobile insurance and so was driving without insurance.

It is good to be proud of our accomplishments, even if its cleaning the house. Those of you with debilitating arthritis, or difficult vision, or other physical problems know how good it can feel to be able to accomplish something that may seem simple to others. But there can come a time when our pride can become detrimental to ourselves and others. It's not always easy to accept our limitations and admit when it's time to give up certain things.

A 93 year-old man purchased a car and drove it for a year. He never drove very far, usually just a few miles from his house. He would drive to church, the grocery store, or to watch a nearby work project. He would take a folding chair, sit and watch a building being constructed, a bridge being built, or a road project. One day, however, he backed into two cars in the church parking lot. He decided it was time for him to give-up driving. He sold his car. Here was a man who knew when it was time to give up driving. He realized his limitations and accepted them.

Prayer can be a way to keep us humble and help us to be more thankful. Remember Paul said, "Have no anxiety about anything, but in everything by prayer and supplication with thanksgiving let your requests be made known to God."

There was a minister who had a parrot. All the parrot would say was, "Let's pray, let's pray." The minister tried to teach him other things, but to no avail. The minister learned that one of his deacons also had a parrot. The deacon's parrot would say, "Let's kiss, let's kiss." The minister decided to invite the deacon and his parrot over to his house. When the deacon arrived the minister put the parrots into the same cage to see what would happen. The deacon's parrot said, "Let's kiss, let's kiss." The minister's parrot responded, "Thank you, Lord, my prayers are answered."

There is a connection between prayer and thanksgiving; that's why Paul included them in the same sentence. Prayer opens us to God's presence and to an awareness of God's love and blessings in our lives. Conversely, if we think of what we're thankful for, we're more likely to acknowledge God as the source of those blessings.

A man went to his doctor complaining of pain in several places. The doctor asked him to indicate where it hurt. He pointed first to his leg, then to his back, then to his side, finally to his head. "Every time I press on these places, it hurts," he said. After a careful examination, the doctor diagnosed his problem. "You have a broken finger," the doctor said.

When we are ungrateful it is usually not our circumstances that are to blame. We are like that man with the broken finger focusing on his leg, his back, his side, and his head when his problem lay in the appendage he was using to examine each of them. The problem is not outside, but inside. The cure is to think about what God has done for us and is doing for us. Let gratitude be your attitude toward life each and every day. It can be if you focus on God.

CHAPTER FOUR
THE POWER OF A POSITIVE
OUTLOOK

"A man's life is what his thoughts make of it." Marcus Aurelius

Gratitude is but one aspect of the way we look at life. How we think about ourselves, about others, about God, about the events and circumstances of life has an effect on our physical and emotional well-being. Many may be familiar with Norman Vincent Peale's classic book, "The Power of Positive Thinking," or with Robert Schuller's possibility books and sermons. Scientists, too, have demonstrated the power of the mind on the body.

When I worked as a student minister in Yellowstone National Park one summer, the general stores celebrated Christmas in July. I thought it was just a gimmick to attract customers. Stores and buildings were decorated with Christmas decorations. I felt the commercialism of the event and had a negative attitude toward the whole thing.

But I had an experience that changed the way I thought. Our staff of six students decided to celebrate Christmas in July by singing Christmas carols out on the walkway that juts out and over the Grand Canyon of the Yellowstone. Perhaps the tourists thought we had been out in the sun too long. But the words and music of such carols as "Joy to the World" reminded me that the true meaning and spirit of Christmas is one that should last all year. We can sing "Joy to the World" at any time of the year because Christ does bring us joy. When we approach life with an optimistic outlook it has the power to change our reaction to life's events and circumstances.

For example, a man pulled into a gas station on the outskirts of town. As he filled his tank, he remarked to the attendant, "I've just accepted a job in town. I've never been to this part of the country. What are people like here?"

"What are people like where you came from?" the attendant asked.

"Not so nice," the man replied. "In fact, they can be quite rude."

The attendant shook his head. "Well, I'm afraid you'll find the people in this town to be the same way."

Just then another car pulled into the station. "Excuse me," the driver called out. "I'm just moving to this area. Is it nice here?"

"Was it nice where you came from?" the attendant inquired.

"Oh, yes! I came from a great place. The people were friendly, and I hated to leave."

"Well, you'll find the same to be true of this town."

"Thanks!" yelled the driver as he pulled away.

"So what is this town really like?" asked the first man, now irritated with the attendant's conflicting reports.

The attendant just shrugged his shoulders. "It's all a matter of perception. You'll find things to be just the way you think they are."

A better example of how the way we think can affect us is the story Norman Cousins tells about himself in his book, Anatomy of an Illness. Cousins was a longtime editor of *The Saturday Review*. At the end of an exhausting trip, Norman Cousins was scheduled to attend an important dinner in Moscow. He left early in a taxi. He assumed the driver knew where to go, but the driver drove around the city as in a daze. Norman Cousins arrived at the dinner three hours late. He was furious.

Still angry, Norman Cousins returned to his hotel room where he climbed into bed and lay awake, tossing and turning. He was so agitated he couldn't sleep. The strong exhaust fumes drifting through his window from the diesel trucks in the streets below didn't help either.

The next day he was still agitated and angry. But now he was also sick. He boarded a plane for New York. By the time he arrived his temperature was 104 degrees. He felt awful.

His condition continued to worsen. His temperature remained elevated. He was becoming weak in his back and legs and he hurt all over. He had to be hospitalized. Numerous tests were done, but the doctors could not determine what was wrong. His condition was steadily deteriorating. It was gradually determined that Cousins was battling a painful and crippling arthritic disease called ankylosing spondylitis.

He began to relive his past, and he made a startling discovery. For the past few months he had been under a lot of stress. Perhaps it was affecting him now. He studied literature on stress, looking for some insight into his condition. He concluded that negative emotions and thoughts produce negative changes in the body. Therefore, positive emotions and thoughts, he reasoned, must produce the opposite.

Norman Cousins checked out of the hospital. He got a movie projector and began watching some old Marx Brothers movies and Candid Camera programs. For hours he watched those films, over and over, laughing all the while.

As Norman Cousins watched, he discovered something about himself. Ten minutes of laughter gave him at least two hours of pain free sleep. The more he laughed, the better he felt. His fever subsided and his illness left him. Norman Cousins' physician could not explain what had happened. But Norman Cousins believed his attitude made a great difference.[23]

As the Bible says, "a merry heart doeth good like a medicine."

Watching a humorous video can increase feelings of hopefulness, according to a study in a 2003 issue of the journal *Humor: The International Journal of Humor Research.*[24]

Preliminary research on the therapeutic value of humor and laughter has found evidence that they may reduce the body's response to stress, perhaps by decreasing levels of stress-related hormones. They may also reduce anxiety and improve mood, self-esteem, coping skills, and pain tolerance. They may even affect the body's production of immune system chemicals.

In the *Humor* study, the goal was to study how watching a comedy video affected one's sense of hopefulness. The subjects were 180 undergraduates who were taking a psychology class. All filled out three questionnaires, which tested their sense of humor, how stressful they found college life, and their level of hope. Then each wrote an essay about a stressful event of the past month. Afterwards, half the students watched a 15-minute so-called "neutral" video. Then they filled out the hopefulness questionnaire again.

The researchers found that the average hopefulness scale score went up in both groups after watching videos, but it rose significantly more in the group that watched the humorous video. Watching the humorous video increased hopefulness scores just as much in people who had had many or severe recent stresses as it did in people with less stress.

The researchers concluded that their study supported the idea that experiencing humor can improve hopefulness. This study looked only at students, and the subjects did not get to choose a video they themselves thought was funny.

Still, the study adds to the growing evidence that humor can bolster physical and mental health.

In another study, researchers at the University of Texas followed 2,478 people ages 65 and older for six years. They found that the subjects who scored high on a happiness questionnaire had a much lower risk of stroke than their negative counterparts. The happier people were, the more protective the effect seemed to be.[25]

Do you remember the story of Pollyanna? In a book which first appeared in 1912, Eleanor Porter described the adventures of a little girl who saw the bright side of everything, even when she was mistreated by her stern aunt and struggling for her life following a serious accident.

In some respects Pollyanna was naïve, but she had learned that a positive attitude brightens the one who possesses it. The Apostle Paul said something similar when he wrote from the misery of a prison cell to the church at Philippi. He said to them: "Finally, brothers, whatever is true, whatever is noble, whatever is right, whatever is pure, whatever is lovely, whatever is admirable, if anything is excellent or praiseworthy, think about such things." (Phil. 4: 8).

The Nun Study, for three decades has collected data from the School Sisters of Notre Dame living in Mankato, Minnesota, as well as elsewhere in the Midwest, East and South.[26]

The goal of the Nun Study was to determine the causes and prevention of Alzheimer's disease and other brain diseases, as well as the mental and physical disability associated with old age.

One of the significant findings has been a study of handwritten autobiographies from 180 nuns, who wrote them, on average, at the age of twenty-two. The writings were scored for emotional content and compared with survival rates from the age of 75 to 95. What researchers noticed is that the nuns who wrote with the most positive attitude at a very young age were 2 ½ times more likely to be alive in late life than the sisters who came across with a more negative point of view at a young age.

We get such a positive attitude by developing the habit of looking for the good when we are tempted to look for the bad. What a difference a positive way of thinking can make in life. Rather than look at the negative when things don't go exactly as we would like, it can be helpful to look for the positive, what do we have, what is there to enjoy, how can we make the best of a situation.

I read somewhere about a salesman who was stuck on an elevator between floors. Nobody in the building knew he was there. Fortunately, there was a telephone in the elevator so the salesman called the fire department to report his plight. While he was waiting for the fire department and an elevator service person to free him, rather than complain and stew about his plight, he decided to put the time to use. He got on the telephone. He called each of his accounts in the building, explaining what had happened and taking their orders by phone. By the time he was rescued some two and a half hours later, he had finished all his business in the building.

One of the ways we can handle the stresses of life is by our attitude, our outlook, the way we think. Like the little boy who kept bragging to his father about what a great hitter he was. Finally the father said, "All right, son, show me"

So the little boy got his softball and his bat and they went out in the back yard. The father stood over to the side while the boy tossed the ball up into the air and then swung the bat with all his might. "Strike one," said the little boy after he had missed the ball completely. "Strike two," he said as he missed the ball again. "Strike three," he said as he missed a third time. Then he turned to his father with a determined glow on his face, and said, "Boy, am I a great pitcher!"

Often what matters is not what happens to us, but the way we interpret what happens. The way we think can make a great difference as to whether an event is stressful or not.

Over a century ago the philosopher William James said, "The greatest discovery of my generation is that human beings can alter their lives by altering their attitudes of mind." As you think, so shall you be.

It is not always easy, however, to maintain a positive attitude. As we grow older, for example, food is likely to be less appetizing. Our sense of taste and smell lessen. Being alone may take away the incentive to eat. Money and economics may influence the choice of diet. Some elderly may have a poor mouth condition, thus making it painful to chew food. There is the discomfort of constipation. Persons with high blood pressure or heart problems may have to avoid salt in their diet. Food without salt can be unappetizing. Added together, or even separately, it may be difficult to have a positive attitude when one has to put up with such changes in regard to eating, which is one of the most essential and enjoyable aspects of life.

Many of us think that other people and the events in our lives cause us to feel the way that we do. Thus, we often blame things external to us for feelings of stress and emotional upset. In doing this, however, we neglect an important factor not only in the cause of our distress, but in the management of stress, and that factor is the way we think or "talk to ourselves" about the events in our lives. For example, someone might say to themselves, "I can't bear to be alone." Such thinking may cause the person to be upset. The truth is, however, that no physically healthy person has ever died merely from being alone. Being alone may be uncomfortable, undesirable and frustrating, but you can live with it, and live through it.

Psychologist Albert Ellis discussed the way our thoughts affect our feelings and actions in his book *A Guide to Rational Living* in 1961. Ellis' basic thesis is that emotions have nothing to do with actual events. In between the event and the emotion is what he calls realistic or unrealistic self-talk. It is the self-talk that produces the emotions. Your own thoughts, directed and controlled by you, are what create anxiety, anger or depression.[27]

Suppose, for example, a grandmother bakes a cake from scratch, not from a mix in a box. Her granddaughter stops by after school and grandma slices her a piece of the cake she has just baked from scratch. The granddaughter takes a few bites and then tells her grandmother that she doesn't want any more. The grandmother feels hurt. The grandmother's self-talk might go something like this: "She only ate a small amount of cake. She must not like my cake. I guess I'm getting too old to bake anymore."

It is not the granddaughter or anything that the granddaughter has done which produces the hurt feeling. It is the grandmother's own self-talk, her interpretation of the event which resulted in her feeling hurt.

If the grandmother had talked with her granddaughter, she might have learned that her granddaughter stopped at a convenience store and had a snack before she got to her grandmother's house and therefore wasn't hungry.

Unfortunately, many of us have learned unrealistic beliefs and perfectionist ideas that can cause us to expect too much of ourselves, leading us to behave irrationally and then to feel unnecessarily that we are worthless failures. For example, a person may continually think, "I should be able to win everyone's love and approval," or "I should be competent in everything I do." Such goals are impossible for anyone. Such unrealistic assumptions and self-demands inevitably lead to ineffective and self-defeating behavior and then to the emotional response of self-devaluation. The emotional response of self-devaluation is thus the consequence, not of real-life events, but of an individual's faulty expectations, interpretations, and self-demands.

Another illustration is an example used by psychologist Dr. Mark McMinn. He asked a client: "How did your week go." The client responded: "It wasn't very good. I felt all right until last night when my husband and I started fighting again. He came home after work and didn't say a word. He just sat down in front of the TV and watched the news. I told him if he wanted a servant, he could hire one. Then he got mad and told me I always nag him. I can't stand living with him any more. He should appreciate all the work I do, but instead he just expects me to do more."[28]

The client's response shows several inaccuracies in her thinking. First she overgeneralized how badly her week went. Her week went well until the night before her appointment with Dr. McMinn. She argued with her husband, but she concluded that her entire week did not go well. Then she jumped to the conclusion that her husband wanted a servant. Next, she used what is called "all-or-none thinking" in concluding she couldn't stand living with him anymore. He might be a challenge to live with, but apparently she had been living with him for a number of years, so she could do it. It would have been nice for her husband to appreciate all her work, but "should" indicates a moral obligation to do so. Finally, she used mind reading to assume he didn't appreciate her and that he expected more from her.

The "Relaxation and Stress Reduction Workbook" suggests five steps to changing the way you think:[29]

1. Write down the facts of the event as they occurred at the time you were upset. Be certain to include only the objective facts.
2. Write down your self-talk about the event. That is sometimes difficult to do because we're not always aware of what we're thinking.
3. Focus on your emotional response. Make a one or two word label such as angry, depressed, felt worthless, afraid, etc.
4. Dispute and change the irrational self-talk.

As an illustration, let's use the example of the grandmother. Her irrational thought was: "She doesn't like my cake. I guess I'm getting too old to bake anymore."

Is there any rational support for the idea that her granddaughter doesn't like her cake? No. The grandmother never asked her granddaughter if she liked or didn't like the cake. The grandmother assumed her granddaughter didn't like the cake because she didn't eat all of the piece she was given. That the granddaughter did eat more than one bite would indicate that she did like the cake otherwise she would have only eaten one piece.

Is there any rational support for the idea that she's getting too old to bake a cake? Nothing in the example is mentioned about the health of the grandmother, but let's assume that her hands aren't arthritic enough to prevent her from mixing the cake, nor is her eyesight a problem that would make it too difficult for her to read the recipe or seeing the ingredients or setting the oven for the correct temperature and time.

Does any evidence exist for the truth of this statement or idea? No, the grandmother's thought is due to her self-talk, how she interpreted the event.

5.Substitute alternative self-talk.

An example might be, "My granddaughter has eaten only a little of my cake. I'll ask her why she only ate a little. I'll ask her if she likes it. If she doesn't like it, I'll ask her what she doesn't like about it. I made a yellow cake. Maybe she prefers chocolate. Maybe she's not hungry. If she isn't hungry, I'll ask her if she would like to finish the cake later, or if she would like to take the cake home."

Or, the grandmother could say to herself, "Just because my granddaughter's not eating all of the cake I gave her, doesn't mean I'm a bad cook."

The authors suggest we realize this:

a. There's nothing special about me. I can accept painful situations when they emerge.

b. Facing the problem is more adaptive than resenting it or running away from it.

c. I feel what I think. If I don't think negative thoughts, I won't feel stressful emotions. At worst I will experience inconvenience, regret and annoyance, not anxiety, depression and rage.

It can be helpful for us to recognize some of the ways we think that can lead to irrational ideas. In his book, *Feeling Good*, psychologist David Burns identifies ten of what he defines as cognitive distortions:[30]

1. 1. All or none thinking. The tendency to see things in absolute, black and white categories. For example, either I am perfectly competent in everything I do or else I'm a complete failure.

2. Overgeneralization. Assuming bad events will happen over and over or that things are always a certain way. For example, "The dogs will always choose my lawn for relief."

3. Mental filter. Focusing on the negative parts of life and filtering out the positive. For example, "My life's awful because I'm in pain from my arthritis" (overlooking a loving spouse, a nice house, financial freedom).
4. Disqualifying the positive. Discounting success or compliments. For example, "I don't really look good in this dress. People are just trying to be nice."
5. Jumping to conclusions. Mind reading. "Everybody is noticing that I spilled something on my tie." Or, fortune telling. "I'm going to fail my physical."
6. Magnification and minimization. Magnifying errors and minimizing successes. For example, "I'm terrible since I just yelled at my grandchildren."
7. Emotional reasoning. Basing thoughts on feelings. For example, "I feel like a loser, therefore I am a loser."
8. Should statements. Setting arbitrary requirements without considering consequences. For example,"I should be friendly with everyone I meet."
9. Labeling and mislabeling. Categorizing people based on limited exposure. For example, "The person in that blue car is really selfish."
10. Personalization. Accepting the blame for some negative events involving others. For example, "My family would be well-adjusted if it weren't for me."

The idea is we need to beware of allowing negative thinking from dominating our way of looking at life. That is not to say we should ignore the negative. If we focus only on the positive then we may overlook or deny things about ourselves that need changing. We can be tempted to overlook the sins that we commit. God gave us life to enjoy and God offers us love and forgiveness. There are some, however, who look only at the negative, who believe that they are terrible sinners and fail to see the forgiveness God offers. That negative outlook carries over into all of life. For example, psychologist Mark McMinn tells of a woman who described her husband as insensitive. She said "he didn't do a thing for our last anniversary." Dr.

McMinn discovered that her husband had sent flowers and taken her out for dinner, but had not gone out of town with her as she had wished. She filtered out her husband's efforts and focused on her disappointment, resulting in anger toward her husband.[31]

According to authors Christopher Peterson and Lisa M. Bossio in their book, *Health and Optimism*, "well-conducted studies support the conclusion that people with optimistic beliefs experience better health than those with pessimistic beliefs." For example, they cite a study conducted by Leslie Kamen and colleagues at the University of Pennsylvania. They were interested in the relationship between optimism and its effect on the body's immune system, which reflects the ability of one's body to fight off foreign cells.

Kamen and her colleagues conducted interviews with 47 mostly healthy adults between the ages of 62 and 87, focusing on major life events, problems, hassles and worries.

A blood sample was drawn from each of the subjects at about the time the interviews were conducted and was analyzed to give an overall estimate of immunocompetence; specifically the ratio between T4 (helper) cells and T8 (suppressor) cells. The helper and suppressor labels reflect the roles that these cells play in turning on and off the body's fight against infection. So, a high ratio meant a robust immune system, with relatively more helper cells and relatively fewer suppressor cells; a low ratio meant a weak immune system, with relatively fewer helper cells and relatively more suppressor cells.

The study showed, as did other studies, that optimistic thinking is associated with good health, and pessimistic thinking is associated with poor health.[32]

Several years ago the American Medical Association carried a story in their Journal that helps underscore the importance of a positive outlook. Jane A. McAdams told the story of her mother in "The Gift of Hope."[33]

"Perhaps the fact that the Great Depression hit just as she and my father were starting to raise their family had something to do with it. But no matter. Already as a small child I was aware that in the handling of money my mother was more than simply thrifty; she was downright frugal. Extravagances and luxuries did not exist. She never bought anything, for example, unless she was certain she would use it. And not only use it, but use it to the best purpose and for the longest time possible. The one exception was a new, frilly, never-worn nightgown that she kept in the bottom drawer of the bureau. But even that had its purpose: 'In case I should ever have to go into the hospital,' she said. And so the gown lay there for years, carefully protected in tissue."

"But one day, many years later, the time came. The nightgown with its now yellowed lace and limp ruffles was taken from its wrappings and my mother entered the hospital, seeking an answer to the mysterious fevers, sweats and malaise that had plagued her since autumn. The time was early January, in the deepest, darkest days of a cold winter, just before her 69th birthday."

"We did not have long to wait for an answer. It came with the finality of a period at the end of a long sentence of strung-out clauses: lymphoma, disseminated, progressive. Privately, her physician told me he was sorry, there were probably only two or three weeks left, certainly less than even a month."

"For days, I agonized over what to do with this information that only I had been given. Should I tell the family? Should I tell my mother? Did she already know? If not, did she suspect? Surely she must after so many months of malaise. Could I talk about it with her? Could I give her any hope? Could I keep up any hope she might have? Was there in fact any hope?"

"Some relief came when I realized her birthday was approaching. The nightgown she had saved all those years she was now wearing, but it was hopelessly old-fashioned. I resolved to lift her spirits by buying her the handsomest and most expensive new nightgown and robe I could find. If I could not hope to cure her disease, at least I could make her feel like the prettiest patient in the entire hospital."

"For a long time after she unwrapped her birthday present, given early so she would have longer to enjoy it, my mother said nothing. Finally she spoke. 'Would you mind,' she said, pointing to the wrapping and gown spread across the bed, 'returning it to the store? I don't really want it.' Then she picked up the newspaper and turned to the last page. 'This is what I really want, if you could get that,' she said. What she pointed to was a display advertisement of expensive designer summer purses."

"My reaction was one of disbelief. Why would my mother, so careful about extravagances, want an expensive summer purse in January, one that she could not possibly use until June? She would not even live until spring, let alone summer. Almost immediately, I was ashamed and appalled at my clumsiness, ignorance, insensitivity, call it what you will. With a shock, I realized she was finally asking me what I thought about her illness. She was asking me how long she would live. She was, in fact, asking me if I thought she would live even six months. And she was telling me that if I showed I believed she would live until then, then she would do it. She would not let that expensive purse go unused. So I returned gown and robe and bought the summer purse."

"That was many years ago. The purse is worn out, as are at least half a dozen others. And next week my mother flies to California to celebrate her 83rd birthday. My gift to her? The most expensive designer purse I could find. She'll use it well."

Our attitude affects our health and our overall happiness with life.

In the July/August 2002 edition of *Modern Maturity* magazine, author Priscilla Grant reports on a survey conducted by AARP Modern Maturity on enjoyment in life. Nearly 30 percent of Americans 55 and over say that the older they get, the more fun they have. The survey of more than 2,000 adults, conducted by RoperASW in July 2001 and January 2002, also found that another 3 in 10 report having the same amount of fun as earlier in life, while 34 percent say growing older means that they're having less fun. The results also show that members of the more-fun group aren't just lucky; they share attitudes and habits that everyone can learn. Here's what makes them different:

1. They make fun a priority. Finding enjoyment in life takes time, and those most successful at it dedicate an average of 24 hours per week to "just having fun."
2. They think of themselves as fun people.
3. They love to learn. Two-thirds of the fun-loving group say they're "always trying to learn new things."[34]

Note how thinking positively is related to having fun. It is never too late to think positively. As we grow older it might be tempting to think negatively. Since my life is nearing an end, why bother about anything. The physical problems due to arthritis, failing vision, hearing loss, or other physical problems can cause pain, discomfort, difficulty in movement, and therefore difficulty in enjoying life. Yet I've known men and women in their nineties who enjoy life even though physical problems may make it difficult for them to do all they would like. Their positive attitude or positive way of thinking enables them to look for what they can enjoy instead of dwelling on what they can't enjoy. They have learned to live with the problems they encounter and find ways to enjoy life in spite of them.

One positive way of looking at the problems associated with growing old is found in the following article that has appeared on the Internet and in Dear Abby. "You Know You're Getting Older When…"

You know all the answers but nobody asks you any questions.

You get winded playing checkers.

You order Geritol on the rocks.

You sink your teeth into a thick steak and they stay there.

You stop to think and sometimes forget to start again.

You don't need an alarm clock to get up with the chickens.

Your pacemaker opens the garage door whenever a cute gal goes by.

The only whistles you get are from a tea kettle.

You finally get it all together, but can't remember where you put it.

You pray for a good prune-juice harvest.

Your little black book contains only names ending with M.D.

You look forward to a dull evening.

Your knees buckle, but your belt won't.

I have a 99 year-old church member who fell about 18 months ago outside his house. Fortunately he fell on the grass and didn't break anything, but he did experience back pain for a long time. Whether from sitting in a chair most of the time due to his back pain, or whether due to his age, his legs are not as strong as they were. He did have polio when he was young, so that may also account for the weakness in his leg muscles. He is reluctant to walk very far due to the weakness in his legs. He is afraid he will fall and break something. So, he spends most of his time sitting in a chair. But, he doesn't feel sorry for himself. Instead, he gets enjoyment from reading, especially reading the Bible and other religious material. His wife is still living, so he also enjoys their companionship and the visits of others. His positive attitude helps him to enjoy life at age 99!

Perhaps most of his positive outlook, and the positive outlook of others at any age is due to his strong religious faith. Belief in God and prayer are an important part of this man's life, and that of his wife.

Christian faith provides a positive outlook. I know there are Christian ministers, preachers, or whatever, who focus on sin, hell and damnation, but while sin can keep us from experiencing God's love, the emphasis in the Bible is on the positive aspects of God: God's love and forgiveness. After all, God created the world and pronounced the creation as good. God created man and woman in the divine image. God established the commandments so that we could live in peace with one another and in a loving relationship with God. God sent the prophets to warn the people when they were going astray. God sent Jesus Christ to let us know how much God loves us, and allowed Jesus to be crucified so that we could experience God's forgiveness and receive eternal life. Those are all positive attitudes by God toward us. That same love of God can allow us to experience God's love in our lives. Experiencing God's love can enable us to have a positive outlook on life.

CHAPTER FIVE
STRESS

"Time spent on the knees in prayer will do more to remedy heart strain and nerve worry than anything else."George David Stewart

One of the medical examinations that many men and women, middle-aged and older, go through is the so-called "stress test." Many of you may have participated in that test in which you walk or run on a treadmill, and the way your heart deals with that test, determines the doctor's assessment of your physical condition. It is always a happy moment when you can say, "I passed the stress test."

That is but one example of what we mean by the word stress, for stress is not simply a testing of the human heart, but stress is something we all encounter everyday of our lives, affecting us physically, emotionally, mentally and spiritually.

In the Biblical story of Jacob and Esau, Jacob cheated his brother Esau out of their father's inheritance and blessing. As a result, Jacob left home and fled to a safe place because his brother had threatened to kill him.

Jacob was under stress and Jacob's reaction was the way God created us to deal with stress. Under a stressful situation our body undergoes numerous physiological changes to prepare us for either flight or fight from the perceived danger. Jacob chose to run away. Once he was away from the danger, Jacob's body would return to a more relaxed state.

The problem with life today, however, is that we cannot always fight or run away. If you're driving along at what you feel is a reasonable speed and cars seem to be backed up behind you, and some are honking at you to go faster, you may feel like yelling back at the drivers, but you hold back because you have been taught that such a reaction is socially inappropriate. Yet, your body still enters into a state of stress preparedness despite your seemingly outward calm. Messages are transmitted throughout the neuroendocrine system which cause significant changes in your biochemistry. Your blood pressure increases, your pupils dilate, blood flows to the muscles of your arms and legs, and adrenalin is pumped into your system. Your body is ready for fight or flight.

When you have taken action by fighting or fleeing, your neurophysiological stress response subsides and your body returns to a state of relaxation. Today, however, people find it more difficult to relax. The stress response continues. Research has shown that when the stress response is prolonged the biochemical changes associated with stress become detrimental to health, resulting in high blood pressure, strokes, heart attacks, diabetes and strain on interpersonal relationships.

The word stress has a long history and is possibly derived from the Latin "stringere", to draw tight. Many people who feel they are under stress talk about feeling tense or tight.

The word is often used in engineering in which stress is thought of as a constraining force acting on an object. One might speak of the stress on a wall or against the piling of a bridge.

However, in recent years, the definition of stress most thought of arose from the work of Dr. Hans Selye, an endocrinologist at Canada's McGill University. His research on the adrenal glands and their relationship with the pituitary gland and other physiological processes laid the groundwork for a great deal of later research on stress.

Selye's use of the term "stress" was significant in that he reversed the prevailing usage. Instead of viewing stress as an agent or force, he regarded stress as the result or response produced within an organism by the presence of some other agent or force.

Selye defines stress as "the nonspecific response of the body to any demand made upon it." He goes on to say that any demand made upon the body is specific. For example, when exposed to cold, we shiver to produce more heat, and the blood vessels in our skin contract to diminish the loss of heat from body surfaces. When exposed to heat, we sweat because of the evaporation or perspiration from the surface of the skin. It has a cooling effect. Cold or heat increases the demand for readjustment. The cold or heat is specific, but the demand is non-specific; it requires adaptation to a problem irrespective of what that problem might be.[35]

It is important to point out that it is immaterial whether the situation or demand we face is pleasant or unpleasant; all that counts is the demand for readjustment or adaptation.

The popular notion of stress seems to have an air of negativity, but a lot of stress is positive. Marriage is often thought to be positive, but it is still stressful. You might be madly in love with someone, but it still requires some adjustment to being with that person. A vacation is thought of as something positive, but a vacation is still stressful. It requires an adjustment to new situations, a new time schedule, etc. Retirement is often viewed as something to look forward to, but retirement can also be stressful. It may mean a readjustment of income, expenditures, time schedules, even readjustment to a spouse. There are many activities we think of as positive, but they are still stressful.

Stress can be beneficial. Although the pressures of life can make us feel uncomfortable, it is doubtful if anyone ever achieved anything worthwhile in life without stress.

The Apostle Paul underwent a lot of stressful situations- shipwrecked, adrift at sea, danger in the city, danger in the wilderness and he complained of a constant thorn in his side.

However, he acknowledged that his sufferings were part of a process of spiritual discipline that gave him inward strength, that made him aware of the grace of God and the power of Christ.

The Gospel itself is a call for us to enter into a stressful situation. The message of Jesus, "Repent for the kingdom of heaven is at hand," is a stressful message because it confronts us with the demand for a change. "Repent" means "turn around". Give up your sinful ways and follow the righteousness of God. That's a demand for change on our part that can be very stressful, yet also very beneficial, even life-saving.

There are many sources of stress. Some may be physical. Some examples might be a speeding car heading toward you, a blizzard or hurricane, a broken washing machine, a traffic jam, or a health problem, such as loss of vision or hearing.

The source of stress may be social, such as a critical spouse, an annoying neighbor, or an appointment to a church committee.

Another source can be psychological, stemming from inner drives and demands. An example might be bottling up resentment toward someone who has hurt you.

It is also important to realize that what may be stressful to me may not be stressful to you, and vice versa. I like to walk. I enjoy being out in nature, the fresh air and the sunshine. I feel better after a nice long walk. To me, walking helps to alleviate stress. To someone else, walking may be difficult to do because of arthritis. They may not enjoy being outdoors at all. To someone else, then, walking is stressful.

As Dr. Selye says, "Our aim shouldn't be to completely avoid stress, which at any rate would be impossible, but to learn how to recognize our typical response to stress and then to try to modulate our lives in accordance with it."[36]

Is there more stress as one ages? At first glance we might be tempted to say, yes. As I think of the physical changes that one must adjust to, the loss of a spouse, often the move to a different home, it might appear there are more stresses. And yet throughout life we encounter changes and must adjust. It may be more of an individual matter. Some people have physical problems in their twenties and thirties and must adjust. Others may not have any problems until in their seventies or eighties. Some people experience the death of a spouse early on in life. Certainly most of us experience the death of parents before we're in our sixties. Some people experience other losses throughout their lives: job loss, divorce, etc. And many people move around the country throughout their lives. Throughout our lives we are making adjustments to the changes in our lives. Some seem to handle such changes better than others.

When I was fourteen we went on a family trip. My parents liked to travel in the Spring during school vacation. My father's job kept him busy during the summer, so an Easter or Spring vacation was ideal. We could get away from the cold and snow of living in Syracuse, New York, and travel to a warmer climate. One year we went to Florida, another year to Virginia, and this particular year, 1958, we went to visit some friends of my father's in Kansas and then on to Paris, Texas to visit my father's brother and family. We took a southern route on our way home, traveling south to visit San Antonio and then over to visit New Orleans. It was on our way to New Orleans that we were in an accident. It was only 9:00 a.m. but it was raining. It was a four lane highway, but a car came across the median and hit us head-on. That car proceeded to go off the road and down an embankment. The driver was drunk. My sister and I were in the back seat. We were both asleep so when the accident happened we were relaxed and were not hurt even though we were thrown against the front seats and onto the floor. My father hurt his chest as he hit the steering wheel, but there was nothing serious. My mother, however, had the most impact and her left knee was crushed from the impact. She was taken by ambulance to a small hospital nearby and then transferred to a hospital in New Orleans. She remained in the hospital for several weeks. She was in a body cast for months after that and then had to wear a brace on her leg to support it ever since. The brace on her leg was difficult enough, but worse has been the brace on her mind. She is now in her late 80's and has never been able to let go of the accident from her mind. She constantly feels sorry for herself. Over the years I have tried to encourage her to see a doctor about an artificial knee. Since 1958 medicine has made progress in so many areas that I'm sure something could have been done to help her, but she steadfastly refuses to see a doctor.

On the other hand, her grandmother, my great-grandmother, had a completely opposite attitude and outlook. She lived independently until about age 90 when she fell and broke her hip. She was put in a nursing home. At age 92 she had part of one leg amputated due to poor circulation. She was confined to a bed most of the day, but her attitude was extremely positive. She wasn't going to let any of the changes she experienced in life get her down!

As you can tell, our attitude toward what happens to us can make a great difference as to whether what happens is perceived as stressful.

While our attitude toward the changes in life can make a difference, there is evidence that too much change within a given time period can also determine the effects of stress.

Thomas H. Holmes and Richard H. Rahe of the University of Washington School of Medicine developed a method of correlating life event changes with illness and tested their hypothesis with more than 5,000 patients. They observed with many patients that life events tended to cluster or increase in intensity prior to the onset of an illness.[37]

From their research, Holmes and Rahe devised a Social Readjustment Rating Scale, which assigned numerical values to events that are typical in people's lives. These events included divorce, marriage, death in the family, change of job, pregnancy, large mortgage, and so on. Many of these events are ones that are considered to be occasions for joy and celebration, but as was mentioned previously, positive life events can produce the same neurophysiological and biochemical reactions as negative events.

To use the Holmes and Rahe scale, a person checks off any of the listed events which have happened within the last year and then totals up the score by adding up the assigned values of these events. Holmes and Rahe determined that a score of 150 based on the past year's events and changes would make one's chances of developing an illness or a health change roughly 50-50. If someone were to score over 300 points within a year, their chances of experiencing a health change go up to almost ninety percent. As the score increases, the probability that the health change will be a serious illness also increases.

Rahe's work with 2,500 officers and enlisted men aboard three Navy cruisers illustrates the validity of the Social Readjustment Scale. Of the 2,500 men, the thirty percent with the highest life-change scores developed almost ninety percent more first illnesses during the first month of the cruise than the thirty percent with the lowest scores. During the rest of the cruise, the high scoring thirty percent consistently developed more illnesses than the lower thirty percent. Too much change within a short period of time can result in health problems.

Another factor in determining the effect of stress is personality and temperament. One of the classic studies in the area of personality and stress was that done by Drs. Meyer Friedman and Ray Rosenman in the formulation of Type A and Type B personality. In their study of the relationship of stress to coronary heart attacks they discovered that men having Type A personalities experienced three times the incidence of new coronary heart disease as compared to their Type B counterparts.

Friedman and Rosenman suggest that the Type A person is characterized by an excessive competitive drive and a chronic, continual sense of time urgency, accompanied by the feeling of always having to meet deadlines. Along with these characteristics, Type A individuals show an easily aroused hostility. The hostility is usually well rationalized and kept under control and externalized only during brief and random outbursts at unexpected times. The Type A person is also very impatient. This type of "hurry sickness," as Friedman and

Rosenman call it, pervades the whole life style of the Type A individual and extends even into leisure time. The individual always feels the need to be accomplishing something so as not to waste a single minute of precious time.

When someone is continuously engaged in a struggle to overcome time, accumulate income and beat competitors on both business and social levels, great stress is the result.

The Type B person, on the other hand, does not have a frantic sense of time urgency, except when it is truly warranted. Type B individuals frequently allow themselves time for quiet contemplation and meditation. [38]

An example from the Bible is the story of Mary and Martha, two sisters, and a time when Jesus was a guest in their house. Martha was busy preparing food while Mary sat with Jesus to listen to what he said. Martha was perturbed because Mary didn't lift a finger to help her. Martha seems to be a Type A personality, while Mary seems to be a Type B personality. "Martha, Martha," Jesus said, "you are worried and upset about many things, but only one thing is needed. Mary has chosen what is better…" (Lk. 10: 38-42)

Our temperament can contribute to stress.

And so can our values. If we think we have to have the newest car, the latest fashion, the best golf clubs, we will put ourselves under stress to acquire those items. Our desires may lead to spending beyond our means to acquire what we want.

I like the story of a lone fisherman sitting on a beach. His fishing pole was planted in the sand. Along came a businessman on vacation. "Why don't you have two poles so you can catch more fish?" the businessman asked. "Then what would I do?" asked the fisherman. "Then you could take the extra money, buy a boat, get nets and a crew, and catch even more fish." "Then what would I do?" asked the fisherman. "Then," said the businessman," you could move up to a fleet of large ships, go wholesale, and become very rich." "Then what would I do?" asked the fisherman. "Then you could do whatever you want!" shouted the businessman. And the fisherman replied, "I am."

The more we want, the more stress we create for ourselves.

The same is true with the demands we put upon ourselves. That can create stress when we think we "should" do something or "ought" to do something. The schedules, too, we set for ourselves can leave us feeling overwhelmed and worn-out when we find we have difficulty keeping up with everything we want to do or think we should do.

We also create stress for ourselves if we have a certain lifestyle. I'm thinking of the person who can't say no to the requests of others, or the person who is a perfectionist, making unrealistic demands of themselves, or the procrastinator, someone who is always late or puts off important matters can create undo stress for themselves.

According to many experts in the field of stress, "it seems quite clear that stress accelerates the aging process. More importantly, there is growing evidence that stress reduction strategies may be effective in slowing down the progression of many of the manifestations of aging. In his later years, in attempting to explain the significance of his research in books for the public, Selye redefined stress as 'the rate of wear and tear on the body'- which is actually a pretty good description of biologic aging."[39]

According to Dr. Paul Rosch in *The Newsletter of The American Institute of Stress*, "Numerous factors can influence different aspects of the aging process. However, the preponderance of evidence suggests that almost all the common manifestations of old age, including atherosclerosis, gray hair, cataracts, wrinkled skin, malignancies, etc., are caused by the cumulative effects of oxidative stress."[40]

Oxidative stress is due to the damage done by oxygen free radicals. You can't see them. You can't feel them, but all our organs and tissues are under constant attack by these biological outlaws known as free-radicals.

When we breathe oxygen into our lungs, it attaches to hemoglobin, and is transported through the blood stream to cells throughout the body. Cells take up the oxygen in exchange for their waste products, which are then carried back to the lungs, and eliminated in the form of carbon dioxide. During this process, hundreds of thousands of changes take place as oxygen enters into various metabolic activities.

Some of the resultant oxygen molecules lack one or more electrons in their outer shell, and thus are termed free radicals. These are highly charged and extremely unstable, and try to find a way to correct the instability. As a result, they race around the body, latching on to and destroying cell membranes, and oxidizing cholesterol, DNA, and anything else they can find.

Keep in mind that there are both unstable and stable oxygen molecules in your body. The stable oxygen is essential to sustain life. Even some unstable oxygen molecules (free radicals) are good in that they enable you to fight inflammation, kill bacteria, and control the tone of your smooth muscles, which regulate the working of your internal organs and blood vessels.

Exercise, eating, stress, or anything that increases metabolism, promotes oxygen free radical production. Conversely, the key to coping with free radicals is balance. Antioxidants are substances which help prevent the devastation and sabotage of free radicals, by supplying electrons that make them stable. Under normal circumstances, natural antioxidants produced by the body block free radical damage, but our ability to manufacture these declines as we grow older. Strategies to prevent this include reducing caloric intake, an appropriate exercise regimen, antioxidant supplementation, and trying to avoid stress.

A recent study from the University of California at San Francisco found that chronic stress appears to accelerate the aging process by shortening the life span of cells. Researchers learned that constant stress causes the telomeres, tiny caps on cells' chromosomes that govern cell regeneration, to get smaller. When a cell's telomeres get too short, the cell stops dividing and eventually dies. [41]

Researchers discovered that the telomeres of women with chronically ill children were much shorter than those of women the same age who weren't caregivers. The cells of people under a lot of stress aged the equivalent of nine to seventeen years more than the cells of people under little stress.

What's more, it wasn't just the stress itself, it was also how stressed people *thought* they were.

We need to admit that stress is working on us all the time, some of it positively and some negatively. We especially need to find ways to deal constructively with those things that affect us negatively, but it is important for anyone to find ways to handle the stresses of life. How much stress we face in a lifetime, and how well we cope with it, is perhaps one of the most significant factors in how well we age.

According to Hans Selye, when faced with stress, people have four main ways of coping: they can remove the stressor or source of stress; they can refuse to allow neutral situations to become stressful; they can deal directly with the source of stress; or they can find ways of relaxing to ease the stress.[42]

As an example of how these methods might work, let us use the metaphor of a mountain, based on Jesus' words: "Truly, I say to you, whoever says to this mountain, 'Be taken up and cast into the sea,' and does not doubt in his heart, but believes that what he says will come to pass, it will be done for him. Therefore I tell you, whatever you ask in prayer, believe that you receive it, and you will." (Mark 12: 23-24)

When a mountain looms in our pathway, one way to deal with it is to remove it by avoiding it. Take a detour and go around it. I have done that. On a trip one time I didn't think the car I was driving could make it over a certain mountain, so rather than try it and worry about it, I took a detour that went around the mountain.

Likewise, when a situation in life looms as large as a mountain in front of us, stop and think if we can avoid the situation. Or, can we change our environment to eliminate stress producing events- changing homes, changing neighborhoods, changing involvement with people who might be the source of our stress.

There are many other examples. Rush hour traffic is stressful to many. We can avoid such stress by not driving during a time when a lot of traffic will be on the roads.

The second possibility is to refuse to allow the mountain to become a cause of stress. It is only a mountain we can tell ourselves.

Many neutral experiences in our lives are turned into stressful experiences when they needn't be. The weather can be a neutral area which can become a source of stress if we let it. A rainy day may be looked at by some as a positive event if rain is needed for lawns, gardens and reservoirs. To someone planning to go boating or on a picnic, the rain may seem aggravating. Most of the time, we tend to look at rain as something that just happens. Its part of life.

When we refuse to allow something to become stressful, we're basically changing our attitude about events, people or circumstances. It may also mean changing beliefs, assumptions or ineffective ways of thinking which make us vulnerable to stress. As I mentioned before, our thoughts and perceptions play a significant role in determining our inner emotional responses.

What do you think about? When a stressful experience occurs do you tend to think in negative terms that can lead to negative emotional reactions? We all talk to ourselves and our self-talk itself can be a producer of stress.

For example, when faced with a health problem, do you say to yourself, "I'll never be able to get through this..." "How can I take care of myself?" Positive statements of self-talk would be, "I'll take one step at a time..." What a difference positive self-talk can make in our lives. It's not self-talk that's unrealistic, but based on what you can do or what you have got going for you.

In Romans 12:2, Paul speaks to this when he says, "And do not be conformed to this world, but be transformed by the renewing of your mind."

The third technique is to deal directly with the mountain. If we're hiking and the mountain is in our path, this may mean mapping out the best route for ascending it and even taking lessons in mountain climbing, if necessary. The important thing is being able to look at a situation, size up the situation, and then plan a course of action that leads to a solution. That is perhaps what Jesus meant when he talked about conquering a mountain.

And the fourth way of coping with stress is to find ways of relaxing to ease the effects of stress. When you can't go around the mountain, nor remove it; when a situation becomes stressful rather than remaining neutral; when you can't find any solution, then you have to find a way to reduce the stress. There are a number of methods that have been proven to be effective in managing stress. These can be divided into three areas: physical, mental and spiritual.

Exercise is one of the simplest and most effective means of stress reduction. Vigorous physical exertion is a natural outlet for the body when it is in the fight or flight state of arousal. After exercise the body returns to its normal equilibrium.

Exercise releases tension. Exercise also acts to reduce stress and illness by cardiovascular and respiratory conditioning and the maintenance of muscle tone. Fitness also encourages a positive self-image.

It is best to talk with your doctor about what type of exercise would be best for you. Some of the best exercises are running, jogging, brisk walking, swimming and bicycling. Even just walking can help. Consult first with your physician.

Nutrition can also help alleviate stress. When you are under stress your need for all nutrients increases, especially the need for calcium and the B vitamins. For example, a diet low in milk and leafy vegetables can lead to a calcium deficiency. Then, when your tense muscles produce a high level of lactic acid, there isn't enough calcium to counteract it. You feel more fatigued, anxious and irritable.

There has been so much in the media about the relationship between cholesterol and coronary heart problems that not much is necessary to say. There are many books on the market with advice on diets, nutrition, etc.

An important consideration concerning eating is to avoid stress while eating. A friend who introduced me to the subject of stress relates how he noticed he would feel uncomfortable about twenty minutes after eating dinner. He thought his wife was a good cook, so he didn't think it was her cooking, nor the food he ate as he tried to watch his diet. The only thing he noticed was he had started to watch the evening news while he was eating. The news was mostly about war and violence throughout the world. Instead of watching the news he watched situation comedies while eating and his digestive problems disappeared!

Under the category of mental, it can be helpful to get our minds off stressful events, thus allowing our body to stop pumping adrenalin into our system. If we can have one or two activities which can captivate our minds and energies, we can detach ourselves temporarily from the parts of our life that are creating stress. Hobbies are a good method of detachment. These might include woodworking, refinishing furniture, rebuilding cars, collecting stamps, knitting, gardening, reading, etc. The list could go on.

Other activities which could serve the same purpose might include poetry writing, painting, ceramics, flower arranging, drama, playing a musical instrument, square dancing, visiting museums, art galleries, lectures, attending plays, concerts or going to the movies. All of these can take one away from the stressor and alleviate the stress response.

For thousands of years members of all cultures have sought inner peace and harmony through one form or another of spiritual meditation.

There are a number of forms of meditation. In the next chapter I will focus on prayer and Christian meditation, but

I will mention here a number of secular forms of meditation that have been proven to be helpful in stress reduction.

Transcendental Meditation involves the repetition of a word, or mantra, for fifteen to twenty minutes each day, while the meditator sits in a comfortable position with eyes closed. TM became popular in the United States a number of years ago from Far Eastern cultures. In Eastern cultures, in Hinduism and Buddhism, one of the purposes of saying a mantra is to attain the ultimate goal of transcendental awareness. Attempts to describe this state defy definition. After long practice of a meditative discipline, through which the practitioner has achieved a total stilling of the mind and total loss of self, he or she becomes open to a whole new order of reality. At this point, practitioners say, he or she is pervaded with the overwhelming and joyous knowledge that all of existence is a unity and that he or she is one with it.

Autogenic training is a form of meditation developed by the German psychiatrist, Johannes H. Schultz in 1932. He devised exercises to teach people deep physiological and mental relaxation. Through a series of mental exercises the participant is able to feel the sensation of warmth or heaviness in his body, which is a form of physical relaxation.

Visualization is the summoning and holding of certain images in the mind for examination and exploration. It involves a detached state of mind, also common to autogenic training and transcendental meditation.

In its simplest form, visualization is a form of day dreaming. Thus, the process of using imagery to relax is simple. Assume a comfortable position, close your eyes and create an image in your mind of some place where you feel truly relaxed, calm and happy.

It can also be helpful to visualize the stress in your life. Try to be aware of what is causing you stress. It may be a troubling situation. Then start to visualize yourself coping calmly and effectively with the stressful situation. As you do this in the scene itself, visualize yourself relaxing emotionally and physically. Start to feel yourself becoming calm and comfortable.

One of the most striking uses of visualization has been its application to healing. One of the early pioneers in this area was Dr. Carl Simonton, a radiation oncologist in Fort Worth, Texas. Since stress has been shown to depress immune system activity, it seemed logical to Dr. Simonton that stress reduction and the mobilization of positive psychological attitudes may be one means of restoring the body's ability to overcome invasive viruses and destroy mutant cells.[43]

By the middle of 1971, Dr. Simonton had evolved a method of treatment using visualization. His first patient was a sixty-year-old man with widespread throat cancer, who had lost a great deal of weight and could not eat. It was decided to use a combined treatment involving both meditation techniques and radiation. For the treatment, the patient was instructed to relax deeply three times a day while mentally picturing his disease and the treatment. Visualization was central to the process and involved picturing the destruction of cancer cells by the body's white cells and disposal of it through the circulatory system. After three months of treatment, the patient recovered completely, and a year and a half later had no sign of throat cancer.

Simonton, and later, Dr. Bernie Siegel, have had considerable success with visualization in the reduction of cancer in a number of patients.

Stress is a part of life. We have never been promised a stress-free, problem-free life. We can allow stress to control us, or we can learn to respond in a healthy manner to stressful situations. This may mean changing ourselves rather than by looking for a change to take place on the outside.

The choice is ours!

CHAPTER SIX
GOD LOVES KNEE MAIL

"Prayer is like a computer - you get out of it what you put into it."

How did Jesus cope with the stresses in his life? One of the most important methods he used was prayer. Matthew relates that after the feeding of the five thousand, "Immediately Jesus made the disciples get into the boat and go on ahead of him to the other side, while he dismissed the crowd. After he had dismissed them, he went up on a mountainside by himself to pray." (Mt. 14:22-23)

Another time Jesus called his disciples to go with him to the opposite side of the lake. On the way over he fell asleep in the back of the boat. Jesus awoke in the midst of a storm. The disciples appeared to be prepared for "fight or flight." Their adrenalin was up to prepare them for the emergency. But what was Jesus' response to the stressful situation? Mark says that "And he awoke and rebuked the wind, and said to the sea, 'Peace! Be still!' And the wind ceased, and there was a great calm. He said to them, 'Why are you afraid? Have you no faith?'"

Jesus knew that to handle stress you need faith. You can handle stress successfully if you believe that God is present to help you.

These passages also show us that Jesus took care of himself. He had faith in God, but he also took time to care for the health needs of his body, mind and spirit. He took time to rest from his work. He was not like the Type A personality, always striving for more success. Jesus was more like the Type B personality. He took time from his work to enjoy life. He took time to visit with children, even when his disciples grew impatient and wanted him to continue on. He took time to admire the lillies of the field. He spent time on the lake, perhaps even fishing with his disciples. He made sure he took time for meditation and prayer, a very important and helpful way to reduce the effects of stress.

A growing body of evidence suggests that religion can be good medicine. Hundreds of studies have been done on the connection between religious faith and health. Most research linking religion and health focuses on how believing in God or belonging to a religious community influences physical and emotional well-being. Among the findings reported in an article by Knight Ridder Newspapers:[44]

- Several studies concluded that people who attend religious services regularly are hospitalized less often and have stronger immune systems than people who rarely or never attend. A longitudinal Yale study also found that churchgoers were less likely to become physically disabled.
- People who go to church or synagogue more than once a week live an average of eight years longer than those who don't, concluded University of Texas researchers who followed 22,000 people over 9 years.
- A 1995 Spokane, Washington, study of 232 heart patients found that those who described themselves as deeply religious were more likely to be alive 6 months after surgery than those who did not.

- A study at Duke University tracked nearly 4,000 North Carolinians age 65 and older for six years and found that those who went to church or any other house of worship once a week or more live an average of seven years longer than those who never go. They also found that the health benefits of regular religious practice translated into stronger immune systems, lower rates of depression and faster recovery after heart attacks.
- Researchers at the Mid-America Heart Institute in Kansas City reported that heart patients who had someone praying for them, even without their knowledge, had 10 percent fewer complications. They used 990 patients in that study.
- A University of Florida study showed that older Americans preferred prayer more than any other remedy to help manage stress. The University of Florida researchers also found that prayer is the most frequently reported alternative treatment used by seniors to improve health and feel better.

These studies also indicate the connection between body, mind and spirit. How we think can affect how we feel, and conversely, how we feel can affect how we think. If we feel tired and depressed long enough we may begin to think negative thoughts which, in turn, add to our negative feelings. But these studies also show the role that the spirit plays in our physical and emotional well-being. This is especially brought out in a type of meditation studied and articulated by Dr. Herbert Benson of Harvard Medical School.

In 1975, Dr. Benson wrote *"The Relaxation Response"* after scientific observations and research in the United States and the Indian Himalayas. Dr. Benson discovered that through meditation the human body can enter a special state characterized by lowered heart rate, decreased rate of breathing, lowered blood pressure, slower brain waves, and an overall reduction of the speed of metabolism. The changes produced by this "relaxation response" counteract the harmful effects of stress.

Dr. Benson said that four steps are necessary to elicit the "relaxation response.[45]

1. A quiet environment. It is important to be free of external noise and distractions. It may be necessary to find a room or a place free of a telephone that may interrupt your concentration. Don't time your session with a loud alarm that would startle you. Instead, keep a watch or a clock in sight and peek now and then when you think about the time. (Jesus taught this, too, when he said, "When you pray, go to your room, close the door, and pray to your Father, who is unseen.")

2. Consciously relax the body's muscles. It's helpful to start with your toes and work up your body to the muscles in your neck and your face. Tense each muscle or muscle group from five to seven seconds and then relax for twenty to thirty seconds. Loosen up your head, neck and shoulders by gently rolling your head around and shrugging your shoulders slightly.

3. Focus for ten to twenty minutes on a mental word or phrase. Repeat aloud or silently the word or phrase you have chosen. If you have chosen a phrase, such as "The Lord is my shepherd," repeat the phrase as you exhale. In other words, breathe in, and then while breathing out, repeat that line from Psalm 23, or whatever word or phrase you have chosen.

4. Assume a passive attitude. As you sit quietly thoughts will inevitably begin to intrude upon your mind. Don't worry about them. It takes practice to clear your mind. The key to dealing with these interruptions is learning to respond to them in an unconcerned or passive manner. If a distracting thought or image comes into your mind, or if a noise disturbs your concentration, or even if a pain in your body becomes bothersome, simply adopt a passive attitude. Don't fight the distraction. Simply let it happen and go back to the repetition of your word or phrase. Even if you're distracted by an itch or

your clothing, go ahead and scratch or rearrange your clothes so that you're more comfortable and continue.

Once your session is over, sit quietly but keep your eyes closed for a full minute or two. Stop repeating the word or phrase you've been using. Allow regular thoughts to enter your consciousness once again. Finally, open your eyes slowly, and sit quietly for another full minute or two. If you stand up immediately, you may feel slightly dizzy. Return to your everyday state in a slow, gradual manner.

Dr. Benson recommends practicing this technique twice daily. He says that the exact time you schedule your sessions is up to you, but the method seems to work best on an empty stomach. A reason for this is that during the relaxation response the flow of blood is directed to the skin and muscles of the arms and legs, and away from the abdominal area. As a result, its effects may compete with the digestion process.

In a later book, *"Beyond the Relaxation Response,"* Dr. Benson tells how the effects of the "relaxation response", *combined with a person's deepest personal beliefs,* "can create other internal environments that can help the individual reach enhanced states of health and well-being."[46]

Dr. Benson claims that his research and that of others has disclosed that those who develop and use what he calls the "faith factor" (a person's beliefs) can:

- relieve headaches
- reduce angina pectoris pains
- reduce blood pressure and help control hypertension problems
- enhance creativity, especially when experiencing some sort of "mental block"
- overcome insomnia
- prevent hyperventilation attacks
- help alleviate backaches
- enhance the therapy of cancer
- control panic attacks
- lower cholesterol levels

- alleviate the symptoms of anxiety that include nausea, vomiting, diarrhea, constipation, short temper, and inability to get along with others.
- reduce overall stress and achieve greater inner peace and emotional balance

It is important, Dr. Benson cautions, to use the "faith factor and relaxation response" in conjunction with modern medicine. It is also important to realize that there are medical limits to what even the strongest positive beliefs can achieve for us. We can't expect super health. It is inevitable that we all must die. We can't use our faith to create immortality here on earth. However, what we believe, our faith, can play a major role in maintaining our health and in healing many physical problems.

When we are stressed, worried, or too concerned about our health, or when we experience a symptom of an illness, we experience anxiety. This turns on our sympathetic nervous system through a mind-body connection and prepares us for "flight or fight." Impulses from your brain cause the nerves of the sympathetic nervous system to release adrenaline or noradrenaline, which produces an increased heart rate, higher blood pressure, a faster respiratory rate, more blood flowing to the arm and leg muscles, and a higher metabolism. Studies have shown that the "relaxation response" blocks or reduces the effect of the hormones of the sympathetic nervous system.

It is important, Dr. Benson stresses, to pick a word or phrase that has special meaning to you. The word or phrase should be short enough to be said silently as you exhale normally. Generally, this means that six or seven words would be the maximum number.

Roman Catholics and related traditions might use such words or phrases as:
- A variation on the prayer: "Lord Jesus Christ, have mercy on me."

- A line from the Lord's Prayer: "Our Father, who art in heaven," or "hallowed be Thy name," or something else.
- A line from the Hail Mary: "Hail Mary, full of grace."
- A phrase from Mary's Magnificat: "My soul magnifies the Lord."
- A line from Zechariah's Benedictus: "Blessed be the Lord God of Israel."
- The final words from the Prayer for the Pope: "Unity in faith and love."

Protestants may use the words or phrases that seem more appropriate to their background, such as:

- Words from Psalm 23: "The Lord is my shepherd."
- Words from Psalm 100: "Make a joyful noise unto the Lord."
- Some of Jesus' teachings or words, such as: "My peace I give unto you" (Jn. 14:27) or "I am the way, the truth and the life" (Jn. 14:6).

Jewish people of any tradition (and many Christians, as well) could be comfortable with words or phrases, such as:

- The Hebrew word for peace: shalom.
- Something from the Psalms, such as Psalm 119:105: "Thy word is a lamp unto my feet."

By combining the faith factor with the relaxation response you will achieve both physical and spiritual benefits.

Is such prayer, however, a way of trying to manipulate God? God can't be manipulated. God is not at our beck and call. However, if we are sincere in what we're doing, the phrase or words we use bring God to mind and in so doing we remember what God means to us. For example, if we use the phrase "The Lord is my Shepherd," it will mean different things to people, but to me it conveys the image of a loving God who cares about me personally, just as a shepherd takes care and looks after each of his sheep. It may help me recall memories and feelings from times in the past when I experienced God as a loving Shepherd.

I think there is more. I think when we begin to use a meaningful religious phrase or words and we think of God we are also putting ourselves in the presence of God. As we do we enter into a personal relationship with God and God can then enter into our minds, our emotions, our spirits, and our bodies to bring comfort and peace to us.

Prayer is basically a personal relationship with God. It is the way we can communicate with God. It's primarily being consciously in the presence of God. Many prayers, however, are asking God to do something for us. Certainly Jesus said, "Ask and it will be given to you; seek and you will find; knock and the door will be opened to you....how much more will your Father in heaven give good gifts to those who ask him!" (Mt. 7:7,11)And we do ask. There are prayers of petition we ask for ourselves. We come before God with prayers for our health, for our problems, for a decision we need to make. Then there are our prayers of intercession which we ask for others. Like the little boy who wanted his grandmother to take him to the park. He was quite disappointed when she explained it was too cold for her rheumatism. That evening, after the boy asked for God's blessings on his mother, father, sister and brothers, his dog and all his playmates, he added..."And, God, please make it hot for Grandma."

There are prayers of thanksgiving. One little girl prayed, "Thank you for the daddies to make the money, and for the mommies to spend the money."

And there are prayers of confession. One mother said she was puzzled to hear her six-year-old daughter's voice from the confessional, admitting to a long and lively group of sins. Afterward the mother confronted the girl and said, "You know you didn't do those things."

"Yes," sighed the girl, "but I had nothing to tell the priest."

Each of these types of prayer have their value, but prayer also means that we are receptive to God's presence. I believe that the faith factor Dr. Benson describes helps us to be receptive to God's presence., to be "with God" just as we might be "with" another person. In a sense, of course, we are with God all the time, but prayer means the time when we are not doing anything else, or thinking about anything else but God.

Whether we use the "faith factor and relaxation response" or use some other form of prayer, God does try to answer our prayers.

A 40 something year-old woman, I'll call Debbie, was in an abusive marriage. Her husband would abuse her physically and verbally. When he would get mad there was no telling what he would do. Debbie had the black and blue marks to show where he had kicked her. She was afraid for her life. She finally had the courage to do something about her problem. During one of their arguments he asked Debbie if she wanted a divorce. That was the opening she needed. She got a restraining order against him but lived in constant fear he would try to break in the house even though she had the locks changed. She couldn't sleep. She couldn't eat. She weighed only 95 pounds. She would sit up at night and talk with a girlfriend on the phone for fear he might try to break in. He would drive by the house even though he wasn't supposed to be near it. He would try to scare her. The night before they were to appear before a mediator, she was at her lowest. Days and months of worry and fear overwhelmed her. She fell to her knees and prayed that God would give her the strength she needed to speak in court the next day. She was afraid she would break down and not be able to go through with the proceedings. She prayed for God's help as her frail body fell on the floor. She cried and cried tears of anguish, pleading for God's help. She finally fell asleep from exhaustion. The next morning she awoke feeling a peace she had never before felt. Calm, confident and composed she went to the hearing, stood up for herself and did what she had to do. God answered her prayer for help and gave her the strength she needed.

God is ever present to help us with our needs and concerns, whether it be help for our problems, or peace of mind. God loves each and every one of us. And prayer is the way for us to connect with God's help and power to help us with our daily concerns. It's like climbing a mountain and looking down at a valley below. You see the full panorama. When you're down in the valley looking up, you're apt to see only tree branches hanging over your head. That's the way problems often are. They hang over you until you find a way to get above them and see the world from a different perspective. We need prayer to lift us up so we can get a better perspective of our problems and find the answers which so often lie hidden right before us.

In order to get the help from God through prayer, we first must humble ourselves by acknowledging that we need help beyond ourselves. We can't do it alone. Let go of the problem by leaving it in the hands of God.

The second step is to pray in depth, like Debbie, the abused wife. Her prayer came from deep within her. The intensity of her prayer touched the great compassionate heart of God. It opened the way to God's unlimited power and help.

Certainly others have prayed with deep sincerity and urgency, and nothing seemingly happened. I don't have the answer. Perhaps the answer was there and went unrecognized. We can be so intent on getting what we want that we may fail to see what God wants, which will be better than what we want!

I do know that some prayers seem to be more effective than others, and intensity often seems to be present when these prayers are answered.

The third step is to have faith that God will answer our prayers. About thirty years ago I was the pastor of two small rural churches in southeastern Ohio. It is beautiful country with high hills and deep valleys. It has been called the Switzerland of Ohio. One day one of my church members, a 40 something year-old man called me in a frantic state. He wife had just been diagnosed with having a brain tumor. They were on their way to a large hospital in Columbus, about a two hour ride from where we were living. The next day I drove to Columbus to see the woman, I'll call Marge. When

I entered her room, her husband was there with her. Both of them looked quite upset. The medical staff wasn't quite sure what they were going to do. We talked awhile and then I said a prayer with them, asking for God's strength to be with them and also praying for healing. I returned home. The next day I received a telephone call from the husband. This time his voice was ecstatic. The tumor was gone! It had disappeared. The doctors had no medical explanation. God had answered our prayer.

At other times I have prayed with people for healing or a cure, and to no avail. Why God seems to answer some prayers and not others, I don't know. Perhaps God answered my prayers in other ways, perhaps giving the person renewed faith in God's love. I don't know. I do know that God does answer our prayers and gives us the answer God feels that we need. The answer may not come right away. The answer may come when God feels the time is right or when God feels that we are right or ready. But if we think of prayer primarily as being with God, getting to know God, getting to experience God's loving presence, discovering God's help, then we are not so likely to be frustrated and depressed when no answer to prayer seems to be forthcoming. We will learn that there really is no such thing as unanswered prayer, for we are drawing closer to One who wants to respond to our needs.

Such closeness with God is especially important for sometimes all we need is God's strength. The Apostle Paul asked God to remove his "thorn in the flesh" (whatever it was). He asked God three times. The final answer he got was: "My grace is all you need, for my power is strongest when you are weak." That answer can be especially comforting to those facing weakness of legs or weakness of spirit. As we grow older we know that there's only so much science and medicine can do. We have to learn to live with aches and pains due to arthritis and other ailments. While we might wish that God would give us the strength and energy of our youth, God can give us the spiritual strength we need to cope with such problems. Perhaps that's what the prophet meant when he said: "But they who wait for the Lord shall renew their strength, they shall mount up with wings like eagles, they shall run and not be weary, they shall walk and not faint." Isa. 40:31

Prayer is important at any age. I have found it especially helpful in reducing the effects of stress, but prayer is also important to help us find answers to our daily problems.

Perhaps an unknown author said it best. Ever wonder about the abbreviation A.S.A.P.? Generally, we think of it in terms of even more hurry and stress in our lives. Maybe, if we think of the abbreviation in a different manner, we will begin to find a new way to deal with those rough days along the way.

There's work to do, deadlines to meet;
You've got no time to spare,
But as you hurry and scurry-
A.S.A.P. - ALWAYS SAY A PRAYER.

In the midst of family chaos,
"Quality time" is rare.
Do your best, let God do the rest-
A.S.A.P.- ALWAYS SAY A PRAYER.

God knows how stressful life is;
He wants to ease our cares,
And He'll respond, A.S.A.P.
ALWAYS SAY A PRAYER

CHAPTER SEVEN
GOD'S ANTIQUE

"We cannot avoid growing old, but we can avoid growing cold."
Unknown

A well-known pastor, filled with his own self-importance, decided to visit a local nursing home. He strolled into the nursing home and announced himself, but nobody seemed to recognize him. He went to one elderly woman in a wheelchair and asked, "Sister, do you know who I am?"

"No, sonny," she replied, "but you check with the lady at the front desk. She can tell you who you are!"

The Psalmist said, "What is man that thou art mindful of him, and the son of man that thou dost care for him? Yet thou hast made him little less than God, and dost crown him with glory and honor." Psalm 8: 4-5

What is man? Who is woman? Who are we?

Humanism is one answer. Believing neither in God, nor in the existence of any supernatural power, the humanist affirms that man is the highest form of being which has evolved in the universe. The humanist is likely to exclaim with Shakespeare's Hamlet: "What a piece of work is man! How noble in reason! How infinite in faculties! In form, in moving, how express and admirable! In action how like an angel! In apprehension how like a god! The beauty of the world! The paragon of animals!"[47]

There are those who think in materialistic terms, arguing that we are simply an animal, an object in nature. That view doesn't do much for my self-esteem. I don't know about yours.

Then there are those who look at us in terms of a number. To the government we are a social security number. To the post office you are known by your zip code. To the phone company and to many others you are known by your phone number.

Many people resent being labeled by a number they have to carry with them. We are more than a number they say. But then business and advertising will be quick to tell you just who you are.

Watch television or read a magazine and you will find that many advertisements trick us into buying a product by making us feel inferior, stupid, lazy, or someone who is always plagued with problems. They tell us gray hair will make us look old, so we need to dye our hair. They tell us that bad breath will keep people away, so we must use their mouthwash. We can't cook, so we need to eat out or bring in food from a fast-food restaurant.

These products all have their valid use, but they also have their place. We should not be so gullible as to believe that all we are is a bundle of problems and needs, measured in terms of what we buy, what we wear or don't wear, what we own or don't own.

When I was on my first job after graduating from seminary, I decided I needed a new car. I went to look at a Pontiac Firebird. I was told by the salesman that all young people wanted a sports car like that and so should I. I did like the car, but I was turned off by the salesman's approach, so I didn't get it.

Is who I am determined by what people may say or think or believe?

It is wrong for someone else to tell us who we are when their only purpose is to use us as a number, a statistic, or a means to making money.

We are more, much more than a physical being with problems, needs and interests. It is important how we think about ourselves and who we are, for how we think and feel about ourselves constitutes our self-esteem. If we think positively about ourselves we tend to have a greater success and enjoyment in life, in our work, in our personal relationships and even in our faith. If we have a low self-esteem; that is, if we tend to think negatively about ourselves, we tend to have a more difficult time trying to live our lives.

Our self-esteem is formed early on in life and can change throughout our lives. The challenges of life can affect how we think of ourselves and how we think of ourselves can affect how we cope with the challenges of life. If we have a negative self-image we are more likely to feel we can't handle or cope with a stressful situation. Conversely, if we have a positive self-image we are more likely to feel we can handle a situation. As we grow older, I think our self-esteem is challenged by several outside influences.

Society's view of aging has tended to be negative. The elderly are rarely portrayed in movies or on television and when they are they tend to reflect the extreme. In the movie, "On Golden Pond," for example, Henry Ford portrayed an elderly man trying to cope with his relationship with his daughter and grandson, all the while trying to cope with senility, if not alzheimer's. His wife, played by Katherine Hepburn, called him, "You old poop!" a term that often characterizes the elderly in the media. Other examples might be Alan Alda coping with alzheimer's in several episodes of ER, or the women in "The Golden Girls," whose lives seem to be characterized by neurosis.

Some primitive peoples like the Eskimos and other nomads respected the elderly but would leave them to die when they could no longer care for themselves. Natives of some South Seas islands paddled away from their families, to leave them for death, when age overtook them. Nor is the idea of abandoning the elderly unique to primitive societies. Marya Mannes' 1968 novel *They* postulated a world in which everyone over 50 was herded into public institutions and eventually killed. A 1966 Rand Corporation study concluded that if the U.S. survived a nuclear war it would be "better off without old and feeble" citizens, and suggested that no provisions be made to care for the surviving elderly.

Advertising is aimed at the young. Youthful actors drive the newest car or wear the newest style. If the elderly are addressed it is to sell products for various problems, such as dentures, incontinence, arthritis, impotence, etc.

And there is a large market for those who think they can reverse the aging process by taking a pill, a potion or a powder. AARP reported in 2001 that Americans spend an estimated $6 billion a year hoping to slow, stop or reverse the aging process. As many as 40 percent are Americans age 65 and over purchasing expensive alternative therapies and herbal supplements. Unfortunately, many of the so-called cures are just worthless. Studies have shown that some products contain harmful contaminants or an active ingredient that is much more potent than is indicated on the label, increasing the risk of overdose for some users. Some supplements may interact adversely with certain prescription or over the counter medicines. And some products contain little or none of the active ingredients listed on the label, making them worthless. In other words, let the buyer beware![48]

Perhaps you've seen the letter that tells how "Seniors Are Worth A Fortune":

"Remember old folks are worth a fortune; silver in their hair; gold in their teeth; stones in their kidneys; lead in their feet and gas in their stomachs. I have become a little older since I saw you last and a few changes have come into my life since then. Frankly, I have become quite a frivolous old gal. I'm seeing five gentlemen every day. As soon as I wake up, Will Power helps me get out of bed. Then I go see John. Then Charlie Horse comes along. When he is here, he takes up all my time and attention. When he leaves Arthur Ritis shows up and stays the rest of the day. He doesn't like to stay in one place very long, so he takes me from joint to joint. After such a busy day, I'm really tired and glad to go back to bed with Ben Gay. What a life!!"

"P.S. My friend came to call the other day. He asked me if at my age I should be thinking about the hereafter. I told him I do all the time. No matter where I am – in the parlor, upstairs, in the kitchen, or down in the basement, I ask myself, 'Now what am I here after?'"

As we age the changes in our physical appearance can affect how we feel about ourselves. Many people don't like it when their hair turns gray, so men and women reach for hair dye. Many don't think they look good so they go for tummy tucks, liposuctions, face lifts, botox, and other types of cosmetic surgery to keep a "youthful" appearance.

When our joints ache from arthritis and we find it more difficult to walk, or we can't read the paper or hear the television like we did a few years ago, we may get mad at ourselves and think less of who we are because who we are physically isn't what we used to be.

Harvey and Gladys are getting ready for bed. Gladys is standing in front of her full-length mirror, taking a long, hard look at herself.

"You know, Harvey," she comments. "I stare into this mirror and I see an ancient creature. My face is all wrinkled, my boobs sag so much that they dangle to my waist, my arms and legs are as flabby as popped balloons, and my butt looks like a sad, deflated version of the Hindenburg!"

She turns to her husband sand says, "Dear, please tell me just one positive thing about my body so I can feel better about myself."

Harvey studies Gladys critically for a moment and then says in a soft, thoughtful voice, "Well, there's nothing wrong with your eyesight."

Services for Harvey Goldman will be held Tuesday morning at 10:30.

It helps if you can laugh at the changes and problems that often accompany growing older, as the following message from the internet attests:

"I'm a senior citizen and proud of it-

I'm the life of the party...even when it lasts until 8 p.m.

I'm very good at opening childproof caps with a hammer.

I'm usually interested in going home before I get to where I am going.

I'm good on a trip for at least an hour without my aspirin and antacid.

I'm the first one to find the bathroom wherever I go.

I'm awake many hours before my body allows me to get up.

I'm smiling all the time because I can't hear a word you're saying.

I'm very good at telling stories...over...and over...and over.

I'm aware that other people's grandchildren are not as bright as mine.

I'm so cared for: long term care, eye care, Medicare, dental care.

I'm wrinkled, saggy, and lumpy and that's just my left leg.

I'm realizing that aging is not for sissies.

I'm walking more (to the bathroom) and enjoying it less.

I'm a walking storeroom of facts...I've just lost the key to it.

I'm a Senior Citizen and I think I am having the time of my life!!

Now if I could only remember who sent this to me, I wouldn't be

sending it back to them. You didn't send it, did you?"

And yet we're still the same person. And we're valuable to God no matter our age or physical appearance.

The writer of Genesis put it this way: "So God created man in his own image, in the image of God he created him;

male and female he created them. And God blessed them."
(Genesis 1:27)

The Bible tells me that I have been created in the image of
God. But what does that mean?

A little boy once asked his mother where he had come
from and who he was. She replied that God had made him
out of the dust and when people die they return to dust.

A little later he came to her again, and exclaimed, that
under his bed there were a whole lot of people either coming
or going!

In Paul's letter to the Colossians, he says that Christ is "the
image of the invisible God."(Col.1:15) Jesus speaks of God as
a Spirit. The word image, then, is not a physical likeness, but
a spiritual likeness.

We are in the image of God in that we, too, are spirit. Our
real self, our eternal self is spirit. We have spiritual powers
like God. We are able to think, to communicate, to look at life
beyond ourselves, to remember, to reflect, to reason, to create
beauty, to contemplate moral values, and above all, to love.

God has created humankind different from all creation. No
other living thing in the Bible is said to be made in the image
of God or to be a little less than God. No other animal, no
other living thing in the world is made in the image of God.

Another way of describing what we mean by the image of
God is written in the letter of John: "See what love the Father
has given us, that we should be called children of God." (1
John 3:1)

We are children of God. And if we are then we are somewhat
like God. Children generally resemble their parents. Our
bodies are not like God, but our spirits are like God's.

God's plan in coming among us as Jesus Christ was so that
through Him each of us would know who we are as a child
of God and who we can become as we seek to live our lives
patterned after Christ's way of life and His teachings.

Look at what Christ did in the lives of the disciples. Jesus
took a faltering, unstable, immature fishing-boat captain, and

suddenly before his friends exclaimed: "You are a rock and upon this rock I will build my church." (Mt. 16:18)

Jesus took a vengeful Saul and changed him into Paul the loving evangelist.

Jesus helped men and women discover who they were and who they could become as God wanted them to be.

One of the unique aspects of Jesus' message was His emphasis on the worth and importance of each individual, including those persons others may consider the least important. No other religion teaches this. Jesus gave a lot of his attention to cheating tax collectors, to people with leprosy, the blind, foreigners, prostitutes, a thief on the cross, even to his Roman crucifiers. This was a new way of thinking. It shattered the old prejudices.

This was especially true in regards to the position of women and children. Because of Christ children were no longer left to die if the child should be born a girl or sickly or handicapped in some way. Because of Jesus women were no longer treated as property, but as persons. Although even after two thousand years children are still being abused and women still don't have the equality they deserve.

Like children, as a child of God, we are to grow in our relationship with God, becoming more adult and mature in our faith, in our love for one another, in leading a life of service for others. But first we need to remember or to discover that we are a child of God and therefore can feel good about ourselves no matter what our age.

Unfortunately, most people judge their worth in terms of worldly values and opinions. Men, especially view their worth in terms of their work. As more and more women are working today, women may also be thinking of themselves in terms of what they do.

We feel good or important, of worth, when we are working. We feel good because of the work we are doing. We feel good and important when our boss or fellow workers tell us we're doing a good job. And our pay is often connected with what we do.

There's a joke about a man who took a job painting yellow lines down the middle of a highway. On his first day he painted ten miles, and the foreman said, "You did well. Keep it up and you'll get a raise."

The next day the man did five miles, and the foreman said, "Well, five miles isn't as good as ten, but keep up the good work."

The following day he painted only one mile. The foreman called him in and said, "First, you did ten miles, then you did five miles, then you did only one mile. You're not doing the work, so I have to let you go."

As the man walked away from the office, he whined, "But it's not my fault. Each day I kept getting farther away from the can of paint."

During the recession of the early 1990's, I was living in New Jersey as pastor of a church. Many companies and businesses in the area were laying-off people. I organized and led an unemployment support group for several years. We met in the church, but anyone was welcome. The purpose of the group was not to focus on how to look for a job, write a resume or hints for a successful job interview, although we did do some of that. The main purpose of the group was to offer emotional support to those who were unemployed and trying to cope and find another job. It was a difficult time for these men and women. They had lost an important part of their life and it was a blow to their self-esteem. It took a while for many of them to accept what had happened and begin to focus on what they could do to find another job. For many it was a time to evaluate who they were, but for many who they were was viewed in terms of the skills and abilities they possessed. Of course, that's only a part of who we are, but so many magnify their skills and abilities so that they view their worth almost solely in terms of what they can do. What we can do, however, is only a part of who we are.

An employer needs to run an efficient business, but there is also the danger that happens so often in which the worth of a person as a person is overlooked and a person is seen only in terms of their usefulness to the company. How many persons, for example, are forced into retirement at age sixty-five even though they still could be useful. Many have more experience and knowledge that would be helpful than someone fresh from college just beginning to work for the company. Why age sixty-five as a cut-off?

Many people have difficulty when they retire because their worth is connected with what they have done for many years. Now they're suddenly in a whole new world and many flounder, not quite knowing what to do with themselves, and not really sure who they really are.

Again, God has something else to say about our worth.

Jesus told a parable about an owner of an estate or farm who went out early in the morning to hire some men to work in his vineyard. He went to what would be the modern-day equivalent of an union hall. A man would come to the market place with his tools and wait until someone came and hired him. Later that same morning the owner again went and hired some more men, agreeing to pay them a fair wage. He went out again at Noon, at three o'clock in the afternoon and again at five o'clock.

When evening came the workers were paid. All were paid the same amount. The ones who started to work at dawn were paid the same amount as those who were hired at three and five o'clock in the afternoon.

Those who had been hired first and worked the longest started complaining. "These men who were hired last worked only one hour," they said, "while we put up with a whole day's work in the hot sun, yet you paid them the same as you paid us!"

The owner then answered, "Listen friend, I have not cheated you. After all, you agreed to do a day's work for one silver coin. Now take your pay and go home. I want to give this man who was hired last as much as I gave you. Don't I have the right to do as I wish with my own money? Or are you jealous because I am generous?" (Mt. 20: 1-16)

In this parable, the owner of the vineyard paid each worker equally. Their worth was not dependent upon their work. Our worth comes from God and according to Jesus'
parable everyone is of equal worth to God.

The parable also says that we cannot earn God's love; God's love is freely given to us because we are of worth to God.

How we view ourselves makes all the difference in the world. If we focus on what we think is wrong, then we'll have a low sense of self-worth, but if we can focus on how God sees us, then we can feel good about ourselves no matter what our age.

Some people concentrate on their mistakes, their failures, their missed opportunities. We replay in our minds the times we looked foolish, the word we wish we had not said. God says, the past is past. All that matters is the future. When we accept Jesus Christ as Lord of our lives we come to discover a new worth about ourselves, one that says we are loved and accepted by God. And that is true no matter what our age.

I remember reading a little devotional article a number of years ago in which the author told of a desk he had in his room at a retirement home. Years before when he had purchased a new desk for his wife, the present desk had been moved onto a sun porch. There it stood year after year. The sun would beat upon it. Now and then a storm would blow open a window and rain would pelt it.

Eventually the time came when he had to sort through his belongings in preparation for the move to the retirement village. He had planned to dispose of the desk in the sunroom. He invited his minister over to sort through his books. There might be some he might find useful. When his minister saw the desk he exclaimed, "Ah, an antique!" The minister told him not to dispose of the desk for it was probably valuable. And so he had the desk cleaned, polished and took it with him to the retirement home. And he asked himself, "Why is it that furniture becomes more valuable as it grows old, while persons seem to be of less value as they grow old?"

If persons seem to be of less value in our society and in our own eyes as we grow old, think about another thought. The man with the desk asked the question: "Why did God permit me to live beyond eighty? Could it be that God regarded me as a valuable antique, as it were?"

It does make a world of difference whether one thinks of himself as a valuable antique as we grow older, rather than an old piece of cast-off furniture.

For example, John Quincy Adams, on his eightieth birthday, responded to a query concerning his well-being by saying: "John Quincy Adams is well. But the house in which he lives at present is becoming dilapidated. It is tottering upon its foundation. Time and the seasons have nearly destroyed it. Its roof is pretty well worn out. Its walls are much shattered and it trembles with every wind. I think John Quincy Adams will have to move out of it soon. But he himself is quite well, quite well."[49]

But how does one come to see himself as valuable? One of the most important things we need to do is to accept both our abilities and our limitations. It is not always easy to accept that one is growing old. It can be difficult, too, to accept the growing old of someone else, for it often brings to mind assorted illnesses, suffering, fear of senility, fear of being left alone, and death.

At various times I've asked people how they cope with some of their physical problems and a typical answer is: "You've got to!" That answer can be a positive response, but in some cases it can also be a cry of resignation. The person who cannot accept growing old, or the person who accepts it grudgingly, "because he's got to," is not open to life in all its fullness.

I suspect that the person who said he accepted old age because "he's got to," was expressing the fear and the dread of many people who live alone. If we could just say, in the words of the poet, Robert Browning, "Grow old along with me," but we often can't say it because there is nobody with us:

Grow old along with me!
The best is yet to be,
The last of life, for which the first was made:
Our times are in His hand
Who saith, "A whole I planned,
Youth shows but half; trust God;
See all, nor be afraid.[50]

We might think, of course Robert Browning could write those words. He had his beloved Elizabeth!

The truth is, when Browning wrote "Grow old along with me," Elizabeth had been dead for three years. The great poet's life was shattered. During those three years he had accomplished very little. At that time he was well past the age of fifty. He wanted to run away and hide, but he began thinking of one whom he had admired for many years, the twelfth century scholar, Rabbi ben Ezra. Among other things Rabbi ben Ezra had written these thoughts: "Approach the twilight of life with joy and hope. Approach the last of life with eagerness, not gloom. For the last of life is the best of life. Trust God and be not afraid."

Browning was inspired to write a poem on the teachings of Rabbi ben Ezra. The point is he was alone when he wrote "Grow old along with me." He saw himself and life as valuable and worthwhile.

God has not meant old age as a curse, but as an added opportunity. We may face limitations of the body and mind as we grow older, but we face such limitations throughout our lives. A baby and children are limited in their capabilities. So are we as adults to some extent. We always have limitations of some kind- limitations of the body, the mind, our environment, our resources, our talents or our abilities.

A Harvard study has shown that the way people view themselves affects how they walk. [51]

When elderly people's walking speed slows down significantly, numerous studies show, they become much more likely to require nursing-home care and much more susceptible to serious illness and earlier death.

An important walking characteristic that affects the ability to balance is known as "swing time," which is the amount of time spent with one foot off the ground. Those who lose the spring in their step and shuffle their feet rather than raising them have less swing time.

Dr. Jeffrey M. Hausdorff, an assistant professor of medicine at Harvard Medical School and a researcher at Beth Israel Deaconess Medical Center in Boston studied 47 men and women aged 63 to 82 who described themselves as healthy. The participants, randomly assigned to one of two groups, were asked to play a 30-minute computer game in which words flashed briefly on the screen. While the words appeared too quickly to be read, they may have stayed long enough to deliver a subliminal, or subconscious message to the participants. Before and after the computer game, each participant was timed walking 300 feet to determine walking speed. Swing time was also measured for two minutes with special equipment.

When the researchers compared walking patterns, the group exposed to positive words about aging, such as "wise," "astute" and "accomplished," showed a significant increase in walking speed and swing time. The other group, which got negative words such as "senile," "dependent" and "diseased," showed no significant differences in either walking speed or swing time.

The study concluded that "negative self-stereotypes of aging" likely play an important role in the loss of walking speed and swing time as people grow older.

How much more important than our outward appearance is our inner spirit. Are you a loving person? Do you enjoy life? Do you have a positive attitude? Are you grateful for God and God's blessings? How do you treat the people around you? Are you kind and compassionate? If your inner spirit is one of beauty, then that is what people will see.

For example, an elderly woman and her little grandson, whose face was sprinkled with bright freckles, spent the day at the zoo. Lots of children were waiting in line to get their cheeks painted by a local artist who was decorating them with tiger paws.

"You've got so many freckles, there's no place to paint!" a girl in the line said to the little boy. Embarrassed, the little boy dropped his head. His grandmother knelt down next to him. "I love your freckles. When I was a little girl I always wanted freckles," she said, while tracing her finger across the child's cheek. "Freckles are beautiful."

The boy looked up, "Really?"

"Of course," said the grandmother. "Why just name me one thing that's prettier than freckles."

The little boy thought for a moment, peered intensely into his grandma's face, and softly whispered, "Wrinkles."

Jo Foxworth, in her book, "Boss Lady's Arrival and Survival Plan," gives several suggestions for boosting self-esteem that I think are helpful at any age. She says:

"Learn something new every day." Even if it's only a new word, or new information, the more interesting you can be to other people. Besides, it helps to keep your mind active.

"Do whatever it takes to make you feel sure of yourself." In other words, wear something new or wear anything that makes you feel better about yourself. Often people feel emotionally secure in the knowledge that they are magnificently dressed.

Certainly there are also other ways. One woman in my congregation who lives alone and has difficulty seeing gains self-assurance by preparing a magnificent dinner every night.

"Cultivate people who give you a feeling of importance." I'm not talking about people you feel superior over, rather it's best to put out of your life anybody who puts you down. Be friends with those whom you enjoy being with and who give you compliments and positive feedback as you do with them.

"Do something every day that you do extraordinarily well." No matter how insignificant it may seem, any accomplishment bolsters self-esteem. It might be something as simple as one of the 'easy' crossword puzzles, preparing a gourmet meal, or even just getting out of bed!

"Concentrate on the things you like about yourself." No matter how down on yourself you may get at times, there must be something about yourself that you can find to like. [52]

Perhaps some of these suggestions taken from the Internet will stir your mind about the perks of being over 45:

"Kidnappers are not very interested in you."

"In a hostage situation you are likely to be released first."

"There is nothing left to learn the hard way."

"Things you buy now won't wear out."

"Your joints are more accurate meteorologists than the national weather service."

"Your secrets are safe with your friends because they can't remember them either."

"If you can change the things about yourself that bother you, do it!" If you need to lose weight, quit smoking, stop drinking so much, start exercising, get out of debt- do it and stop talking about doing it. But if what bothers you is something you can't do anything about, stop brooding about it. Accept it and focus on what you can do.

It is important, too, to see ourselves as God sees us, as like a valuable antique. As we see ourselves as one of God's children we can feel important and good about ourselves no matter who we are or how old we are.

Certainly in the Bible age was no barrier to value in God's sight. Abraham was seventy-five when God called him to move to Israel; he was 100 and his wife Sarah is reported to have been 90 years old when their son Isaac was born.

And God said to Abraham, "You shall go to your fathers in peace; you shall be buried in a good old age." (Gen. 25:8)

God values the aged. God said to the prophet Isaiah: "Hearken to me, O house of Jacob, all the remnant of the house of Israel, who have been borne by me from your birth, carried from the womb; even to your old age I am He, and to gray hairs I will carry you. I have made, and I will bear; I will carry and will save." Isaiah 46:4

As the years pass, as the seasons come and go, as we change outwardly, as many of our friends and loved ones leave us, we need to realize that there is one thing that never changes and that is our worth to God. This assurance of God's eternal help and love should help us to accept middle age, old age, and any age as part of God's plan and love.

Perhaps that's why the Apostle Paul could say, "Therefore, we do not lose heart. Though outwardly we are wasting away, yet inwardly we are being renewed day by day…" 2 Cor. 4: 16

You tell me I am getting old;
I tell you that it is not so;
The "house" I live in is worn out,
And that, of course, I know.
It's been in use a long, long time;
It's weathered many a gale;
I'm really not surprised you think
It's getting somewhat frail.

The color's changing on the roof;
The window's getting dim;
The wall's a bit transparent…
And looking rather thin.
The foundation's not so steady,
As once it used to be;
My "house" is getting shaky,
But my "house" isn't me.

My few short years can't make me old;
I feel I'm in my youth.
Eternity lies just ahead,
A life of joy and truth.
I'm going to live forever there;
Life will go on – it's grand.
You tell me I am getting old?
You just don't understand.

The dweller in my little "house"
Is young and bright and gay;
Just starting on a life to last
Throughout eternal day.
You only see the outside,
Which is all that most folks see;
You tell me I am getting old?
You're mixing my "house" with me![53]

CHAPTER EIGHT
LIFE AFTER DEATH

"The truest end of life is to know that life never ends." William
Penn

The most popular television show of the 1999-2000 season
was a game show entitled, "Who Wants to Be a Millionaire?"
Contestants were asked a question and given a choice of
four possible answers. Only one was the correct answer.
Contestants could use a lifeline if they had some uncertainty
about the answer. They could poll the audience; have two of
the answers deleted, leaving one correct and one incorrect
answer; or they could telephone someone. Contestants could
keep going and receive more money for each correct answer
until they reached one million dollars, or they could stop at
any time and take what they had won up until that point. The
host for the show was Regis Philbin, a long-time television
entertainer. In response to each contestant's answer, Regis
would ask, "Is that your final answer?"

Suppose you are a contestant on "Who Wants to Be a
Millionaire?" and for one million dollars, Regis asks you this
question: "When a person dies, they: A. Cease to exist. B. Are

reincarnated. C. Go to purgatory, or D. With God's grace, go to heaven."

If you had lived in Jesus' time the answer given by many would have been A, cease to exist. Most people believed that death was the final answer. When you died, that was it, except to live on in the memory of those who loved you.

Oh, there were intimations of immortality. Numbers 16:30 describes men going down to Sheol, the realm of the dead. Sheol seems to have been located in the depths of the earth. It did not sound like a pleasant place. Job speaks of Sheol as "the land of gloom and deep darkness, the land of gloom and chaos, where light is darkness." (Job 17:13)

Extraordinary individuals like Enoch (Genesis 5:24) and Elijah (2 Kings 2:1-11) might escape by being transported to the heavens by God, but other individuals went the way of all flesh and went to Sheol.

What survived in Sheol, however, was but a shadow image of the whole person. Death was considered as a state in which the forces of life were at their lowest, a state similar to fatigue or sleep. The dead continued to have the same physical aspect as when they were alive, but they had no life as we tend to think of it. They were like a vapor, a misty shell, or a ghost.

Nor was there anything to look forward to in Sheol. In Psalm 116:3, the Psalmist said: "the snares of death encompassed me; the pangs of Sheol laid hold on me; I suffered distress and anguish." In Psalm 31:12, the Psalmist said: "I have passed out of mind like one who is dead; I have become like a broken vessel." Death and Sheol came to be thought of as things to be dreaded. Where this conception of Sheol came from is unkown since the dead do not normally come back from Sheol. The witch of Endor called up the spirit of Samuel at Saul's request, but he did not mention anything about the nature of Sheol.

One reason may be in the thought, as expressed in Psalm 6:5 that "in death there is no remembrance of thee (God); in Sheol who can give thee praise?" In Sheol, "in the land of forgetfulness " (Psalm 88:12) and "the land of silence" (Psalm 94:17) all things are forgotten, even God.

Worst of all, perhaps, is the conviction expressed in Psalm 88 that God ceases to remember those who have gone to Sheol. The Psalmist says in verses 4b-5: "I am a man who has no strength, like one forsaken among the dead, like the slain that lie in the grave, like those whom thou dost remember no more, for they are cut off from thy hand." However, in Psalm 139:8, the Psalmist exclaims: "If I ascend to heaven, thou art there! If I make my bed in Sheol, thou art there." Such a statement is the exception, rather than the norm concerning life in Sheol. Were God to be present in Sheol, perhaps a more hopeful idea of immortality would have arisen.

A few Psalms are on the brink of belief in something beyond or instead of Sheol. Psalm 16 is a song of trust for God's protection and continued presence. In verses 9-11 the Psalmist says: "Therefore my heart is glad, and my soul rejoices; my body also dwells secure. For thou dost not give me up to Sheol, or let thy godly one see the Pit. Thou dost show me the path of life; in thy presence there is fullness of joy, in thy right hand are pleasures for evermore." (RSV)

Peter used these verses in his sermon at Pentecost to refer to a belief in immortality. Scholars vary in their interpretations of these verses. Some feel that the verses refer only to God's protecting care through this life.

Next is Psalm 49. The important verses here are 14 and 15: "Like sheep they are appointed for Sheol; death shall be their shepherd; straight to the grave they descend, and their form shall waste away; Sheol shall be their home. But God will ransom my soul from the power of Sheol, for he will receive me."

The psalm itself is concerned with the prosperity of the wicked. The psalmist cannot understand why such things should be. The psalmist realizes that all must die, rich and poor alike. Riches will do one no good beyond the grave, so in the end their wealth is no good. Our hope in life rests in God. Yet, the author seems to be saying that God has another plan for the righteous. The righteous will not go to Sheol with the wicked, but they will continue to live. Where or how one will live is not indicated, but there is hope that God will take care of one after death.

From my experience Psalm 23 is chosen frequently by people at the funeral of their loved ones. The Psalm, as a whole, seems to convey a message of peace, hope and an assurance of God's love. The last verse seems to convey a message of eternal life. The Psalmist says in the RSV version of the Bible: "Surely goodness and mercy shall follow me all the days of my life; and I shall dwell in the house of the Lord for ever." However, in his commentary on the Psalms, Artur Weiser translates the verse: "Only goodness and lovingkindness will follow me all the days of my life; and I may dwell in God's house to the end of the days." Such wording conveys a different interpretation. The Psalmist seems to be talking about the happiness he receives from his relationship with God in God's Temple. It is not a reference to an afterlife, but to a lifelong relationship with God. No mention is directly made to an afterlife. However, my personal thought is that the Psalm can also refer to an afterlife as we look at it today.

Psalm 49 still seems to be the most plausible reference to a belief in immortality in the Psalms, and in the Old Testament time period. How or where such an existence is like is not mentioned.

A hundred years or so before the birth of Jesus, a special class of literature known as apocalyptic emerged. Apocalyptic literature abounds with strange visions, symbolism and supernatural events. Written in times of persecution, it was meant to give readers hope that God would prevail. Usually the writer envisions a time when God would usher in His Kingdom. It will be preceded by cataclysmic events in nature. There would be a judgment of all people and God's people would prevail. The book of Daniel is one such book, as is Ezekiel. Perhaps from about the same time comes a section of the book of Isaiah often called "the little apocalypse" (Is. 24-27). The writer portrays the Last Judgment, when God will judge all the nations by bringing about a cosmic catastrophe. But in the midst of these natural disasters "the righteous nation that keeps the truth" (26:2) will remain secure. The righteous of earlier generations will be raised from the dead in order that they too may participate in the consummation of history (26:19). Here we have the first clear evidence in the Old Testament to the resurrection of the individual. Ezekiel had spoken of the resurrection of Israel (Ezek. 37), but here in Isaiah is the first reference to individual resurrection. Such a future life beyond the grave is expressed in terms of the resurrection of the body. Isaiah says: "But your dead will live; their bodies will rise." (26:19). The doctrine of the immortality of the soul comes from a later Greek influence.

According to Hebrew thought, the individual cannot experience fullness of life without participating in the Kingdom of God. Therefore, the resurrection of the body occurs at the end-time when God's victory over the powers of evil is complete.

The resurrection of Jesus solidified that view among the early Christians. Paul tells the Corinthians that the resurrection of Jesus is only the beginning or "the first fruits" (1 Cor. 15:20) of the resurrection that is yet to be for everyone. At his "coming" again (15:23), the rest of his own people will be united with him in the resurrection life.

In the first century AD the Hellenistic world believed that only the soul could survive death. Certain men might after death be raised to heroes and live among the gods, but there was no expectation that the bodies of most of humanity had any other prospect than death and decay. Even in those philosophies and religions that believed in the transmigration of souls from one body to another, in each case the body returned to the earth following death, freeing the soul to enter a new body. In none of these systems of belief was there any place for the idea of bodily resurrection.

Paul argues that one cannot assume that a resurrection body will be identical with the way we know an earthly body. He draws an analogy between a self that dies, is buried and is to be raised from the dead and a seed that is sown in the soil, decays, but brings forth new life. Paul writes, "But God gives it a body as he has determined, and to each kind of seed he gives its own body. All flesh is not the same: men have one kind of flesh, animals have another, birds another and fish another. There are also heavenly bodies and there are earthly bodies; but the splendor of the heavenly bodies is one kind, and the splendor of the earthly bodies is another. The sun has one kind of splendor, the moon another and the stars another; and star differs from star in splendor. So will it be with the resurrection of the dead. The body that is sown is perishable, it is raised imperishable; it is sown in dishonor, it is raised in glory; it is sown in weakness, it is raised in power; it is sown a natural body, it is raised a spiritual body. If there is a natural body, there is also a spiritual body." (1 Cor. 15:38-44)

Paul does not tell us what a spiritual body is, though he does state that it does not consist of "flesh and blood" (15:50) and is therefore not subject to the limitations of bodily existence as humanity knows it.

The transformation that occurs in various aspects of nature has often been used as a metaphor for what might be the change from a physical body to a spiritual body. The butterfly, for example, has been a symbol because of its metamorphosis from a caterpillar to a cocoon to a butterfly.

An example from nature I have long enjoyed is a story Cecil B. DeMille, the great motion picture producer and director reputedly told to his children and grandchildren. One summer day he was in Maine, in a canoe on a lake deep in the woods. He was all alone. He wanted to do some work on a movie script, so he let the canoe drift idly while he worked. Suddenly, he discovered that he was in low water, about four inches deep, near the shore and he could see the bottom of the lake. He told the story of what he observed: "Down below the surface of a quiet pond lived a little colony of water bugs. They were a happy colony. For many hours they were busy, scurrying over the soft mud on the bottom. They did notice that every once in a while one of their colony seemed to lose interest in going about with its friends. Clinging to the stem of a lily pond it gradually moved out of sight and was seen no more.

'Look!' said one of the water bugs to another, 'one of our colony is climbing up the lily stalk. Where do you suppose she is going?'

Up, up, up, slowly it went. As they watched, the water bug disappeared from sight. Its friends waited and waited but it didn't return. 'That's funny!' said one water bug to another.

'Wasn't she happy here?' asked a second water bug.

'Where do you suppose she went?' wondered a third.

No one had an answer. They were greatly puzzled. Finally, one of the water bugs, a leader in the colony, gathered its friends together. 'I have an idea. The next one of us who climbs up the lily stalk must promise to come back and tell us where he or she went.'

'We promise,' they said.

One Spring day, not long after, the very water bug who had suggested the plan found himself climbing up the lily stalk. Up, up, up, he went. Before he knew what was happening, he had broken through the surface of the water, and fallen onto the broad, green lily pad above. When he awoke, he looked about with surprise. He couldn't believe what he saw. A startling change had come to his old body. His movement revealed four silver wings and a long tail. Even as he struggled, he felt an impulse to move his wings. The warmth of the sun soon dried the moisture from the new body. He moved his wings again and suddenly found himself up above the water. He had become a dragonfly.

Swooping and dipping in great curves, he flew through the air. He felt exhilarated in the new atmosphere.

By and by, the new dragonfly lighted happily on a lily pad to rest. Then it was that he chanced to look below the surface to the bottom of the pond. He was right above his old friends, the water bugs. There they were, scurrying about, just as he had been doing some time before. Then the dragonfly remembered the promise: 'The next one of us who climbs up the lily stalk will come back and tell where he or she went and why.'

Without thinking the dragonfly started down. Suddenly he hit the surface of the water and bounced away. Now that he was a dragonfly he could no longer go into the water. And so the dragonfly flew off happily into the wonderful new world of sun and air."

Do you think that if God would do that for a water bug, God wouldn't do so much more for you and I? If there is a physical body, there is a spiritual body.

Paul seems to think that the resurrection will not occur, however, until the second coming of Christ. In 1 Thessalonians 4:13-17, Paul offers words of reassurance to those Christians who are upset that some of their family and friends have died before Christ comes again and therefore may not be able to take part in His coming. We should note that the early Christians expected Christ to return during their lifetime. Paul tells them not to worry. God will bring along those who have "fallen asleep," the Christian euphemism for dying, when Christ comes again. In fact, they will have precedence over those living at the time of the end. That event will consist in the Lord's appearing from heaven to defeat the powers of evil. Then all the faithful, both those who have been raised from the dead and those who never died, will be joined with the Lord forever.

And yet in his letter to the Philippians, Paul writes as though he expected to be taken to the presence of Christ immediately when he died. He says: "...I desire to depart and be with Christ, which is better by far..." (Phil. 1:23)

The evidence of a spiritual body seems to be corroborated by many who have had near-death experiences. In his 1975 book, "Life After Life," Dr. Raymond A. Moody describes case histories of men and women who were medically dead, but who came back to life and told what they experienced.

In a summary of his stories, he pieced together a composite picture. He says that all persons experienced a floating out of their physical bodies. They were aware of another person who helped them in their transition to another place of existence. They were greeted by loved ones who had previously died. They experienced a loving, warm spirit, a being of light. At some point they found themselves approaching some sort of barrier, apparently representing the limit between earthly life and the next life. Yet, they find that they must go back, that the time for their death has not yet come. At this point they resist, for by now they are taken up with their experiences and do not want to return. They are overwhelmed by intense feelings of joy, love and peace. Somehow they become reunited with their old body and live.[54]

In a 1990 Gallop poll, it was reported that more than 22 million U.S. adults have had a near-death experience.

I vividly remember a man dying of cancer who told me about his near-death experience. One time while he was in the hospital his heart stopped and he remembered floating over his body, seeing white light and loved ones calling him. He was resuscitated, however, and restored to life. He told me he no longer feared death because when he died he felt peace, joy and no pain.

Since people have been more willing to talk about their near-death experiences, scientists have sought to find a scientific explanation. According to an article in "U.S. News & World Report," Michael Persinger, a neuroscientist at Laurentian University in Sudbury, Ontario, has induced many of the characteristics of a near-death experience- the sensation of moving through a tunnel, the brilliant white light, by stimulating the brain's right temporal lobe with mild electro-magnetic fields. And the U.S. Navy has managed to replicate many of the sensations of a near-death experience by subjecting test pilots to massive centrifugal force. Such physical stress can induce the presence of a patriarchal figure interpreted by some as God.

In the same magazine article, Sherwin Nuland, author of "How We Die," is quoted as ascribing near-death experiences to the actions of opiate-like compounds in the brain known as endorphins, which are released by the brain at times of great stress. He scoffs at those who view near-death experiences as a temporary bridge to an afterlife. [55]

Yet there are scoffers who say that finding a chemical change in the brain does not necessarily prove that it causes near death experiences.

We know from the experience of the disciples that Jesus returned to earth with a new kind of body, a form of being that defied description. In John's Gospel he had an ability to appear and disappear. But he wasn't a ghost, for the risen Lord came and took food and offered his body for inspection to the doubting Thomas.

Words fail us when we try to describe life beyond this one, for we see only through a mirror and dimly. But I believe that in Paul's attempt to describe the resurrection body, he was trying to say that in the world to come God's love will not separate us from God nor from those we love who have gone before.

What that "heaven" will be like, we don't know. The Bible is vague on that matter. The Old Testament portrays heaven as a celestial sphere above the earth from which God rules creation. But there is no suggestion that heaven is the final destination of earthly souls.

The most vivid and familiar images of heaven appear in the New Testament book of Revelation. It is there that we find the often popularized descriptions of pearly gates and streets of gold, of a vast white throne, and throngs of angels gathered around God. But the meaning and significance of those images are widely debated. For one thing, the holy city, the new Jerusalem is depicted as coming down from heaven to earth.

Some Christian theologians have viewed Revelation as a description of future events with a final Judgment Day and the end of the present world. Other theologians view Revelation as literature intended to give hope to first-century Christians living in Asia Minor who were facing Roman persecution. No matter, no one has come back to accurately describe an afterlife. It is more important to state that for the believer, heaven means dwelling forever in the presence of God. The particulars we won't know until we experience them.

Many, however, have made jokes about the afterlife. One of my favorites is the story of a woman who died after a long illness and arrived at the Gates of Heaven. While she is waiting for St. Peter to greet her, she peeked through the Gates. She saw a beautiful banquet table. Sitting all around were her parents and all the other people she had loved who had died before her. They saw her and began calling greetings to her: "Hello." "How are you! We've been waiting for you!" "Good to see you."

When St. Peter came by, the woman said to him: "This is such a wonderful place! How do I get in?"

"You have to spell a word," St. Peter told her.

"Which word?" the woman asked.

"Love."

The woman correctly spelled "love" and St. Peter welcomed her into heaven.

About six months later, St. Peter came to the woman and asked her to watch the Gates of Heaven for him that day. While the woman was guarding the Gates of Heaven, her husband arrived. "I'm surprised to see you," the woman said, "How have you been?"

"Oh, I've been doing pretty well since you died," her husband told her. "I married the beautiful young nurse who took care of you while you were ill. And then I won the lottery. I sold the little house you and I lived in and bought a big mansion. And my wife and I traveled all around the world. We were on vacation and I went water skiing today. I fell, the ski hit my head, and here I am. How do I get in?"

"You have to spell a word," the woman told him.

"Which word?" her husband asked.

"Czechoslovakia."

We learn through Jesus that at the heart of the universe is a heavenly parent, who is kind, compassionate and loving. Jesus described heaven as like a loving home. He tells us in the Gospel of John: "Let not your hearts be troubled; believe in God, believe also in me. In my Father's house are many rooms, if it were not so, would I have told you that I go and prepare a place for you? And when I go and prepare a place for you, I will come again, and will take you to myself, that where I am you may be also."(John 14:1-3)

The apostle Paul adds to that when he says :"For we know that if the earthly tent we live in is destroyed, we have a building from God, a house not made with hands, eternal in the heavens." (2 Corinthians 5:1)

If we think of death as going from one home to another where we will meet family and loved ones, then death does not seem so apprehensive or foreboding.

In 1800, a boy named John Todd was born in Rutland, Vermont. Shortly afterward the family moved to the little village of Killingsworth. And there, when John was only six years of age, both his parents died. The children in the home had to be parceled out among relatives and a kindhearted aunt who lived in North Killingsworth agreed to take John and give him a home. He lived with her for fifteen years until he went away to study for the ministry. When he was middle-aged, his aunt became ill and thought that she would soon die. In great distress she wrote her nephew a letter asking what would death be like? Would it mean the end of everything or would there be beyond death a chance to continue living? In reply John Todd wrote:

"It is now thirty-five years since I, a little boy of six, was left quite alone in the world. You sent me word you would give me a home and be a kind mother to me. I have never forgotten the day when I made the long journey of ten miles to your house in North Killingsworth. I can still recall my disappointment when, instead of coming for me yourself, you sent your servant, Caesar, to fetch me. I well remember my tears and my anxiety, as perched high on your horse and clinging tightly to Caesar, I rode off to my new home. Night fell before we finished the journey and as it grew dark, I became lonely and afraid."

"Do you think she'll go to bed before I get there?" I asked Caesar anxiously. "Oh, no," he said reassuringly. "She'll sure stay up for you. When we get out of these woods you'll see her candle shining in the window."

"Presently we did ride out in a clearing and there, sure enough, was your candle. I remember you were waiting at the door, that you put your arms close about me and that you lifted me- a tired and bewildered little boy- down from the horse. You had a big fire burning on the hearth, a hot supper waiting for me on the stove. After supper, you took me to my new room, you heard me say my prayers and then you sat beside me until I fell asleep."

"You probably realize why I am recalling all this to your memory. Someday soon, God will send for you, to take you to a new home. Don't fear the summons, the strange journey, or the messenger of death. God can be trusted to do as much for you as you were kind enough to do for me so many years ago. At the end of the road you will find love and a welcome waiting, and you will be safe in God's care. I shall watch you and pray for you until you are out of sight, and then wait for the day when I shall make the journey myself and find you waiting at the end of the road to greet me."[56]

If we can believe that God loves us so much that God will eternally care for each of us, it makes each day of our journey through life more hopeful, more meaningful, more joyous. Death is not the final answer. As Paul said, "Neither death nor life…nor anything else in all creation will be able to separate us from the love of God that is in Christ Jesus our Lord." (Rom. 8:38-39)

CHAPTER NINE
HAPPY HOLIDAYS

"Each day comes bearing its gifts. Untie the ribbons." Ann
Schabacker

The following letter appeared in a Dear Abby column. "Dear Abby: My husband and I are senior citizens living on a fixed income. It has become harder and harder to purchase gifts or give money (which we have done in the past) to all our beloved family members. Recently a grandson called to inform us they are expecting their first child. Instead of being happy for them, we were filled with dread, because now there will be another gift to buy! During the year, I try to save for Christmas gifts, but it's never enough. I have told my husband that we are going to have to be honest with the family. He is too embarrassed to tell them that we cannot give like we have in the past. How have other senior citizens solved this problem? I lie awake nights worrying. The holidays should be a happy time, but I don't look forward to them anymore."

The holidays are projected as "happy" times, especially Christmas and New Year's, but holidays are not always happy occasions. As the above letter indicates, finances can keep us from doing what we think we should, and when we can't we are likely to feel guilty. My mother-in-law solved such a problem by giving an equal amount of money to each grandchild. She would tell them or their parents that that was all she could afford and that was it!

Holidays can be difficult for another reason. My first year in seminary, I spent Thanksgiving by eating a turkey dinner by myself at a Howard Johnson's restaurant. I was in Boston and my parents were in Pittsburgh. I didn't have enough vacation time to drive home, nor enough money to fly home. Most of the other students had gone home, the school cafeteria was closed, and so I found myself alone with nowhere to go. Being alone does not mean one has to be lonely, but holiday times are often lonely times for many people. The loss of a spouse or other loved one during the year can be especially difficult at holiday times or at birthdays, wedding anniversaries or the anniversary of the loss. At Christmas, an awareness of the empty place at the table, the absence of presents under the Christmas tree, and other missing ingredients tends to heighten the sense of loss related to the holidays.

Holidays tend to stir memories of previous holidays and can bring a sense of sadness with the loss of the loved one. At the same time, talking about past memories can be a healing experience as you relive a favorite food that was always prepared, or items that were hung on the tree, or customs followed. Even as a teenager, I fondly remembered Christmases while growing-up. We moved from Syracuse, New York to Long Island when I was sixteen, but at Christmas I would remember our house in Syracuse. My sister and I would be up early but we would have to wait for our grandmother and great-aunt to get-up and dressed before we could go downstairs to see what Santa had brought. At the time we were anxious to go downstairs, but looking back, memories of time spent with my grandmother and great-aunt were comforting when we didn't have them with us.

Even if a spouse is still living, many older adults find themselves living far away from children and grandchildren. They may not be able to be together with them at holidays due to finances or health. The sense of separation can also be difficult at holiday times, especially at Christmas, which has come to mean so much in our society.

Having a loved one die near a special holiday, such as Christmas, can heighten the sense of loss. From then on Christmas will always be remembered as the time we lost so and so.

Our expectations can also magnify our sense of loss, especially at Christmas, which is idealized as a happy time. Songs and advertisements depict Christmas as a time of peace, love and joy. If we've recently lost a spouse, it's difficult to feel any joy and yet we may feel guilty because we're expected to be joyful at Christmas.

I have found that people may have selective memory at Christmas or other occasions. They may idealize times spent with a loved one and overlook, forget or deny times when the occasion was one of arguments, disappointments or difficulties. I remember one woman, Eva, a friend of my mother-in-law. When her husband was alive she constantly complained about him. He could do no right. After he died, he could do no wrong. We forget the "bad" times.

There are steps you can take, however, to help give the holidays a new meaning. The holidays, especially Thanksgiving and Christmas, can become a time of peace and reflection, a time to cherish the gift your loved one has been, and continues to be, in the life of your family. Even if you have no family left and were never married, you can still make the holidays a meaningful time. Here are a few ideas that may help you:

1. Be realistic. In the past you may have filled the house with decorations, sent out a hundred cards, baked dozens of cookies. And so we still have a mental picture of how things ought to be. If we're grieving or if physical problems make it difficult to do all we've done in the past, be realistic. Perhaps this year just decorate a room, a corner or a table. Send out only a few cards. Buy some cookies. There is nothing wrong

with simplicity. Decide what is important to you this holiday season, and forget the rest. You can always add things back in years to come.

2. Take care of yourself physically. Eat wisely. Avoid the temptation to overindulge in the season's many culinary delights. For some, it can be tempting to numb the pain of the loss of a loved one, or the pain of loneliness, through alcohol, but you will only feel worse later. Make time for exercise and rest. Exercise is an important stress reliever and a healthy mood elevator.

3. Do something for others. There are many ways to help others at the holidays. If you're physically able there are numerous opportunities to help at soup kitchens, and community agencies. Usually local news media inform people of places volunteers are needed. Or, contact agencies in your community. Your church may also be a place. Many churches deliver food and/or gifts to others, especially at Thanksgiving and Christmas. Visit a nursing home. If you are not physically able to do the necessary work, you can always contribute financially to some area of interest. If you're limited financially perhaps you could write a card or phone someone who has meant a lot to you and tell them how much you appreciate their friendship, their help or whatever.

4. Acknowledge your feelings. If you don't feel the joy you think you're expected to feel, it's ok. Let yourself cry if you feel sad. If you're sad because of the loss of a loved one, try to remember all the joyous times you spent together and how your loved one brought you the gifts of love, joy, companionship. You might even want to write these gifts on strips of paper to be placed in a gift box or hung on a tree. They will be positive reminders of the joy your loved one has brought into your life.

5. Be present oriented. In other words, live one day at a time, but don't spend that day reminiscing or longing for the past or worrying about the future. We can't bring back the way things used to be. If we spend all

our time focusing on the past, no matter how enjoyable it was, we miss opportunities for enjoying the present. Likewise, if we worry about the future, we also miss what we can do in the present. I know of many people in their seventies and eighties who refuse to spend their money because they are saving it for their old age. Unfortunately, one spouse often dies before they use any of their money to travel or do something they have dreamed about doing for many years, but put off. We can waste the present by using up the present moment planning, figuring, hoping, wishing, dreaming, or whatever, about a future time or event. Ask yourself what it is that you want out of this holiday. Give yourself permission to try new things.

6. Focus on the spiritual dimension of the holidays. The word holiday comes from the idea of a "holy day." The Hebrew word for holy, kadosh, means to set apart from sin; to devote to God. Whenever we celebrate a holiday, we should recognize it as a day set apart for God's purposes. Any holiday, religious or secular, should be a time in which we look for the spiritual significance of what we are celebrating. The sights and sounds of the holidays, especially Thanksgiving and Christmas, can be meaningful as we allow them to remind us of the spiritual meanings of these days. Take time to attend church services, read stories from the Bible or religious works that pertain to the holidays. Take time for prayer and quiet meditation and reflection. Express your feelings to God. Utilize the therapy of thanksgiving. "Count your blessings" by making a list of all God's benefits (Ps. 103:2). Review this list regularly, especially when you feel an attack of "If only..." coming on.

In their book, How To Say Goodbye, authors Joanne Smith and Judy Biggs offer some suggestions shared by other bereaved people on planning for the holidays or other special occasions. They say, ask yourself these questions: [57]

What can I handle comfortably?

Do I want to talk about my lost loved one at holiday celebrations?

Can I handle the responsibility of the family dinner and/ or holiday parties or do I need for someone else to take over some of these traditional tasks?

Will I stay home for the holidays or "run away" to a totally different holiday environment this year?

Have I involved or considered my children in holiday planning?

Do I really enjoy doing this? Do other family members really enjoy this?

Is this a task that can be shared by other family members?

Would Christmas be Christmas without doing this (baking Christmas cookies, sending cards, other traditions)?

The authors also suggest not being afraid to make changes. They say that making changes can make things less painful. They say you might want to:

Open presents Christmas Eve instead of Christmas morning, or vice versa.

Eat dinner at a different time.

Attend a different church for your Christmas Eve service.

The authors also suggest your greatest comfort may come in doing something for others such as:

Giving a gift in memory of your loved one.

Donating the money you would have spent on your loved one for a gift to a particular charity.

Adopting a needy family for the holidays.

Inviting a guest to share holiday festivities.

Hopefully, these suggestions will enable you to cope with the holidays and find new meaning in them.

Sometimes people want to be alone and not celebrate what they don't feel like celebrating. If you have family, however, it can be helpful to spend holidays with them for they can provide needed support and love. As time goes on and you can focus on happy memories of previous holidays, the holidays may become less a time to dread.

CHAPTER TEN
WHEN DEATH TOUCHES
YOUR LIFE

"The fear of death keeps us from living, not from dying."   Paul C.
Roud

As a pastor for over thirty years I have officiated at hundreds
of funerals. It is never an easy task. It is especially difficult the
more you know the person. Yet, it is still difficult when trying
to provide a service for someone you've never known, but
whose family wants to have a service for their loved one. I
always try to find something personal to say about the person,
what they were like, what they meant to the family, what
their occupation was, or their hobbies and special interests.
It seems to help the family and friends to put the life of their
loved one into the larger picture of God's love and help them
make sense of their grief, or at least cope with their grief.

Throughout our life we experience many kinds of losses,
but the most profound loss most people experience is the
death of a loved one, whether it be a spouse, a parent, a child,
or someone close to them.

As the writer of the Old Testament book of Ecclesiastes exclaims, "For everything there is a season…a time to be born, and a time to die…"

Death is a reality for which we are never quite ready or prepared, no matter what our age.

When death comes to a person who has lived a long and active life, we are not ready. We may wish we could have the person with us for many more months or years. My great-grandmother lived to be 102! Her mind was still sharp. Her health was still fairly good. Her body simply wore out. I always remember her with a smile on her face and a happy outlook. It was a joy for me to visit her. I wish she could have lived forever in this world.

When death comes mercifully, after a person has been terminally ill for weeks, or months, we are still not quite prepared. We may have mixed feelings. We don't want to see them suffer, yet we may want them to live, hoping a cure might suddenly be discovered.

When death comes suddenly, people usually find themselves in a state of shock, as if they were in a dream world, unable to fully comprehend what has happened.

No matter when death comes or how it comes, we are never ready for the grief, the sadness, the pain and the sense of loss it brings.

It can be important and helpful to understand the feelings and reactions that often accompany grief, both for our own self-understanding and so that we may be more understanding of others experiencing grief. Many of these reactions to grief have been reported in numerous books and literature, so I won't dwell on them, but briefly mention them.

Psychiatrist Elizabeth Kubler-Ross's book, *On Death and Dying*, described five stages one may experience on one's journey through grief. [58]

Denial, she says, is the first response. We are in a state of shock. "This cannot be true," we say to ourselves. God has made us so that we can bear pain and sorrow, but when the sorrow is sudden or overwhelming, we may find ourselves in a state of disbelief. We just can't believe that he or she is dead. We may experience a feeling of numbness or unreality. This initial stage may last for hours or even days.

Denial may take the form of immobility. I have seen individuals who seemed totally drained of energy, virtually unable to move. Others may throw themselves into a whirlwind of busyness, going from one thing to another, with seemingly endless energy.

It can be especially painful to clean-out clothing and other articles of the deceased. At that time death can become real as we face the task of deciding what to do with the deceased's personal belongings. Such a task quickly brings to mind our feelings of grief.

In the Biblical account of the death of Lazarus and Jesus' raising of Lazarus, we find a number of the stages of grief, including denial. When Jesus told his disciples, in figurative terms, "Our friend Lazarus has fallen asleep; but I am going there to wake him up" (John 11:11), the response of the disciples was, "Lord, if he sleeps, he will get better" (vs. 12). John explains that Jesus had been speaking of his death, but his disciples thought he meant natural sleep. There is some confusion on the part of the disciples, and perhaps denial, as well. Jesus finally breaks through their denial by stating plainly, "Lazarus is dead" (vs. 14).

Anger comes next. As the reality of the loss begins to sink in, our emotions begin to surface. Anger is a common response. Our anger may be displaced outwardly. We may blame the medical profession, such as the doctors and nurses who cared for our loved one. "They're no good. They don't know what they're doing. If the doctors had really been on top of things, they would have found the cancer before it spread and he wouldn't have died."

We may also find ourselves angry at God. When Jesus' friend Lazarus was ill, Jesus didn't come to visit Martha and Mary for several days. When he did arrive, Martha's greeting could be taken as anger. "Lord," Martha said to Jesus,"If you had been here, my brother would not have died." Jn. 11:21

We may even be angry at the person who died. The thought is that they died and left us here by ourselves to pay the bills and cope with life.

We want to know why God didn't do something to help our loved one. We may wonder if God really cares about us. At the time it may not seem so.

Anger can also occur if we learn that we have a life-threatening illness. At such times we can also experience disbelief and then anger. And we have a right to be angry. There's nothing wrong with being angry at our loss or threatened loss.

It is important to learn how to release anger constructively. Blow off steam to someone who will listen, such as a relative, a friend, a neighbor, your pastor, priest or rabbi. Exercise is another way to use up the energy created by anger. Writing your thoughts and feelings down in a journal can also be helpful.

We may turn our anger inward at ourselves. Guilt usually follows. Having or expressing anger toward others or God often leaves us feeling guilty. This kind of guilt may be expressed in such thoughts as, "I didn't spend enough time with him." "If only I had told her more often I love her."

Often such feelings of guilt will involve true guilt, since no relationship is perfect. It may be guilt for things that were said or done in the past that were hurtful. Some of those words might have been said shortly before the loved one died. These need to be acknowledged and forgiven. It can be helpful to talk to a clergyperson, a counselor, and certainly God. You could also write a letter to the one who died, confessing your sorrow and asking them for forgiveness. Then forgive yourself.

You might wonder how writing a letter to the deceased would help, but it's purpose is to help you sort through, express and deal with your feelings, which such a letter can do.

On the other hand, much of what we may feel can be termed false guilt. It is unrealistic. To say that we didn't spend enough time with our loved one is something only our loved one could determine. One might want to spend as much time as possible with someone, but that is an unrealistic expectation.

Perhaps guilt is alluded to when Martha said to Jesus: "But I know that even now God will give you whatever you ask" (John 11:22). We may be reading more into Martha's mind than we should, but her words may indicate she felt, "If only I had prayed more." In times of grief, we may say to ourselves, "If only I had prayed more, or gone to church more, or you fill in the blank, my loved one would not have died."

A third stage is bargaining. This is apt to occur more when death is imminent, either our own, or the death of a loved one. It is an attempt to postpone death. Sometimes it is a promise of "good behavior." It may be a deadline, asking God to wait until after a grandson's wedding, or the next birthday or holiday.

Bargaining may also occur as a result of guilt. We may feel guilty for not attending church very often, for example, and ask God for more time so we might have a chance to "suddenly" become more religious.

There usually comes a stage of depression, a feeling of loneliness and isolation. We may feel uncertain about the future. What will happen? Can I handle life? We may feel that no one understands what we're going through. We may prefer to be alone, refusing to see family or friends. There may even be the feeling that God doesn't care, or even that there is a God. Jesus faced this loneliness when on the cross he cried out, "My God, my God, why have you forsaken me?"

I don't believe that God purposely sends illness, suffering or death to punish us, keep us humble, or strengthen our character. At times I've heard people give one of these explanations as to why their loved one died.

The fifth stage is one of acceptance. It "should not be mistaken," says Kubler-Ross, "for a happy phase." It is "almost void of feelings." It seems to be a time when the struggles of the other stages has finished. If we believe, however, that God does not purposely send grief-producing situations, then we can move from the "why" questions- "Why is this happening to me?" "Why did this happen to my loved one?" to the "how" questions- "How can I make it through this difficult time? How can I cope?"

Critics have argued that Kuber-Ross's stages are not as pat as she believes, although she has said that not everyone experiences these stages in exactly the same way or the same sequence.

There does seem to be a consensus among those working with grief that an emotional release is important to coping with death. We need to allow ourselves to express the emotions we feel. William Shakespeare in *Henry VI* said, "To weep is to make less the depth of grief." Jesus wept when he learned that his friend Lazarus had died.

There are various manifestations of grief that we may experience as we mourn the loss of a loved one, a friend, or try to deal with our own impending death. Some of these have already been mentioned, but it might be helpful to list them according to the ways they are expressed, rather than as stages, which are limiting and too mechanical:

Feelings: Sadness is felt over the death of a loved one or friend. There is also anger. Anger comes from many sources. There is a sense of frustration that there was nothing one could do to prevent the death. There is anger at the loved one leaving us. Such anger many come from a tendency to feel helpless, to feel unable to exist without the person. Sometimes anger is directed away from the deceased toward someone else. If someone else can be blamed, such as a doctor, family member, or even God, perhaps the loss could have been prevented. There may also be feelings of guilt. We may feel guilty for not being loving enough towards the person, or perhaps guilt over something we said and now regret. There can also be anxiety. There can be a fear that we won't be able to take care of ourself on our own. The death of a loved one also makes us more aware of our own mortality, and that can also cause anxiety. The great writer C.S. Lewis also knew this anxiety and said after losing his wife Joy, "No one ever told me that grief felt so like fear. I am not afraid, but the sensation is like being afraid. The same fluttering in the stomach, the same restlessness, the yawning. I keep on swallowing."[59]

One may also experience feelings of loneliness, fatigue, yearning, numbness and relief, especially if a loved one suffered a lengthy or painful illness. Relief doesn't mean you didn't love the person. It simply means that you're glad their suffering is over, though its okay to feel some relief yourself if you've spent a lot of time caring for the person. Its a natural reaction.

<u>Physical sensations.</u> Most commonly reported were hollowness in the stomach, tightness in the chest, tightness in the throat, oversensitivity to noise, shortness of breath, weakness in the muscles, lack of energy, dry mouth and a sense of depersonalization, in which nothing seems real, including oneself.

<u>Cognitions.</u> These are thought patterns. Usually the first thought to occur is disbelief, especially if death is sudden. One may be confused and have difficulty concentrating. There may be a preoccupation of thoughts about the deceased. There may be a sense of presence of the deceased.

<u>Behaviors.</u> One may have difficulty going to sleep and/or may wake up early. You may not feel like eating. You may call out for the person. Usually this comes from habit. You're so used to the person that you absent-mindedly look for them or call out for them. You may withdraw socially. You may cry. You may treasure objects that belonged to the deceased and resist parting with their belongings. You may dream about the deceased. For example, Dr. J. William Worden tells about a patient, Esther, who was filled with remorse over the death of her mother. Although she had visited her ill mother faithfully every day, she had left to get something to eat. While she was out, her mother died. In therapy, she had a dream about her mother. In this dream she saw herself trying to assist her mother to walk down a slippery pathway so she would not fall. But her mother fell and nothing Esther could do in the dream would save her. It was impossible. This dream was a

significant turning point in her therapy because she allowed herself to see that nothing she could have done would have kept her mother from dying. This important insight gave her permission to shed the guilt which she had been carrying for years. [60]

For some people, grief is a very intense experience; for others, it is mild. For some, grief begins at the time of loss; for others, it may be delayed. For some, grief lasts a brief period of time; for others, grief seems to go on forever. There is no one way to say how grief will be for each person. It is an individual experience. Don't try to compare your grief with what anyone else has gone through or allow others to place a timeline on your recovery period.

Dr. J. William Worden feels that there are four tasks involved in the grief or mourning process: to accept the reality of the loss, to experience the pain of the loss, to adjust to an environment in which the deceased is missing, and to reinvest one's emotional energy.[61]

To speak of "tasks of mourning," implies taking action. The "stages" of grief mentioned by Dr. Kubler-Ross, and others, seem to be more passive, something one passes through, and is acted upon. To speak of grief as a "task" can give one hope. In times of grief one feels helpless. To know there is something you can do to be better gives one hope and encouragement that someday life will seem better. This is not to deny the love one feels for the deceased or to diminish it. The love we have for loved ones will always be a part of our lives and our memories. It is important to allow ourselves to grieve, but it is also important not to get "stuck" somewhere in our grief, so that we become fixated on the deceased the rest of our life. A classic example of this involved Queen Victoria, who after the death of Prince Albert, had his clothes and shaving items laid out daily and often went around the palace speaking to him

Or, remember the story of Miss Havisham in Charles Dicken's book, *Great Expectations*.. She was engaged to be married. Dickens describes all the preparations she makes for the wedding- the dresses, the arrangements with the church, the reception and all the other preparations. When she arrives at the church, however, she learns that her boyfriend has decided not to marry her. She is literally left, jilted, at the door of the church.

When Miss Havisham returns home, she pulls down all the blinds in her house. She stops the clock at the moment when the wedding was scheduled to take place. She dresses in her wedding gown every day until it is in tatters. The wedding cake is left on the table until it is dust. Miss Havisham brings her life to a standstill.

The twenty-third Psalm says, "Yea, though I walk through the valley of the shadow of death." The important words are "walk through."

Bereavement is like a journey. We are traveling from a place of happiness, searching for another place of happiness to make our home. It may seem like no such place exists. Yet along the way we may find glimpses.

There is no clear cut guideline for when the journey will end. Usually after a year or two life seems more like living once again. You will find it a little easier to get back to the demands of everyday living. Give yourself time. In America, we are such a fast-paced society. We are used to instant this and instant that. We eat instant breakfasts, go to drive-through restaurants for lunch, and microwave dinners. We can find quick answers via the internet and computers. We have pills to give us quick relief from pain. All this can have a carry-over effect on our emotions and feelings, and we think we should also achieve instant release from the pain of grief. But there is no short-cut to the healing of grief. It takes time.

"One day at a time" is the motto of many self-help groups. It can also be very helpful to those who are mourning. Take each day for what it is. Try to get through each day as it comes rather than worrying about what tomorrow will be like. Try to find meaning in one day at a time.

The more dependent a person has been on a spouse, the more difficult adjusting to their loss can be. One woman I knew never learned how to drive. She let her husband do all the driving. When he died suddenly she was left in her late 60's with a car, but didn't know what to do with it. She lived several miles from any stores. What did she do? She took driving lessons and got her driver's license!

It's important, I think, for spouses to help one another learn what they need to know should they find themselves independent. That may include getting a driver's license, doing the checkbook, learning where all the important papers are kept, knowing the financial situation, knowing how to cook, to clean, to do laundry, even to work at a computer. Maybe there are other items you can think of that are important for your spouse to know. Don't wait until it may be too late!

The pain of grief is the price we pay for loving someone. Whenever we choose to love someone, we are also choosing to be hurt, for someday they will leave us, or we will leave them.

Here are some suggestions for helping you adjust or cope with the death of a loved one:

1. Take time to accept death. We may initially hope it was all a bad dream and that we are going to wake up and everything will be all right. It is difficult to accept the reality of death, but it is important to gradually let the reality sink in and come to accept that our loved one did die.

2. Take time to let go. From birth to death, life is a process of letting go. Death is the ultimate form of letting go of someone we love. Letting go means adjusting to a new reality in which our loved one is no longer physically present. Letting go can be easier when we are willing to entrust our loved one to God's care and also entrust our needs to God's care.

3. Take time to make decisions. Often we can't think clearly for some time. Well-meaning advice and invitations can come to us. Our mind may be filled with questions. Should I sell my house and move into an apartment or move in with a relative? Give yourself time to make any major decisions.

4. Take time to share. It can be helpful to join a grief support group. Sharing memories and feelings with people who are also grieving can be especially helpful. You can learn you're not crazy because you feel or behave a certain way. You can learn how they are coping. Talking about your loved one can be therapeutic.

In our society, men seem to have more difficulty showing and expressing their emotions and feelings, while women seem to be better at having a support system of friends and others with whom they can talk.

It may help to keep a journal. Each day write down your thoughts, your feelings, your dreams, your behavior, whatever you want. This is an excellent way to document daily experiences. Reviewing such a journal periodically can help you to see where you are in the grieving process.

5. Take time to believe. Grief can shake our faith. We may wonder if God has forgotten us. We may be angry at God for taking our loved one. It may be difficult to go to church, or to pray. I remember a woman who wouldn't go to church for the longest time because singing the hymns reminded her of her mother and she was afraid she would begin to cry and she didn't want to cry in public. Yet, in our grief, God is with us. Give God a chance to work in our lives and with our grief.

6. Take time to forgive. As we have said we may feel guilt about something we said or did, or about what we didn't say or didn't do. We need to make peace with ourselves. We need to realize we're not perfect. We can't change anything by dwelling on our imperfections. It only makes us miserable. God forgives us. We need to forgive ourselves. We may also need to forgive the deceased if we find ourselves feeling angry at them.

7. Take time to feel good about yourself. The death of a loved one can affect how we feel about ourselves. We may not feel like doing anything or going anywhere. We may not take care of ourselves like we should and that can lead to feelings of low self-esteem. We can feel

sorry for ourselves and that can also lead to a negative self-image and outlook. This is especially true if we were dependent on the other person to drive or to handle the finances. And so, as you learn new skills, be proud for your accomplishments, no matter how insignificant they may seem. They can help to build confidence in yourself.

8. Take time to socialize. You may not feel like being with others, and you may not feel like you fit in anymore with your old social group. Widows and widowers often think they don't fit into the couple-oriented model of our society. It can be helpful to try to meet new friends. Perhaps learning something new or taking up a hobby can lead to new friendships. Church or civic groups can be places to meet people. If there is a Y in your community, it can also be a great place to meet new friends.

9. Take time to laugh. You may consider laughter to be an inappropriate response to grief, but laughter can help to bring about healing to our spirit as we recall, smile and laugh at memories that come to us. You may recall humorous times together. I remember a time with my parents when I was a child. My parents, my sister and I were walking home one winter night after a movie. The sidewalks were slippery so we were holding on to one another. One slipped and all four of us fell on the ice together. All we could do was laugh!

10. Take time to give. One of the best ways to overcome our loneliness and sorrow is to be concerned about the loneliness and sorrow of others. In a grief support group you can share your experiences with others which can enable them to learn ways to cope and to learn that what they are feeling and experiencing can be normal. There are other ways to help others. One woman, whose husband died from cancer, became active with the American Cancer Society as a volunteer. At Christmas she helped out at an American Cancer

Society booth in a shopping mall wrapping Christmas packages. A widower became involved as a leader with a 4H group of boys. He loved photography and shared his knowledge with a group of boys who were interested in photography as a 4H project. There are many ways to give. Being able to help someone gives us meaning and helps us feel good. It takes us away from focusing on our sorrow and gets us involved in thinking about others.

The journey of grief is often a painful and seemingly lonely one. The road to recovery can be helped by exploring these ten suggestions. They can help us begin a journey of discovering new meaning about ourselves and about life. They can help us to love again; love ourselves, love others and love life.

All of us come to a time when we must contemplate our own death. It can be a frightening experience and one we may try to deny or put off. Youth seem more willing to take chances with their lives, driving too fast, smoking or drinking, using drugs, participating in death-defying activities, often with the attitude that "I'm too young to die," or "It won't happen to me." Perhaps as we grow older and see our bodies change, and family and friends die, we take more seriously our own mortality.

When you begin to contemplate your own death there may be feelings of regret for how you have lived in the past, or guilt for how you have treated others. You may wonder if your life has been worthwhile.

If you've been suffering because of health problems, you may come to a point where you look forward to dying. I have known many Christians who have told me they were ready to die. They believed a better life, a life free of pain, was awaiting them.

I have found that people are often not so much afraid of death itself as they are of whatever pain may accompany death.

To contemplate our own mortality often means experiencing some of the stages or phases of grief we experience when a loved one dies. We don't want to believe it will happen. We may experience anger and sadness. We may try to bargain with God. But it is in our relationship with God that we find the answer to coping with our own mortality as well as coping with the death of loved ones and friends.

A former church member, who was in his seventies, had lost his wife the year before and was now diagnosed with bone cancer. He had one son who lived out of state. Eston wanted to remain at home rather than live with his son. He sold his house and moved into an apartment. He knew he was going to die; he knew his time was limited. When asked about his situation, Eston would respond, "What're you going to do?" He had accepted his situation.

I thought it might help him if he participated in a program sponsored by the American Cancer Society entitled, "I Can Cope." It was a six or eight week program involving weekly group meetings held at a local hospital. Its purpose was to educate cancer patients on ways to cope with their cancer, but also as a means of support.

I drove Eston to and from the weekly meetings and stayed with him at the meetings. Eston, it turned out, didn't need to find ways to cope. His faith in God enabled him to cope very well. He ended up helping others in the group finding ways to cope!

It can be important for you to think about your own death. For one, it can be helpful to your family if you can plan for arrangements at your death. Some people make arrangements with a local funeral home as to what they would like done when they die. Some pick out a casket and a burial site. Others make arrangements for cremation. Even if you don't go that far, it can be helpful for family or those who will take care of your body to have your wishes in writing and know where they are located. I officiated recently at the service for a man who died after a lengthy illness. He had made all the arrangements with a local funeral home, but he never told his wife. She found out when she called the funeral home to make arrangements! It's good for you to plan ahead, but share those plans with your family!

You may also want to have a living will which expresses your desire to keep a hospital and doctors from taking extraordinary measures to save your life. I sat in a hospital waiting room all night with a man whose wife lay in the next room kept alive by a respirator. Her doctors had concluded that she was being kept alive only by machines. Yet he had to make the life-death decision as to whether she should be kept on the machines.

Imagine yourself in a coma, if you can, unable to communicate with your family or doctors about the machinery being used to keep you alive. Would you want to stay on a respirator indefinitely? Would you want to be kept alive on a feeding tube for years with an unknown chance of recovery? Does your family and/or physician know what you would want in such a situation?

How much easier if we can make such decisions in writing before a loved one is put in the position of having to decide. Make certain, though, you write down in clear, specific language exactly what kinds of medical treatment you want or don't want, so there is no room for misinterpretation. A living will should also say whether or not you would like to receive medication for pain.

Appoint someone who will be legally responsible for carrying out your wishes. Choose a family member or person you trust. It might also be helpful to have in mind a backup in case your first choice dies before you do. Fill out a form for durable power of attorney for health care so the person can make decisions on your behalf. Give that person and family members a copy of your living will. Forms can be obtained from your doctor's office, or a local hospital.

If we think about death at all, most people I talk to say that they want to die quickly, mostly, in their sleep. Unfortunately the more common process is a slow decline as our system or organs gradually give out. Most of us would like to die at home; most of us won't. All of us hope to die without pain; many will be kept alive, in pain or discomfort. Without instructions from us or our family, a doctor's obligation is to provide life-sustaining treatment.

Another task is to prepare a list of relatives, friends and others who should be informed of our death.

It is also helpful to decide if you want a service, and if so, where it should be. Most funeral homes have chapels. If you are religious, I am a firm believer that the service should be held in the church, synagogue or place of worship. A service can be conducted within a few days of death, or at a future date as a memorial service. A memorial service at a later date sometimes allows more time flexibility for friends and relatives to attend the service. A service, with or without calling hours, is not for the deceased. It is more for the living. It offers family and friends an opportunity to say good-bye. It offers the chance for family and friends to provide emotional support for one another.

If you do decide on a service, it can be helpful for the officiating cleric for you to think about possible scripture readings, poems, hymns, etc., you might want included. My wife would like to have a Dixieland band playing, but that is another story.

With the help of a funeral director you can decide in advance if your body is to be in a family burial plot or one you need to purchase. If cremated, will your ashes be interred somewhere, or given to a relative? Also, if there are to be calling hours or a service, if people want to give contributions, should they be given to a favorite charity in lieu of flowers? Sometimes, it may be better to have no designation for contributions, but left to the discretion of the family. In a particular *Dear Abby* newspaper column I recall letters from widows describe how they couldn't have made it financially in the weeks following their spouse's death if it hadn't been for financial contributions at the time of death. Benefits from insurance companies or social security may take a few months. What do you do in the meantime? Contributions to the surviving spouse can be very helpful.

Funeral expenses can vary widely from place to place and the type of funeral desired. But if you plan ahead it can save your family a lot of anxious moments. Check with a local funeral director to get an idea of the costs involved.

Also make sure your will is updated. If you don't have a will it is essential to get one especially to save problems for family members. Be sure to have it done by an attorney.

Many people have wills, but they are not up to date. Tax laws change. If you have moved to another state, the laws in the new state may affect your will. Maybe the good friend or family member you named as executor has died, become incapacitated, or moved. Are distributions to beneficiaries the way you want them now, or the way you wanted them when the will was drawn up? You may have acquired some new things since a will was done that now need to be added or changed. Also, talking with family members about what they would want may help to avoid problems later.

In a broader sense we need to clean our house, so to speak, as we approach the end of life. Leaving a mess to be sorted out by children and others does not help them in their grief. We may want some of our possessions left to a church or preferred charity or to friends rather than being trashed. This means we need to think about them in advance and let our wishes be known.

A safe deposit box in your bank may be an invaluable place to keep important documents together, such as veteran discharge papers, naturalization, adoption and divorce papers, marriage and birth certificates, passports, titles to your automobile(s), insurance policies, deed to your house, investment papers, bank accounts, the original copy of your will, etc. There is often much confusion at the time of death. A safe deposit box can ease the search for important and needed documents.

While it may be obvious, it is essential to let someone else know about your end of life decisions and wishes. Certainly a spouse, child or other family member should know where you have stored your papers and documents. You may do all the planning for your own death, written down instructions and stored them away either in a safe deposit box or somewhere in your home, but if no one knows where they are they're not very helpful when you do die.

Writing an autobiography can also be helpful. While it may sound like a conceited thing to do, it can be helpful for future generations. Most of us may feel our lives aren't important enough to be known by others, but our grandchildren, great-grandchildren and other generations may want to know about us. I wish I knew more about my ancestors. Writing about ourselves can help future generations know what life was like during our time. It's important that we include in our autobiography not just facts about our lives, where we lived, what work we performed, but more of what were the major events of our time and how did we feel about them. What gave meaning to our lives? Think about what you would like your future generations to know about you and about life.

Preparing for death is something no one really wants to do. Experiencing the death of loved ones is also something no one wants to go through. We know, however, it is something we each must do. As Christians, we know that we have a loving God who travels with us on our journey through death. As the 23rd Psalm proclaims, "Yea, though I walk through the valley of the shadow of death, I will fear no evil, for thou art with me."

CHAPTER ELEVEN
ENDINGS OR BEGINNINGS

"What we call the beginning is often the end
And to make an end is to make a beginning.
The end is where we start from."

T.S. Eliot
"Little Gidding"

Remember when you graduated from high school? For many it is a thrilling moment. Exams were over. No more studying. No more getting up early to get to school on time. No more teachers to listen to. It seemed like a happy ending. But it was only the beginning. If you went on to college, you soon discovered that exams were not over. You might be lucky enough to escape 8:00 a.m. classes, but there was still a schedule to maintain and there were still teachers to listen to. If you went on to get a job, you soon discovered you probably had to get up early and there were new people to listen to, such as your boss. What seems like an ending is usually a beginning. However, it may not seem like it at the time. It may seem like an ending, or a loss.

By the time we have aged to sixty-five, seventy, or later, we will have experienced losses in our life. Any change can result in a loss of some kind, and any loss can trigger a grief response, similar to the response we discussed in the last chapter. It depends on the type of loss and the significance of the loss to us.

Some of the losses we experience can occur when we go from grade school to junior high to high school and college. We leave behind old friends and need to adjust to new friends, new teachers, and a new environment. It can be a sad experience to leave behind friends, classmates and playmates if you go to different high schools or colleges.

Loss occurs when we leave an old community to move to a new community; or from one job to another.

Loss also occurs when children enter new phases of their lives. I remember crying when one of our sons entered kindergarten!

There is also loss and grief in a time of divorce, being laid-off from a job, or the loss of finances.

Usually a divorce will bring about a greater amount of grief than moving to a new community, depending upon the situation. So will being laid-off or fired from a job bring about a greater amount of grief than leaving friends at one job to take on a new job.

In a previous chapter I mentioned that in the early 1990's, I led an unemployment support group that met at the church I was serving in New Jersey. It was a time of recession in our country. Most of those who participated were engineers who had worked at a plant involved in parts for airplanes. It was difficult for most of them to adjust to the loss of their job. Most of them had worked for the same company for many years, and now to be let go was a blow to their self-esteem, as well as their finances. So many people, especially men, equate their work with their self-esteem. Since more and more women are working, we may see the same result, but in the early nineties, it was the men whose self-esteem was shattered. I saw these men go through many of the responses to loss that we see in a grief reaction. They were mourning the loss of their jobs. There was denial at first that it could happen to them. There was anger that management could do such a thing to them. There was guilt that perhaps they could have done more to keep their job, or guilt that they should have foreseen the lay-offs. There was sadness at their loss. I am happy to say that most of the men were able to obtain new jobs, but it took many months to do so, and a concentrated effort on their part. Some took longer than others to become mobilized and go job hunting.

Another serious potential for grief comes when we enter retirement. After years of the same and familiar routine, you are suddenly on your own. You are free to do what you want and when you want. This can be difficult for many. They don't know what to do with so much time on their hands. I have a friend who recently retired and finds he is at a loss as to what to do. There are days when he doesn't shave. When he had to get up to go to work he would shower and shave, but now that he doesn't have to go to work, he says he hasn't worked out a new schedule for himself.

Former President Jimmy Carter remembers clearly when he knew he had become a senior citizen, a state he had rejected until then as only for older folks.[62]

He and his wife, Rosalynn, and some friends had ordered identical breakfasts at a restaurant in Georgia, but when the bills came, Carter's was less. An honest man, Carter called the waitress over and told her she had made a mistake. She hadn't charged him enough.

A farmer sitting at the next table spoke up and said, "That ain't no mistake, Mr. President. They give free coffee to senior citizens."

"Everybody roared with laughter," says the President, but for him it was a watershed, "...the first time I ever realized that I was a senior citizen. At first, it was really disturbing to me. But now, I've gotten to kind of enjoy it because there's some privileges that go with being older."

Retirement from work can affect our self-esteem. Judith Viorst, in her book, *Necessary Losses*, says that "work shores up our identity; it anchors both the private and social self; it defines that self to itself and to the world. And lacking a workplace to go to, a circle of colleagues to connect with, a task to confirm our competence, a salary that puts a value on that competence, a job description that serves as a shorthand way of telling strangers who we are, we may, when we have retired, start to ask, with growing anxiety, 'Who am I?'"

She quotes a doctor, age 79,who said, "I was depressed at the thought of retiring, because I wasn't quite sure what would happen to me. You see, I had had my position for so long- my specialist work, my hospital staff, my professional travels, my teaching. All these things which I had were what I *was*, and to have to give them up at sixty-five left me with something quite unrecognizable."[63]

Authors Leland and Martha Bradford discovered that it would have been helpful for them to prepare for the inner turmoil they experienced at retirement. They encountered three problem areas: the unexpectedly shocking and deep emotional reactions many feel as they retire; the many displacements, disengagements and losses accompanying retirement; and the need for a sensibly planned transition from one phase of living to another very different one. They feel that the extent to which these areas are recognized and the effectiveness with which they are handled determines whether the years of retirement will be happy, involving, growth and self-rewarding, or whether they will be unhappy, depressive and non-productive in terms of self-growth. They say: "No matter how acutely an individual after long years in a career or with an organization is aware of approaching retirement, and may indeed be looking forward to it, when the moment arrives there may be a sinking feeling that something very important, even crucially so, is suddenly, radically, surgically ending. Relief and euphoria at the release from burdensome responsibilities or unrewarding work may be engulfed in the painful realization that tomorrow and all the tomorrows to follow- will include no job to go to, no organization to be a part of, no colleagues with whom to share easy comradeship. One will no longer belong and will, in fact, quickly become an outcast…a termination to a major portion of life is occurring. What lies ahead? These are thoughts difficult to deal with-thoughts laden with painful emotions...It is so easy when one retires to feel unwanted, undervalued, disposable. Self-approval, self-respect and sureness of identity can be easily shattered. This way lies self-doubt, emotional stress, apathy and depression."[64]

Sometimes people are pressured into retirement. Health problems can force people into retiring before they really want to retire. Sometimes companies pressure people into retiring early. My father retired early. The company he was working for was letting people go so they wouldn't have to pay pension benefits. The government changed the situation, but my father was afraid he might be let go early so he retired. This was before the government stepped in.

Many, who in youth, set high and often unattainable goals for themselves, may be filled with bitterness at retirement that eats away at them because their goals were not attained.

If you have a hobby, it can help a lot. It often means cultivating new interests and activities. Many find part-time jobs just to keep busy for boredom can become a problem.

Retirement can also be difficult for a spouse. If both have worked and retire it can mean new adjustments will have to be made. If the wife (or, it could be the husband), has stayed home while the husband worked, with a husband around all the time, it changes the wife's routine. I have often heard of spouses getting on one another's nerves. Adjustments need to be made. If there were problems in the marriage prior to retirement they could be put-off due to one or both spouses away at work much of the time, but in retirement there is less escape from the causes of interpersonal tension. Irritations, hurts and hostilities, previously smoldering, can now become active. Retirement offers the opportunity for a deepening relationship, but it may take time, work and communication.

Retirement comes at a time when losses in one's health are becoming greater. Those losses can mitigate other losses, compounding the situation. For example, loss in vision may mean losing a driver's license and having to find new means of transportation. Loss of one's job through retirement can mean a loss of income. You may depend on a pension, savings and social security income, which may be considerably less than one's salary. On the other hand, those who have managed to save money, invested wisely and/or receive a pension may find that they have more money in retirement.

For some, retirement and growing older may seem like a time to "give up," to do what one can with one's time until we die. It may seem like the end of one's youthful dreams and goals. Receiving that first social security check is a signal to many that they're approaching the end of their life. There are others, however, who have used retirement to begin a new career or a new time of creativity.

For example, "Dear Abby" printed a letter from a grandson extolling the achievements of his grandmother. He writes, "This May (2000), my grandmother...will receive her Ph.D. in art therapy from the University of Tennessee. At graduation, she will be 90 years old! Abby, she received her bachelor's degree at age 69 and her master's at age 81. She has been attending classes the last two years in spite of macular degeneration (she is nearly blind). Our entire family is extremely proud of her, and she is an inspiration to all who know her. If you print this letter, it may inspire others to continue their education no matter what stumbling blocks may be in the way."

In the Bible, God frequently chose the "elderly" to do His work. Abraham was 75, when God called him to move from Haran to the land of Canaan. When Abraham was 100 and his wife Sarah was 90, she gave birth to a son, Isaac.

Some of the ages of people mentioned in the Bible may lead us to question how age was determined. Noah, for example, is mentioned as being 500 years old when he became the father of Shem, Ham and Japheth (Gen. 5:32). All the men listed in Chapter 5 of Genesis enjoyed long life-spans, Methuselah's 969 years (verse 27) being the longest. While those ages are questionable, and the average lifespan in Biblical times was not as long as it is today, still those we would consider "elderly" were a part of God's plan and God's work. The Bible is clear, for example, that "Abraham and Sarah were already old and well advanced in years, and Sarah was past the age of child-bearing." (Gen. 18:11)

Moses and Aaron were 83 when they went to Egypt to free the Hebrews from slavery.(Exodus 7:7)

Anna was an 84 year-old widow who prayed constantly for the Messiah and had the vision to recognize him when he came. (Luke 2:36-38)

Lois, a grandmother, is praised by Paul for her religious influence on her grandson Timothy, a friend of Paul's and an important leader in the early church.(2 Tim. 15,3:15)

John is reputed to have been banished to the island of Patmos where he wrote the last book of the Bible, the Book of Revelation, about AD 90. At that time he would have been well-up in years.

I like what General Douglas MacArthur said when he was 78: "Nobody grows old by merely living a number of years. People grow old by deserting their ideals. Years may wrinkle the skin, but to give up interest wrinkles the soul."[65]

An eager and active mind with the desire for new knowledge and new experiences need never age. It is not age that makes us old. It is life changes, and how we react to them.

Change is a part of life. It is inevitable. An article in the Wall Street Journal a few years ago said: "A new century is at hand, and a fast spreading technology promises to change society forever. It will let people live and work wherever they please, create dynamic new communities linked by electronics, improve the lot of the poor and reinvent government, unless, its use for illicit purposes sparks a crackdown."[66]

You might think the article was referring to computers and the internet. But it wasn't. The fast spreading technology being described was the telephone. The article was taken from the Wall Street Journal a century ago.

What else would the telephone do for us according to this article? Supposedly it would eliminate southern accents, revolutionize surgery, stamp out heathenism abroad, and save the farm by making farmers less lonely.

They might have been overly optimistic, but change is inevitable.

A snail was going down the road one day when it got run over by a turtle. When the paramedics came, one of them asked the snail, "What happened?" The snail replied, "I don't know. It all happened so fast."

We live in a fast changing world. Just think of all the changes that many of you have encountered during your lifetime.

There have been changes in technology. Certainly the advent of computers has been a challenge for many of us.

Words can change their meaning, and that's something to get used to. For example, in my day, pot was something you cooked in; grass was mowed; coke was a cold drink; aides were helpers; closets were for clothes, not for "coming out of;" and hardware meant hardware; software wasn't even a word.

Sometimes we resist change. For example, in 1832 the people of Lancaster, Pennsylvania, refused the use of a school house for the discussion of the desirability of a railroad for that locality, because the school board felt that "Railroads are impossible and a great infidelity. If God had intended that his intelligent creatures should travel at the frightful speed of seventeen miles an hour by steam he would have clearly foretold it in the Holy Prophets. Such things as railroads are devices of the Satan to lead immortal souls down to Hell."[67]

Or, in 1867 the following news item appeared in the Chicago Federation News, a leading Chicago newspaper: "Joshua Coppersmith has been arrested in New York for attempting to extort funds from ignorant and superstitious people by exhibiting a device which he claimed will convey the human voice any distance over metallic wires, so that it will be heard by listeners at the other end. Well informed people know it is impossible and of no practical value. The authorities who apprehended this criminal are to be congratulated."[68]

We can resist change, too, when it comes time for retirement. For example, President Jimmy Carter admits he was devastated when he was "retired" involuntarily at age 56 after a single term.

"We went back to our tiny town (Plains, Ga.). I didn't have a job. We were deeply in debt. We thought the best time of our life was over.," a feeling that millions of Americans share upon getting that first Social Security check. "Just because we had lived in the White House didn't make us any different."

"And we went through a very difficult time with each other. Rosalynn was almost physically ill. I think I looked on the bright side of things more to combat her despair than (because that was how) I really felt."[69]

We can deny change. Black hair gone gray goes black again, or blonde. The chin gets tucked. Breasts get a lift. Joints get replaced. Some of the changes really are for health reasons, but how many changes are to try to preserve a youthful appearance.

In 1990, actress Zsa Zsa Gabor was pulled over by police for having expired registration tags. Police reports of the incident reveal a bizarre exchange between the actress and the police officer. First, she claimed to have over-paid her registration, so the DMV didn't give her any tags. Then, the officer discovered a number of discrepancies in Gabor's driver's license. Her date of birth and weight were wrong (the stout actress claimed to be 110 lbs.). Zsa Zsa claimed that illegal Mexican immigrants stole her license, changed her personal stats to make her seem younger and thinner than she really was, then returned her license to her. Finally, the actress slapped the officer when he tried to arrest her.

Now, I don't want to judge Ms. Gabor. Perhaps we don't have all the relevant details. She has been a famous actress, and it wouldn't be surprising if a person in her situation would do something like that when you are not as youthful as you once were.

We can resist change. We can deny change. Or, we can accept change. We can look at the changes in our lives, not as endings, but as beginnings, just like the countless men and women who have used their "senior" years for creative endeavors.

The first thing we need to do is to assess our situation. President Carter said that "Things looked grim until we finally had the courage to do what everybody needs to do: to sit down in a time of quiet contemplation and say, 'OK, what is there that I have? What are my talents? What are my abilities? What have my experiences given me on which I can build for my future? What are some of the things we did when we were young that we really enjoyed and have never had a chance to pursue because we were too busy making a living? What are the talents that I thought I had when I was young that I never was able to develop?'"

"Out of that analysis," Carter says, "has come almost everything that we do now," none of which has to do with politics, but with writing books, teaching at Emory University, teaching Sunday School and a dedicated and visible volunteer for Habitat for Humanity, an international nonprofit organization that helps the needy build homes for themselves.[70]

He also heads the Carter Center in Atlanta, Georgia, whose programs worldwide include monitoring democratic elections in developing countries, helping African farmers improve crop yields and mediating conflict in countries from Haiti to North Korea.

It's not just the outer events of our lives that can change from endings to beginnings, but also our inner self can change. I've seen a bumper sticker that reads, "Be patient. God isn't finished with me yet."

According to Judith Viorst, "…although our present is shaped by our past, personality changes are possible, even unto the seventh, eighth, ninth decade. We are never a 'finished product' - we refine and we rearrange and we revise. Normal development doesn't end, and over the course of our life, important new tasks- or crises- will arise. We can change in old age because every stage of our life, including our last one, affords new opportunities for change."[71]

Often we need to change inwardly if we are to change outwardly. That is especially true if we are holding onto the endings in our lives and feeling sorry for ourselves. Rather than letting go of the endings and searching for new beginnings, they are like baggage that weighs us down. If you've ever packed a car with so many things that when you see something new you would like there may be no room for it because of all the baggage.

Its like the story William Bridges tells. "Once there were two monks who were traveling through the countryside during the rainy season. Rounding a bend in the path, they found a muddy stream blocking their way. Beside it stood a lovely woman dressed in flowing robes. 'Here,' said one of the monks to the woman. 'Let me carry you across the water.' And he picked her up and carried her across. Setting her down on the further bank, he went along in silence with his fellow monk to the abbey on the hill. Later that evening the other monk said suddenly, 'I think you made an error, picking up that woman back on our journey today. You know we are not supposed to have anything to do with women, and you held one close to you! You should not have done that.' 'How strange,' remarked the other. 'I carried her only across the water. You are carrying her still."[72]

Endings must be dealt with if we are to move on to whatever comes next in our lives.

We always have a choice as to what comes next. We can decide how to turn endings into beginnings. Sometimes the choice is more open and clear. Retirement, for example, may provide a long list of opportunities we can choose from.

Sometimes our choices are limited. Our health may prevent us from doing certain things. But always the choice is there, no matter where we are.

I officiated at a funeral for a woman who had been living in a nursing home for several years. For many people moving to a nursing home can be viewed as an ending. But not for this lady. She viewed it as her new home. Over her closet there was a big sign which read, "I love you grandma." Next to the sign she hung pictures of her family. She would say good-night to those pictures every night.

One time her grand-daughter wanted to bring her to her house for Christmas, but she didn't want to go. Her grand-daughter said she needed her to peel potatoes. Her grandmother's response was, "Bring them here."

When a nurse in the nursing home felt ill because she was pregnant, Heddy offered her bed to the nurse.

Endings are often a time of confusion. We may not be certain who we are at first. Endings can threaten our identity and self-esteem. It is important at such times to remember that we are a child of God and that God is with us.

Jesus' experience in a wilderness area was an ending. It was a time to question who he was and what he was going to do next with his life. It was a spiritual struggle for him. It was a time of testing. How was he going to go about his ministry. It shows us Jesus rejecting the way of power and glory and accepting the way of suffering and the cross.

For Jesus, his wilderness experience was a battle with temptation. The first temptation was to turn stones into bread. The wilderness was covered by little bits of limestone exactly like loaves of bread. According to noted Biblical scholar, Dr. William Barclay, "the Tempter said to Jesus, 'If you want people to follow you, use your wonderful powers to give them material things.' The Tempter was suggesting that Jesus should bribe people with material gifts into following Him."

In the second temptation, Jesus, in his imagination, stood upon a mountain from which the whole civilized world could be seen. The Tempter said, "Worship me, and all will be yours."

In the third temptation Jesus imagines Himself on the pinnacle of the Temple in Jerusalem. There was a drop of 450 feet down into the Kedron Valley below. Dr. Barclay says that "this temptation was the temptation to give the people sensations."[73]

In each of the temptations Jesus remembered a quote from Scripture. Those words strengthened him to resist doing his own will rather than God's will. From his experience in the wilderness, Jesus embarked on a new beginning in his life.

Much as we may wish to make a new beginning, some part of us may resist doing so. The fear of taking the first step may prevent us from doing so.

William Bridges tells of a man whose forty-year marriage was on the rocks, and it was all because his wife could not adjust to the new situation resulting from his recent retirement. He began to think that his wife just wanted him for a paycheck, and now that he was there as a person, she really didn't care for him.

He had reorganized the kitchen for his wife, and she had kicked him out of the house. He was a very precise and orderly man who had been used to supervising others. He discovered in the empty first days of his new leisure a fresh field for his talents- the kitchen cupboards. His wife had come home from a trip to the city to find everything in the kitchen in some new place, with a label on each shelf and a list on the back of each cupboard door.

The man never used to help around the house before. He thought he was making a new beginning. Instead, he was just perpetuating his old style and activity in a new way. He was avoiding an ending and calling the result a new beginning.[74]

In south Florida, where I live, there are numerous assisted living facilities. They vary in financial arrangements and costs, but usually for a monthly fee, you can rent a room/apartment, receive three meals a day and numerous other amenities. Many of them have a nursing section for those needing health care or rehabilitation. Transportation is often available to doctors offices, shopping centers, etc. Many people retire and move to Florida to live in a house, condo, apartment or trailer. There often comes a time when these same people need to relinquish some of their independence. Usually it is because of health reasons. Some move back north to live with or near their children. Others choose to move into an assisted living facility. For some it is not an easy decision. Giving up one's living facility and independence is often viewed as an ending. It can be difficult to make a new beginning in a new place.

Even though we may look forward to something new, change can be difficult. It is not always easy leaving behind places, people and memories. Even though we may look forward to a new beginning there is usually a sense of uncertainty. Will I like it? Will I feel comfortable?

The important thing is to look at endings as beginnings of new possibilities. Endings need not necessarily be seen as "bad." Sometimes we need to bring an end to a job, a relationship, or an activity. Sometimes endings are to be relished. Many people look forward to retirement from a job to pursue an activity or hobby. All endings can be forerunners of the beginning of something new for our lives.

A grandmother took her three-year-old grand-daughter onto her lap and began reading to her from the Old Testament book of Genesis. After a while, noticing that the little girl was unusually quiet, the grandmother asked, "Well, what do you think of it, dear?"

"Oh, I love it," answered the child. "You never know what God is going to do next.!"

We never know what is going to happen next in life. And when life brings changes in our lives, changes we might not always like, we need to have the ability, the mental attitude and faith to adjust to the change and be open to new ideas or new ways of doing things.

Sarah was ninety years old when she was told by God that she would have a child. She and Abraham laughed in disbelief. Abraham, the Bible says, "fell on his face and laughed, and said to himself, 'Shall a child be born to a man who is a hundred years old? Shall Sarah, who is ninety years old bear a child?'" (Genesis 17:17)

But Abraham and Sarah had an open mind, a faith that enabled them to accept the many changes they encountered in their lives, and to them was born a son, Isaac.

We may not have to worry about having more children at age ninety, like Sarah, but we will have a good many changes to face in our lives. If we can do so with a flexible mind and faith, we will be able to endure and overcome many of our problems.

One clear Biblical principle is that God is always pushing us forward. The people of Israel were always being pushed forward to a new discovery, to a new place, to a new relationship with God, and to a new commandment about how to live together. In this life we never arrive at a point where we can stay and that's it. Some people choose to stand still and stagnate. But God is always calling and challenging us to move forward through all the changes of life, from endings to beginnings. There is always the possibility to do new things, to learn new things, to make new friends, to be of service to God.

My great-grandmother lived to the age of 102. She was married when she was fourteen and divorced a few years later. She remarried but her second husband died. At age eighty-five she went into a nursing home. At age ninety-two she had one leg amputated because of poor circulation. At age ninety-eight her daughter died. Her body was weak, but her mind was sharp. Everyday she read the newspaper because she wanted to know what was going on in the world.

What I remember most about her life was her ability to accept the changes of life that came her way. No matter what seemed to happen, she seemed content to accept her lot and make the best of it

I think her ability to stay young in spirit, to turn endings into beginnings, was built above all upon her strong faith in God.

Through all the changes of life and through all the years of life we can receive the courage we need to face our endings and beginnings from God who is with us. When the people of Israel were getting ready to cross the Jordan River to go into their promised land, Moses says to them: "Be strong and courageous. Do not be afraid or terrified...for the Lord your God goes with you; he will never leave you nor forsake you." (Deut. 31:6)

There need be no fear as we age, but rather a savoring of the times, acceptance of the changes, and a sense of reverence about the wonder of it all.

A newspaper article told the story of a woman of 68 and the courage she mustered up in the face of life's changes. Eleven years before, when the last of her four children moved away, she had a husband to comfort her. Eleven months ago when her husband died, she had only friends and faraway children to comfort her.

Now she is regrouping. Her house is for sale. She's called her kids home to claim most of her possessions. She is hunting for an apartment in a big city near a big airport. And she's planning a road trip.

"I don't have to do this, I know," she tells skeptical friends. "I could sit in this house and wait for the next event in life to happen to me. But that seems like deteriorating. Why should I stop growing and advancing and planning?"

God is always calling us to go forward. The future may be unknown. The future may be frightening. It may seem like an ending. But if we trust in God, what may seem like an ending may be the beginning of a whole new and wonderful time. That is true with death, as well.

A beloved grandmother, who became ill, was taken into the home of her daughter and family. She enjoyed the bedside visits with loved ones, especially her four-year-old great-granddaughter, Jill. Jill smoothed the covers, discussed the things she and her doll had been doing, and often brought her doll with her to visit.

One day the door to the bedroom was closed and Jill's mother told her as gently as she could, "Your grandmother just went to heaven."

"In her nightgown?" Jill exclaimed. "She should have gotten ready first!"

What Jill didn't understand was that her great-grandmother had been getting ready for years. She had spent much time in prayer for family and friends. She had stored up knowledge of God's greatness and had shared it with many people. She had given her love, her time, her faith to Sunday School classes, to strangers, to her family, and to anyone in need.

Faith in God can reassure you that God is with you as you seek to cope with the changes of life. Faith can help what seems like endings into the hope of new beginnings.

CHAPTER TWELVE
LIVE FOR THE JOURNEY

"It is good to have an end to journey towards; but it is the journey that matters in the end." Ursula K. LeGuin

If you've ever been on a trip with children, sooner or later the question is asked, "Are we there yet?" Children are often impatient with the time it takes to get to where you are going. But many adults are also impatient. That is true not just with the taking of a trip, but with many other things in life, and sometimes with life itself. People can't wait until the next event. We look for the end results. But in the process we miss so much of the journey.

The newspaper columnist, Ann Landers, once ran an essay entitled, "The Station," written by Robert Hastings. He writes, "Tucked away in our subconscious is an idyllic vision. We see ourselves on a long trip that spans the continent. We are travelling by train. Out the windows we drink in the passing scene of cars on nearby highways, of children waving at a crossing. But upermost in our minds is the final destination. On a certain day at a certain hour we will pull into the station. Bands will be playing and flags waving. Once we get there so many wonderful dreams will come true and the pieces of our lives will fit together like a completed jigsaw puzzle. 'When we reach the station, that will be it!' we cry. 'When I'm eighteen.' 'When I put the last kid through college.' 'When I have paid off the mortgage.' Sooner or later we must realize there is no station, no one place to arrive at once and for all. The true joy of life is the trip. The station is only a dream. 'Relish the moment is a good motto, especially when coupled with Psalm 118:24- 'This is the day which the Lord hath made; we will rejoice and be glad in it.' It isn't the burdens of today that drive men mad. It is the regrets over yesterday and the fear of tomorrow. Regret and fear are twin thieves who rob us of today.

So, stop pacing the aisles and counting the miles. Instead, climb more mountains, eat more ice cream, go barefoot more often, swim more rivers, watch more sunsets, laugh more, cry less. Life must be lived as we go along. The station will come soon enough."

Too many times we get caught up in endings and destinations; we put our efforts and thoughts on the future and miss the joys, relationships and inspirations of the present moment. Live and enjoy life one day at a time.

I have found that to be true in my experience with traveling. I have traveled to the West Coast of the United States by airplane, and I have been to the West Coast by car. While I reached my destination in only a few hours by plane, I couldn't experience the beauty of our country from the East Coast to the West Coast except in traveling by car and stopping each night along the way.

We can get into trouble sometimes if we don't focus on the present. For example, a professor at an eastern university driving to the west coast one summer had been invited to stop en route at the homes of half a dozen of his former students. A methodical man who prided himself on efficiency, he wrote all his thank-you notes beforehand. He sealed, addressed and stamped the letters, bundled them up with a rubber band and put them in his overnight bag.

His first stop was in Buffalo, New York. The following night, unpacking in a hotel room about 300 miles father west, he discovered the thank-you notes were missing. Telephoning his Buffalo host, he asked with studied casualness, "Did you by any chance find a bundle of letters in the guestroom?"

"Why, yes," said his friend. "I mailed them for you this morning."

Live and enjoy life one day at a time. But someone will wonder how we can possibly enjoy life one day at a time while living with sickness or pain. Perhaps Morrie Schwartz can answer that question.

Tuesdays With Morrie is the best-selling book about the lessons sports columnist Mitch Albom learned from his former college professor, Morrie Schwartz, some twenty years after graduation. Morrie was Mitch's mentor in college at Brandeis University. Mitch Albom rediscovered Morrie in the last months of the older man's life.

Morrie developed asthma in his sixties. A few years later, he began to have difficulty walking. At times he stumbled inexplicably. It was in his seventies, after undergoing a battery of tests, that Morrie was diagnosed with amyotrophic lateral sclerosis (ALS), also known as Lou Gehrig's disease, an illness of the neurological system. There is no known cure.

Knowing he was dying, Morrie traveled to Mitch's home every Tuesday to visit. Their rekindled relationship turned into one final class lesson in how to live.

In one of their visits, Morrie and Mitch talk about death. Morrie says to Mitch, "Everyone knows they're going to die, but nobody believes it. If we did, we would do things differently."

"So we kid ourselves about death," Mitch replied.

"Yes. But there's a better approach. To know you're going to die, and to be *prepared* for it at any time That's better. That way you can actually be *more* involved in your life while you're living."

"How can you ever be prepared to die?"

"Do what the Buddhists do. Every day, have a little bird on your shoulder that asks, 'Is today the day? Am I ready? Am I doing all I need to do? Am I being the person I want to be?'"

"Why is it so hard to think about dying?" asked Mitch.

"Because," Morrie continued, "most of us all walk around as if we're sleepwalking. We really don't experience the world fully, because we're half-asleep, doing things we automatically think we have to do."

"And facing death changes all that?"

"Oh, yes. You strip away all that stuff and you focus on the essentials. When you realize you are going to die, you see everything much differently."

"He sighed. 'Learn how to die, and you learn how to live.'"

Morrie continued. "We are too involved in materialistic things, and they don't satisfy us. The loving relationships we have, the universe around us, we take these things for granted."

"He nodded toward the window with the sunshine streaming in. 'You see that? You can go out there, outside, anytime. You can run up and down the block and go crazy. I can't do that. I can't go out. I can't run. I can't be out there without fear of getting sick. But you know what? I *appreciate* that window more than you do.'"

"Appreciate it?"

"Yes. I look out that window every day. I notice the change in the trees, how strong the wind is blowing. It's as if I can see time actually passing through that window-pane. Because I know my time is almost done, I am drawn to nature like I'm seeing it for the first time."

"He stopped, and for a moment we both just looked out the window. I tried to see what he saw. I tried to see time and seasons, my life passing in slow motion. Morrie dropped his head slightly and curled it toward his shoulder."

"'Is it today, little bird?' he asked. 'Is it today?'"[75]

Morrie knew he had a limited time left. He wanted to use his time to enjoy what he could of life. In spite of the progressive nature of his illness and no matter how uncomfortable he was, Morrie tried to live each day to the fullest until the day he died.

We also find such advice in the 118th Psalm. This Psalm is a litany of thanksgiving for God's help and has long been a favorite of many. In verse 24 the Psalmist declares: "This is the day which the Lord has made; let us rejoice and be glad in it."

The Psalmist didn't say that yesterday was the day or tomorrow will be the day. Today is the day!

We never know when the time of death will be for each of us. As we grow older, we know that death is growing closer. Each day should become more important and more significant. Each day should be lived to the fullest and made the most of because we don't know how much longer we have.

No matter what our age, we can die at any moment as the result of an accident, catastrophe, or heart attack. When we're young we tend to ignore the importance of time because we tend to think we have a lot of time left.

A university professor was invited to a military base one December. A soldier named Ralph had been sent to meet him at the airport. After they introduced themselves, they headed toward the baggage claim. As they walked down the concourse, Ralph kept disappearing. Once it was to help an older woman whose suitcase had fallen open. Once it was to lift two toddlers up to where they could see Santa Claus. And another time it was to give directions to someone who was lost. Each time Ralph would come back with a big smile on his face.

"Where did you learn to do that?" the professor asked.

"Do what?" Ralph said.

"To be so helpful and considerate to others," said the professor.

"Oh," Ralph said, "during the war, I guess."

Then he told the professor about his tour of duty in Vietnam. It was his job to clear minefields. He told of watching his friends being blown up before his eyes, one after another. "I learned to live between steps," he said. "I never knew whether the next one would be my last, so I learned to get everything I could out of the moment between when I picked up my foot and when I put it down again. Every step I took was a whole new world, and I guess I've just been that way ever since."

We need to be aware of and awake to the possibilities that exist in the world around us each and every day. How often, however, do people sleep through the day, sometimes literally.

One of my favorite stories in the Bible is also a very humorous one. It comes from the 20th chapter of the Book of Acts. The story gives us a picture of what life was like in the early church. Most services took place at night. That is probably so because it was only at night, when the day's work was done, that people would be able to come to church. However, church in those days was in someone's house.

The setting is someone's house in Troas, a city in Greece. Paul has come to speak, and because he intended to leave the next day, he kept on talking until midnight.

In the room of the house where the service was held it was dark and probably warm. The many lamps and torches used for lighting would have made the air stuffy and perhaps, oppressive.

A man named Eutychus was there. No doubt he had come from his day's work and was tired. Perhaps he had eaten more than he should have for dinner. Just as many of us sit down after a good dinner and get drowsy, so did Eutychus.

He was seated in a window, either because there was no room elsewhere, or perhaps to get some fresh air to keep awake. In either case, Eutychus succumbed to sleep and fell out of the window. It reminds me of a slap-stick comedy one might see on television.

And there is no end to stories about people falling asleep in church. For example, a husband and wife went to a prayer meeting where, during a testimony period, the wife became so wound up that her husband dozed off. She talked about crime in the streets, immorality throughout the country, war, deceit, and evil everywhere. "In fact," she declared, "I fight with the devil all week long." At that moment her husband woke up, jumped to his feet, and exclaimed: "Reverend, I can't help it. She's just hard to get along with."

When we fall asleep in church we can miss what God might be trying to say to us. By falling asleep, Eutychus missed the report of a great missionary's work. He missed the chance to have his own life uplifted through the words of Paul.

Each day, though, we can miss what God is saying to us if our bodies and spirits are asleep. Many people take pills or drugs to get away from the pains and anxieties of life, but life can be an exciting adventure, no matter what our age.

There is a story about a famous rabbi who once took his student, a wealthy miser to the window of his living room and asked him to look out. "What do you see?" asked the teacher. "People," replied the rich pupil. Next the rabbi took his student to a mirror and asked the same question. "What do you see?" "Myself," came the reply. "You see," explained the teacher, "both the window and the mirror are made of glass. Yet the mirror is covered with silver. As soon as the silver is added, you stop seeing others and can only see yourself."

Many people are unhappy today, and I think it is because they see only themselves. They are so worried about material things, or their health, or other things, that they have lost sight of the simple things in life. We get so busy with worries and activities that we can lose our awareness of what God is saying to us. But God's love is present all around us. Be awake and aware of how God might be trying to awaken you to a new and deeper experience of that love.

If we fail to see God's love for us in a beautiful sunset or in the birth of new life or in blooming flowers and trees, it is perhaps because we can only see ourselves. Take time to go for a daily walk early in the morning or at sunset in the evening. If walking is too difficult, spend some time just sitting outdoors. Plant some flowers. If that is too restrictive where you live, get some house plants and tend to them and enjoy their beauty.

If you live near a park, take time to visit it. Go for a walk, or sit on a bench and let the sights, the sounds and the smells refresh and renew you.

I love to be near the ocean and I feel fortunate that I am able to live within a few miles of the ocean on the east coast of Florida. I also love the rocky coast of Maine. I love to watch the waves as they roll in upon the rocks and send their spray high into the air. Here in Florida I love to walk along the sandy shore and watch as the ocean gently comes and goes upon the shore, leaving behind treasures from its deep.

Sometimes I become almost overwhelmed with how large the ocean is and how insignificant I am compared to it. Looking at the ocean, one almost feels a sense of helplessness. I remember how the Psalmist has said, "In his hand are the deep places of the earth...The sea is his and he made it." (Psalm 95:4,5) There is One who is greater even than the ocean, there is a God who is not helpless nor insignificant before it. There is a God who can control the sea. Thinking about that, my faith is strengthened.

There is always the opportunity for new learning. Elder hostels are an increasingly popular way to learn something new, as well as make new friends and have a good time. If there is a community college in your area, why not check out the courses offered. Many communities also offer courses through adult education programs sponsored by the School Board.

Community senior centers also offer many programs for seniors in education, hobbies, sports, physical fitness and travel.

Many senior communities also offer opportunities for learning, fun and fellowship. For example, in Boynton Beach, Florida, Leisureville is a community of individual houses for anyone 55 years of age and older. Several clubhouses are located throughout the community with individual swimming pools. There is also a nine-hole golf course. Throughout the year there are programs at the clubhouses that feature movies, musical entertainment, bazaars, dances and other social activities. The clubhouses are also places one can go to play cards, pool, shuffleboard or just to sit and talk.

If there is a YMCA or YWCA in your community, there are usually activities in the areas of education and fitness.

Churches, too, usually offer opportunities for Bible study, fellowship groups, fellowship dinners and programs, worship and service.

Marc Freedman, in his book, *Prime Time: How Baby Boomers Will Revolutionize Retirement and Transform America*, argues that retired Americans can and should be a powerful social force in a country that in recent decades has seen a serious erosion in the time and effort available for volunteer work by older adults.

For example, in his book, he tells the story of Dr. Jack McConnell, a pediatrician who later became a pharmaceutical company executive who retired to Hilton Head, South Carolina, where he planned to play golf, dine out and catch up on his reading. But he soon realized that his "fulfillment would not occur on the golf course."

One thing led to another, and through his ingenuity, caring, persuasiveness and persistence, Dr. McConnell created Volunteers in Medicine, a medical clinic staffed almost entirely by unpaid retirees, to provide free health care for the uninsured working poor and their families.

Dr. McConnell's project was so successful that he soon received almost five hundred requests for guidance from communities around the country wanting to create similar clinics. His full-time job now is helping these communities follow his example.[76]

Freedman also cites the case of Marv Welt, a man in his early 70s. Upon retiring from his career as a management consultant, Welt parlayed his passion for fishing into an environmental education program for youngsters in poor neighborhoods.

His project, the Waterworld Program, now operates in nine public schools in Portland, Oregon. It started with Welt teaching children in housing projects how to fish. But soon he realized more was needed. So he went back to school and took biology courses so he could take groups of children on field trips and teach them something about the environment. After all, Welt said, "these kids are going to decide what happens to our environment."[77]

Taking time to volunteer to help others can be personally fulfilling and socially rewarding.

"There's a population out there all dressed up with no place to go," he said in an interview. "Most of the opportunities available to senior citizens were designed for a former generation of older adults, to get them out of the rocking chair. But this is not the retirement of their parents. We need activities that would capture people's imagination, use their skills and give them a sense of purpose."[78]

Some organizations do just that, besides our churches. In one of her columns, Jane Brody, of the New York Times gives some examples. One example is the Experience Corps, now in more than two dozen cities, which provides schools and other youth organizations with older adults who help improve academic performance and foster the development of youngsters. There is also the National Senior Service Corps, which operates the Foster Grandparent Program, the Senior Companion Program and the Retired and Senior Volunteer Program around the country. For more information, contact the Corp. for National Service, 1201 New York Ave. NW, Washington, D.C. 20525, (202) 606-5000, www.cns.gov.[79]

Also, Habitat for Humanity has built more than 100,000 houses around the world, with the help of volunteers of all ages, for families in need. The national headquarters is at 121 Habitat St., Americus, Georgia 31709-3498, (912) 924-6935, www.habitat.org.

The appendix of Freedman's book describes 21 groups that provide productive volunteer opportunities for older Americans. You can also check what's needed in your local community. That can be done through local churches, the newspaper, or perhaps your Chamber of Commerce.

My wife and I have become active in our local Humane Society of Martin County, Florida. We are a part of their pet therapy program with our standard poodles, Tiffany and Toby, and our Cardigan Welsh Corgi, Stormy. We visit area nursing homes with our dogs. The residents love to have them come. It gives them an opportunity to interact for awhile with the dogs. Many of the residents had dogs at one time. Pets are good for people. We even take our dogs to church on Sunday where they always receive a welcome.

They are wonderful companions. Studies have shown that pets can help lower blood pressure in people. Of course, some people may have physical difficulty in caring for a dog or a cat, but I highly recommend having a pet companion. Unfortunately, many senior living communities frown on pets.

People of all ages volunteer with the Pet therapy program. In addition to visiting nursing homes, there is a program called "Paws to Read." Volunteers go with their dog to an area public library once a week. Children with reading problems spend time reading to a dog. It has been found that children have improved their reading skills by doing so. The dogs just sit or lay there while the child is reading to them.

Take time to enrich your life by helping others through the many volunteer opportunities that are available.

Take time, too, to be aware of the beauty and joy of our beautiful world and relationships.

Take time each day to be aware of God's presence in the world and in your life.

For example, the Rev. Charles Allen, in his book, *All Things Are Possible Through Prayer,* tells the story of a woman who was sick and went to Florida to recuperate. Each day she would go out on the beach alone and there, in the midst of nature, she would turn her mind toward God.

One day she became acutely aware of the deep silence of nature. The quietness was such that she could feel her heart beating. She began to notice the steady undeviating rhythm of her heart.

As she was conscious of her heart beating, she turned her eyes and looked through the beach grass near her. She noticed how clean it had been washed by the tides. Also, she noticed that the grass moved slowly and gracefully to and fro with the gentle breeze. As she watched she became conscious that the grass, too, had a rhythm, the same rhythm as her heart beat.

Then she lifted her eyes to the sea and she watched the waves rise and fall and roll up on the sand. She suddenly became aware that it, too, had a rhythm, a rhythm like the waving of the grass and the beating of her heart. She began to realize that there is one fundamental harmony throughout the universe. She realized she was in tune with nature and she realized that God is the great Creator and, thus, she was in tune with God. She said, "Now I know there is a power by which life can be recreated- one must be attuned to that power."[80]

In the story of Eutychus in the Book of Acts, when Eutychus fell out of the window he was "taken up for dead." Then, Paul went out and discovered he was still alive. God would not let him die. Thus, the name Eutychus means "fortunate one." We are indeed fortunate when we allow the Spirit of God to awaken us to life.

Another value in learning to live for the journey, or living one day at a time, is that it enables us to get more control over our worries. People waste so much time worrying. They worry over past misfortunes and regrets. They worry over future events.

We worry over insignificant things, things that don't matter, and end up with greater problems as a result.

A number of years ago an Eastern Airlines jumbo jet crashed in the Everglades of Florida. The plane was bound from New York to Miami with a full load of holiday passengers. As the plane approached the Miami airport for its landing, the light that indicates proper deployment of the landing gear failed to light. The plane flew in a large, looping circle over the swamps of the Everglades while the cockpit crew checked to see if the gear actually had not deployed, or if instead the bulb in the signal light was defective. When the flight engineer tried to remove the bulb, it wouldn't budge. The other members of the crew tried to help him. As they struggled with the bulb, no one noticed the aircraft was losing altitude, and the plane simply flew into the swamp. Dozens of people were killed in the crash. While an experienced crew of high-priced pilots fiddled with a seventy-five cent light bulb, the plane with its passengers flew right into the ground.

We can lose sight of what really matters.

Jesus would take time out of his never-ending schedule for spiritual renewal and refreshment. One of his special places of retreat was the home of Mary and Martha and their brother Lazarus. Their home was located in the village of Bethany just a short distance east of Jerusalem. It was a place where Jesus could rest and relax among friends.

When we first encounter Mary in the story she is "sitting at the feet of Jesus." She was listening to his wisdom and his teachings.

While Mary was sitting at the feet of Jesus, Martha was in the kitchen slaving over a hot stove. But the stove was not the only "hot thing" in the kitchen. One can imagine that she was thinking to herself, "When is my sister going to get in here and help me finish?"

Finally, Martha can't stand it anymore. She bursts into the other room, her face flushed with anger, as she says, "Lord, do you not care that my sister has left me to serve alone? Tell her then to help me!"

And Jesus replies, "Martha, Martha, you are worried and upset about many things, but only one thing is needed. Mary has chosen what is better, and it will not be taken away from her."

The word "worry" means "to be torn in two directions; to be pulled apart." That is what worry does to a person. It pulls us in different directions. That is what happened to Martha. As a result she was falling to pieces.

The thing about worry is that most of what we worry about never happens.

Now Martha was just trying to be a good hostess. I wonder how many women, or men, would not do the same thing.. We want to make our guests feel comfortable. We have been taught to be good hosts. Jesus, however, was trying to tell Martha that she was more worried about the details of being a host than taking time to enjoy his visit and their friendship.

Martha was allowing the distractions of life to get in the way of what was really important.

Someone once said, "It's not the crosses we bear that get us, but the splinters."

In other words, it's not necessarily the great crises that get us down, but the everyday little hassles of life. It's the accumulation of the little everyday frustrations and annoyances that seem to wear us down and wear us out. We let the little things get the best of us.

Somewhere I read about an English homeowner who declared war against a mole that had been burrowing unsightly tunnels throughout his property. Moles are nocturnal animals, so one night he drove his car onto his lawn to hunt the mole with the aid of the car's headlights. The car stalled. When he got it started again, it lurched into gear and out of control. Onward it rolled until it crashed into his house. The car's fuel tank ruptured and burst into flames, which quickly reached the house and burned it to the ground.

He couldn't even phone for help. The telephone cable was burned through before he could call the fire department. This is an example of truly making mountains out of molehills.

We can get that way, too. As we grow older there probably are more things to concern us and its easy to worry about the future. We can worry about our health. We may worry about our mind, afraid we'll get Alzheimer's. We can worry about having enough money in the future to live. We may worry about falling and breaking something. We may worry about death. These may be realistic worries, but if we let them, they can get the better of us and we can find ourselves thinking and worrying about them every day.

If we can learn to focus on one day at a time and enjoy the day we have, we will find it will help us cope so much better. Why worry about our health if we're doing all right today? Alcoholics Anonymous, and other self-help groups, have long used this "one day at a time" principle. If one is trying to abstain from drinking alcohol, abstinence may seem impossible if one thinks of it over a life time, but when you think about abstaining for just one day, the task becomes much more manageable. Then tomorrow you do the same thing, and the next day, and so on. Don't worry about a lifetime, just think about today and how you can make the most of your time today. Problems will not disappear, nor will they necessarily be solved, but we will find that our worries don't seem as overwhelming.

I like the illustration that Corrie ten Boom uses in her book, *Nestle, Don't Wrestle.* She tells an old Dutch parable about the clock that had a nervous breakdown.

The little clock had just been finished by its maker, who put it on a shelf in his storeroom. Two older clocks were busy ticking away the noisy seconds next to the young clock.

"Well, " said one of the clocks to the newcomer, "so you have started out in life. I am sorry for you. If you'll just think ahead and see how many ticks it takes to tick through one year, you will never make it. It would have been better had the maker never wound you up and set your pendulum swinging."

"Dear me," said the new clock. "I never thought about how many ticks I have to tick in a year."

"Well, you'd better think about it," the old clock said.

So the new clock began to count up the ticks. "Each second requires 2 ticks, which means 120 ticks per minute," he calculated. "That's 7,200 ticks per hour; 172,800 ticks per day; 1,209,600 ticks per week for 52 weeks, which makes a total of 62,899,200 ticks per year!" The clock immediately had a nervous breakdown and stopped ticking.

The clock on the other side, who had kept silent during the conversation, now spoke up. "You silly thing! Why do you listen to such words? That old grandfather clock has been unhappy for years. Nobody will buy him, and he just sits around the shop gathering dust. Since he is so unhappy, he tries to make everyone else unhappy, too."

"But," the new clock gasped, "he's right. I've got to tick almost 63 million ticks in a year. And they told me I might have to stay on the job for more than 100 years. Do you know how many ticks that is? That's 6 billion, 200 million ticks! I'll never make it!"

"How many ticks do you have to tick at a time?" the wise old clock asked.

"Why, only one, I guess," the new clock answered.

"There now. That's not so hard, is it? Try it along with me. Tick, tock, tick, tock. See how easy it is? Just one tick at a time."

A light of understanding formed on the face of the clock, and he said, "I believe I can do it." And he began ticking again.

"One more thing," the wise old clock said. "Don't ever think about the next tick until you have your last tick ticked."[81]

Live life one day at a time.

Too many of us, when the pressures of life seem to overwhelm us, react by feeling sorry for ourselves. The more we think of ourselves, the more tired and worn we become and the greater our worry of being unable to cope with the future.

The prophet Isaiah had some good advice when he said :"Thou wilt keep him in perfect peace, whose mind is stayed on thee." (Isaiah 26:3)

If we leave God out of our lives, if we leave God out of the day-to-day concerns of our life, then our problems will grow bigger and bigger and overwhelm us. Faith in God helps us to keep an accurate perspective on life.

There may even be a time when taking time to enjoy the day may actually save our life as the following story illustrates.

There once was a young man who, with his father, farmed a little piece of land. Several times a year they would load up their ox-cart with vegetables and drive to the nearest city.

Except for their names and the patch of ground, father and son had little in common. The father believed in taking it easy and enjoying the day, while the son was always in a hurry.

One morning, they loaded the cart, hitched up the ox and started out. The young man figured that if they kept going all day and night, they would get to the market by next morning. He walked alongside the ox and kept prodding it with a stick. "Take it easy," said the father. "You live longer."

"If we get to the market ahead of the others," said his son, "we have a better chance of getting good prices."

The father pulled his hat down over his eyes and went to sleep on the seat.

Four miles and four hours down the road, they came to a little house. "Here's your uncle's place," said the father, waking up. "Let's stop in and say hello."

"We've lost an hour already," complained the anxious son.

"That's the nicest thing you've said in a long time," smiled the father. A minute later he was asleep.

A little before sunrise, the young man shook his father awake. They hitched up and went on. A mile and an hour away they came upon a farmer trying to pull his cart out of a ditch. "Let's give him a hand," said the father.

"And lose more time?" exploded the son. "Relax," said the father. "You might be in a ditch sometime yourself."

By the time the other cart was back on the road, it was almost eight o'clock. Suddenly a great flash of lightning lit up the sky. Then there was thunder. Beyond the hills, the heavens grew dark.

"Looks like a big rain in the city," said the father.

"If we had been on time, we'd be sold out by now," grumbled his son.

"Take it easy," said the old gentleman. "You'll last longer."

It wasn't until late in the afternoon that they got to the top of the hill overlooking the city. They looked down at it for a long time. Neither of them spoke. Finally the young man who had been in such a hurry said, "I see what you mean, father."

They turned their cart around and drove away from what had once been the city of Hiroshima.

Worrying less can save us from physical and emotional problems. Worry can lead to ulcers and other gastrointestinal problems. Worry can lead to high blood pressure, to perhaps strokes and heart problems. Less worry can save your life.

Suppose, for example, that you were a great organist and were suddenly thrown into jail without having committed any crime. What would you do?

That happened to Dr. Albert Schweitzer, the leading organist of his day when he went to German West Africa as a missionary during the First World War. The French captured the territory and as one of the precautions of war, jailed all the Germans they found there.

What did the great organist do to spend his time? Did he think about all the accomplishments of the past, or did he feel sorry for himself for all that we was not doing, or did he worry about his future? No. He took a piece of white chalk, drew an organ keyboard on the step of his cell, and practiced the organ, just as though the drawings were real keys.

As he rehearsed day after day, his fingers kept nimble and his mind was occupied. When he was released from prison, his technique was just as good or better than when he had been locked up.

We can be glad each day no matter where we are, or no matter what has happened to us. Don't let the circumstances or surroundings of your life affect your enjoyment of each day.

When you face problems and you begin to feel overwhelmed, and when you find yourself living more in the past or future than you live in the present, remember you have an alternative. You can live happier and more effectively by taking life one day at a time.

Are you making the most of the days God has given you? Remember these words of the 118th Psalm: "This is the day which the Lord has made; let us rejoice and be glad in it."

CHAPTER THIRTEEN
THE GOOD OLD DAYS

"The beauty of memory is that it still sees beauty when beauty has faded." Paul Boese

Three sisters ages 92, 94 and 96 live in a house together. One night the 96 year old draws a bath. She puts her foot in and pauses. She yells to the other sisters, "Was I getting' in or out of the bath?" The 94 year old yells back, "I don't know. I'll come up and see." She starts up the stairs and pauses. "Was I going up the stairs or down?" The 92 year old is sitting at the kitchen table having tea listening to her sisters. She shakes her head and says, "I sure hope I never get that forgetful." She knocks on wood for good measure. She then yells, "I'll come up and help both of you as soon as I see who's at the door."

We can laugh, but many know how true that can be. One of the fears of growing old is the fear of losing our memory. When people have memory problems they tend to forget recent events but have the ability to remember people and events from many years ago.

Even if people don't have problems with their memory, sometimes people will have selective memories. They will look at the past as "the good old days." They will think back to a time when life seemed easier or happier.

A number of years ago while on vacation I thought it would fun if all of us climbed a mountain I had ascended many years before while a student in seminary. And so my wife,Gail, and myself and my son, Patrick, traveled to Mount Monadnock, 3, 165 feet high, in southwestern New Hampshire. As I remembered the climb it was very easy. There were several smooth trails one could hike and make it to the summit in fifteen minutes. On top there was a spectacular view of the surrounding countryside.

It was a clear, warm July afternoon when we arrived at the parking lot at the base of the mountain. We asked a ranger how many miles it was to the top and he replied: "It is two and a half miles to the summit. Plan on a round trip time of three to four hours."

We decided to start out as I still thought we could reach the top in fifteen minutes. However, as the trail became more difficult, steeper, and the rocks more difficult to climb, my family began to doubt my memory. As the sweat ran down my face I began to wonder the same thing. We finally stopped and turned around one and a half miles up, too tired to go on. I thought of the good old days and wondered if it had been as good as I remembered it to be. Perhaps I hadn't climbed it as quickly as I had thought, nor as effortlessly.

If we look back upon what we think were "the good old days," they were not really as good as we would like to remember. We tend to forget the work, the sweat, the hardships that were a part of those days.

Depending, too, on how far back we go, life was very difficult for many people. Think how much easier life is today for people since the advent of modern appliances, such as the automatic washing machine, electric clothes dryer, dish washing machine, stove, microwaves, automatic coffee maker, electric iron, electric hair dryer, and on and on.

People complain about rising prices, but according to financial writer Louis P. Cain, in the 1890's it cost the equivalent of 12 ½ cents to mail a letter, butter was $1.39 per pound, and a three minute phone call from Chicago to New York cost $31. And that was over 100 years ago!

While we may exaggerate our memories, some things in life ought to be remembered.

Todd Outcalt, in his book, *The Best Things in Life Are Free,* tells about a short story authored by Charles Dickens, titled, "Tale of a Chemist." It is a futuristic tale in which a famous chemist is tortured by the painful memories of his past. He tries desperately to shake these memories from his mind, for they haunt him constantly. But his efforts are to no avail. Eventually he decides that he will undergo a series of experimental shock treatments, which will obliterate his memory. This he does, and the shock treatments are a success.

However, the chemist soon discovers that the obliteration of his memory has had some dire consequences. Because his entire memory has been erased, he has no past. He cannot remember where he was born, who his parents were, who his friends are or where he has come from. Not only are the painful memories gone, but also the memories that compose his identity.

At the end of the story, the chemist cries out for his past-painful memories and all. He wants what he has lost, for without his memories he is nothing. He cries out again and again, "Keep my memory green. Keep my memory green."[82]

We do cherish our memories, don't we. And some memories are important to remember, memories of those we once loved who are now with God, memories of our wedding day, memories of the birth of our children, memories of vacations, memories of important events in our lives. Some memories are important to remember because they bring us comfort and happiness as we recall them.

A woman by the name of Elaine Pondant wrote in a *Reader's Digest* article about an old bed that belonged to her parents. She inherited it after her father's death. Elaine noticed a list of dates and names faintly scratched in the surface of the wooden headboard. Elaine's mother explained that she and her husband had used the headboard as a memory album; these names and dates made up the story of their lives. For example,

September 18, 1946 – the day they got married.

Elizabeth, October 22, 1947 represents the day their baby daughter, Elizabeth, died.

Ralph, February 18, 1966. Ralph was a young soldier who had saved their son's life during the Vietnam War. Ralph died a couple of years later while on a tour of duty.

Since that day, Elaine and her husband have added new names and dates to the headboard, and new stories to the family history.[83]

There are some things that need to be remembered. That is why God told the people of Israel to "Remember how the Lord your God led you all the way in the desert these forty years…" (Deuteronomy 8:2) The people were to remember all that God had done for them in freeing them from slavery in Egypt.

One of the important reasons for religious holidays is that they remind us of God's actions in history in significant events.

Whenever the Lord's Supper is celebrated it is among other things a reminder of Jesus and all that he means to us

There are some things that need to be remembered.

There are some things that need to be forgotten. Our memories are a wonderful gift to us, unless they cripple our ability to function as whole persons, as families, and as nations.

There are tragedies carried out in the world today because people refuse to forget ancient grievances, ancient resentments, and ancient hatreds.

But it is also true on an individual level as well. How many people live in misery because they can't let go of hurtful memories?

A man was proud of his children. For years he and his wife worked hard, even sacrificed, to give them a good life and opportunities, and now the children were grown and getting married. Soon he would be a grandfather. His oldest son and his wife were expecting their first child, the first grandchild.

The man was so excited he could hardly wait. "Surely it will be a boy," he thought, "and they'll name him after me. After all it's an old family tradition." But more than tradition, it was a way of showing honor and appreciation.

When the first grandchild was born, it was a boy, but the child wasn't named after him. The grandfather was deeply hurt. Disappointment turned to anger which began to build until finally he confronted his son. There was a bitter argument, many harsh words were exchanged between them, and they parted. For fifteen years the man did not speak to his son or see his grandson.

How sad and wasteful. How tragic that a hurt can be so damaging.

In *A Prayer for Owen Meany,* John Irving says, "Your memory is a monster; *you* forget—it doesn't. It simply files things away. It keeps things for you, or hides things from you...and summons them to a recall with a will of its own. You think you have a memory; but it has you!"[84]

And for some people that is true. Someone insulted us, someone didn't give us the job we wanted, someone hurt our feelings. Rather than forgive and try to forget we keep our resentments stored away in our memory and bring them out from time to time to relive them.

Abraham Lincoln once explained why he could be almost absent-minded about the slurs of his political foes: "I do the best I know how, the very best I can. I mean to keep on doing this down to the very end. If the end brings me out all wrong, then ten angels swearing I had done right would make no difference. If the end brings me out all right, then what is said against me now will not amount to anything."[85]

Lincoln was so busy with the important business of the nation that there was no space left for memories of unpleasant things said about him.

Yet, how many people waste a lot of time looking back to the past. It can be dangerous. I remember reading somewhere, for example, about Roger Banister, the first man to officially run a mile in less than four minutes. A lot of people have done it since, but Roger Banister was the first. A month after Roger Bannister broke the record, an Australian, by the name of John Landy topped his record by 1.4 seconds. Soon after, the two athletes met in British Columbia to compete against each other. As they moved into the last lap, the other contestants were trailing far behind. Landy was ahead. It looked as though he would win. As he neared the finish line, the story goes that he was haunted by the question, "Where is Banister?" Finally, he could not stand the strain any longer. He looked back over his shoulder. When he did that, his step faltered and Banister surged by him to break the tape and win the race. As Landy supposedly said to a reporter, "If I hadn't looked back, I would have won the race."

Perhaps the ultimate danger in looking back is exemplified in the Old Testament by Lot's wife, who, according to the story was turned into a pillar of salt because she looked back upon the destruction of Sodom when she was warned by God not to look back.

Many geologists believe that the cities of Sodom and Gomorrah were destroyed when an earthquake ignited the minerals and gases in bitumen pits, causing an immense explosion which engulfed four of five cities in the area, leaving only the most southerly, Zoar, untouched.

Caught in the open by falling hot sulphur, Lot's wife was incinerated on the spot, and it was this that led to the tale of her being turned into a pillar of salt.

Whether she was, or not, it is true that those who turn back for one reason or another, often lose their lives.

Sometimes we may wish we could live our lives over so we could change some of the mistakes we made or perhaps do something in a different way. If you could live your life over, what would you do? Would you marry the same person? Would you look for a different job? Would you do anything different if you could go back and change your
life?

Lowell Thomas was once asked what he would do if he could live his life over. And he replied, "I would give more attention to my college studies. If I had my life to live over again I would study Greek, Latin and Sanskrit, the base of all the languages of western Europe and of this continent. It would help me speak more meticulouosly."[86]

Perhaps we all wish we could live some part of our lives over again when we make a mistake or get into trouble. Like the little boy who wished his mother had lived her life over by marrying someone else after he received a spanking from his father. The boy climbed into his mother's lap and said, "Mama, I wish you had married Jesus. He loves little children!"

Instead of dwelling on past pleasantries or past mistakes, learn from them. There are times when in talking with people, sometimes at important times in moments of crisis, I will later think of a word or a phrase or a verse from the Bible that I wished I had thought of at the time of our conversation for it might have been helpful. Why didn't I think of it at the right time, I ask myself?

But we need to realize that as humans we all will make mistakes. None of us is perfect. And so use your successes and your mistakes of the past as ways to learn. If I later think of what it would have been helpful to say to someone in need I can try to remember to say it in another similar situation.

The important thing is not to dwell on the past, either the "good old days" or the hurts we have endured, for these only prevent us from the life that is to be lived today. Jesus said, "No one who puts his hand to the plow and looks back is fit for the kingdom of God." (Luke 9:62)

Those who would follow Jesus are called by him to look ahead, with their vision not on the past, not on the days that used to be, but on the days that are and that will be.

Perhaps it's like the 103 year-old woman who checked in at her doctor's for her annual physical, just after her birthday. The doctor found her in good health. As she was leaving, she turned to the doctor and said: "Doctor, see you next year!"

The doctor replied: "What makes you so confident about that?"

She replied: "How many 103 year-olds do you see dying?"

After her 104th birthday, she reported again for her annual checkup. Her regular doctor was on vacation so a young doctor gave her her physical. When he had finished the examination he reported to her: "I find you in excellent health, but your pulse is just a little high."

To which the woman replied: "What do you expect with a young man like you holding my hand?"

Look at Moses and the Hebrews, who were told by God to go out from slavery in Egypt to a land God would show them. They had no idea what the future would be like, but they were willing to go because they trusted God. They were willing to put the past behind and look forward to new experiences..

It may be difficult to believe that there can be good things waiting for us in the future. As we age we may think only of a future filled with negative experiences, such as the death of a spouse, our own death, health problems and perhaps having to live in a nursing home.

Those things will happen, at least in the case of death, but why dwell on them? When we do we may be missing out on many opportunities for enjoyment and inspiration.

I think of my great-grandmother Gardiner, who died just two weeks shy of her 102nd birthday. Her mind was sharp until the day she died. She would read the newspaper every day. When she was one hundred she received a letter of congratulations from then President Nixon. It was shortly after Watergate. She tore up the letter because she was angry with the President for his involvement in Watergate!

What I remember most about her life was her ability to accept the changes of life that came her way. No matter what seemed to happen, she seemed content to accept her condition and make the best of it. She didn't complain or whine. She tried to see something positive in her situation.

Trust in God to guide you and be with you into an unknown future, just as Abraham and Sarah did and Moses and the Hebrews. Rather than complain or condemn or find fault with new situations, look to God for help and guidance.

I am reminded of the story of a boy who lived in Decatur, Illinois. He was deeply interested in photography. He carefully saved his money to buy a certain book. When he had enough money he ordered the book. The publisher, however, made a mistake in his order and instead of sending the book on photography, he sent a book on ventriloquism. This boy was not interested in ventriloquism. In fact, he didn't even know what it was.

He didn't know he could send the book back. He could have simply put the book aside and nursed his disappointment and hurt. Instead, he began reading it and he became interested. He learned to throw his voice and eventually got a wooden dummy which he named Charlie McCarthy. Out of a mistake, Edgar Bergen built a great career. Was it a mistake of the publisher or was it the providential hand of God that he was sent the wrong book? Who can say? The important thing is that he turned his disappointment into an appointment for new life. We, too, can turn our disappointments into appointments for new meaning and new happiness.

We cannot bring back the past, nor relive it. We change. People change. Life changes. If we have made mistakes or been hurt we cannot change the past, but we can hope and try to make the present and the future a better one. No matter how meaningful or how difficult life may have been in the past, God gives us so much to live for today and in the days to come. In some ways it is often easier and safer to look to the past, but God is always calling His people to look ahead- to new life and what might be.

The Associated Press had a story one time about a man who had entered our country illegally. The immigration authorities had discovered it and took steps to deport him, to send him back to where he belonged. Getting down into the case, they found themselves confronted with an international dilemma. The alien stood there waving his arms, trying in his broken English to tell them they couldn't deport him because the country he was born in had slid off the map. He had come from a small country in Central Europe, and, in the shifting of boundaries after the war, his country was wiped out; it just wasn't there any more.

That is true of us, too. The land of our birth, the land of our childhood, the familiar world we grew up in, has slid off the map. It isn't there. We can never go back to it for life has gone beyond it. We may have some marvelous memories of that time but we should never let our memories, whether good or bad, keep us looking back into the past. There are many new and wonderful lands and experiences waiting for us in the days to come. They will be made even more wonderful for God will be with us.

CHAPTER FOURTEEN
ROAD RAGE

"All of us could take a lesson from the weather. It pays
no attention to criticism."
                              North Dekalb Kiwanis Club Beacon

So many times I have heard people talk about a loss as part
of God's will. Why people do this I don't know, other than it
is the only explanation that they can come up with in the face
of their loss. When something tragic happens people seem to
want to know why it happened and why it happened to them.
Why they don't ask the same question when something good
happens, I don't know.

Rabbi Harold Kushner was concerned with "When Bad
Things Happen to Good People." He wrote his book in
response to the death of his son. When his son, Aaron, was
only three years old, he was diagnosed with progeria, or
"rapid aging." He would never grow much beyond three feet
in height, would have no hair on his head or body, would
look like a little old man while he was still a child, and would
die in his early teens.

Why do people suffer? Or, as Rabbi Kushner asks, "why
do bad things happen to good people?" We tend to ask these
questions when we see or hear of children who die, but we also
ask them of others who die at a young age. We are especially

conscious of those whose lives make a difference for good in the world. In the 1960's, for example, that question concerned our nation at the deaths of President John F. Kennedy, his brother, Robert Kennedy, and the Rev. Martin Luther King Jr. But do we not also ask those questions at the death of a loved one, no matter what their age. My mother-in-law died suddenly at age seventy-nine of a stroke. Was her death any less of a loss to those who loved her and miss her?

One of the ways in which people have tried to make sense of the pains and suffering we encounter in life has been by assuming that somehow our misfortunes are a punishment from God for sin. In the Old Testament the two are linked together. If you led a good and righteous life, you would be rewarded by God with riches, health and/or a long life. If you sinned, then you would be punished by poor health and other misfortunes.

In the New Testament, this same mind-set was behind the question some people brought to Jesus. They brought up a recent news story about some Galileans who had been cruelly offered as human sacrifices by Pilate. Were they greater sinners than others in Galilee that they should suffer so? Also, a tower had fallen in the town of Siloam and crushed eighteen bystanders. Was it because of their sin?

Jesus dealt with that question a number of times. At one time he was confronted with a man who had been blind from birth. Jesus' disciples wanted to know was it the man's parents' sin or his own that was responsible for his blindness?

Jesus consistently condemned the notion that human tragedy is punishment for sin. In the Sermon on the Mount, for example, Jesus said: "God makes His sun rise on the evil and on the good, and sends rain on the just and the unjust."

In other words, God does not reward us according to our virtues, or punish us for our transgressions. At least not in this world.

Many of the purest saints who ever lived have suffered the deepest sorrows. As Jesus suffered on the cross, he did not say he was being punished by God. Paul suffered from an unknown illness. Some think it was epilepsy. He, too, did not believe that God was punishing him for his earlier life when he was persecuting the early Christians. Instead he looked at his illness or ailment as a means of glorifying God.

There are some things in this world that just happen as a consequence of the physical laws which govern this universe. And sometimes they happen to the best of people. Church buses loaded with Christian young people get hit by drunk drivers. Christian men and women and children die with cancer. Some things just happen. Somebody was in the wrong place at the wrong time. Some things in life we cannot control. And yet we want to control them. We want to try to make sense of what has happened. We search for some explanation. Therefore we're willing to blame ourselves, if necessary, even though we may not be responsible at all.

This, too, is what superstition is all about. People carry around a rabbit's foot or hang a horseshoe or consult a horoscope in order to try to control fate. Maybe something good will happen to us, we think. At least, maybe the bad will somehow be warded off. Sometimes our efforts are absurd.

A number of years ago there was a tragic incident in which the top was ripped off of a jet flying out of Hawaii and a flight attendant was sucked out to her death. When the mangled jet landed, another flight attendant on that same flight made plans to fly home on the next available plane. Someone asked if she was not nervous flying again so soon after her harrowing experience? Her answer was that she felt her number had already been called once and she didn't feel it could be called again so soon.

Her reasoning reminds me of the man who was nearly panic-stricken on his first flight. The pilot came back personally to calm him down. "Are you a religious man?" the pilot asked. "Yes," the man replied. "Don't you believe that when your time is up, you'll go and not until then?" the pilot asked. The man said grimly, "It's not me I'm worried about. I'm afraid your time will come before mine."

Superstition is an attempt to manipulate that part of our lives that is beyond our personal control. If I carry a rabbit's foot with me, I am trying to control my luck. Christian faith, however, is not an attempt to use God, but a willingness to surrender control of our lives to God. We need the spiritual maturity to pray, "Not my will, but yours be done."

Jesus did not want his interrogators to get bogged down with this question about why bad things happen. He wanted them to understand their responsibility for making good things happen. He tried to get them to see that we are not to concern ourselves with those things in life which we cannot control. Rather we need to concern ourselves with those things which we can control.

Some people sit around and speak sadly about what life has done to them. Jesus says to them and to us that on the Day of Judgment we will not be asked what life has done to us but what we have done with life!

Jesus used the parable of the fig tree and said that if it does not bear fruit, cut it down. He was saying to his listeners and to us that we are responsible for bearing fruit, for making a difference, for taking responsibility for that part of life that we can control.

Now in some cases, people may be to blame for the tragic things that happen to them. If we act irresponsibly, then bad things may happen. That should be obvious. If we drink several beers and then get in our car to drive home, the alcohol may impair our judgment so that we have an accident and injure ourselves or a passenger.

People may also blame someone or something else for the tragic events in our lives. We may blame the government, or the manufacturer, or the doctors, or whomever.

Some people blame a supernatural presence, such as the Devil, for what happens. Sometimes others are at fault. A doctor who made a fatal mistake on a loved one because he was drunk, should be to blame. In the case of the Devil, however, I find it too easy to blame a supernatural power when we may be at fault. Comedian Flip Wilson used to have a comedy routine in which he would jokingly say, "The devil made me do it." Its easy to blame a devil and escape our own personal responsibility.

A third source of blame when bad things happen is to get angry at God. I am reminded of the story of a young boy and his doting grandmother walking along the shore in Miami Beach when a huge wave appeared out of nowhere, sweeping the child out to sea. The horrified woman fell to her knees, raised her eyes to the heavens and begged the Lord to return her beloved grandson. And, lo, another wave reared up and deposited the stunned child on the sand before her. The grandmother looked the boy over carefully. He was fine. But still she stared up angrily toward the heavens. "When we came," she snapped indignantly, "he had a hat!"

Dare we admit that we get angry at God? Some may think getting angry at God to be blasphemous, but if we admit it, we do get angry at God…when a loved one dies or becomes incapacitated, or when we have an accident, or whatever "bad" thing happens to us or a family member, many will ask, "why God, why?"

Sometimes people try to console themselves with the idea that God has His reasons for making "bad" things happen to them. In his book, "When Bad Things Happen to Good People," Rabbi Harold Kushner tells the story of a woman named Helen.

The trouble started when Helen noticed herself getting tired after walking several blocks or standing in line. She thought it was just because she was getting older or because she had added a few pounds. But one night, coming home after dinner with friends, Helen stumbled when she entered her house and fell to the floor. Her husband joked she had had too much wine, but Helen suspected it was no joking matter. The next day she made an appointment to see a doctor.

The diagnosis was multiple sclerosis. The doctor explained that it was a degenerative nerve disease, and that it would get worse, maybe quickly, maybe gradually over many years. Eventually Helen would be confined to a wheelchair, lose bowel and bladder control, and become more of an invalid until she died.

Helen broke down and cried when she heard the news. "Why should this happen to me? I've tried to be a good person. I have a husband and young children who need me. I don't deserve this. Why should God make me suffer like this?" Her husband tried to console her by telling her that God must have His reasons for doing this, and its not for us to question Him. There must be some purpose to it.

Helen tried to find peace and strength in what her husband said. She tried to be comforted by the knowledge that there was some purpose to her suffering. She wanted to believe that it somehow made sense.

Helen didn't want to question God or be angry at Him, but her husband's words only made her feel more abandoned and more bewildered. What kind of higher purpose could possibly justify what she would have to face? How could this in any way be good? Much as she tried not to be angry at God, she felt angry, hurt, betrayed. She felt she had been a good person; not perfect, perhaps, but honest, hard-working, helpful, as good as most people and better than many who were walking around healthy. What reasons could God possibly have for doing this to her?[87]

We wonder the same thing when we go through suffering. Have you ever noticed that in the language of insurance companies such natural catastrophes as tornadoes, hurricanes, earthquakes, and floods are called "acts of God," while sunshine, gently falling snow, and Spring flowers are the works of "Mother Nature?"

Somewhere along the line people have conceived that suffering is somehow tied to the will of God.

Leslie D. Weatherhead, in his book, "The Will of God," attacks that kind of thinking when he relates the following incident from his life:

"When I was in India I was standing on the veranda of an Indian home darkened in bereavement. My Indian friend had lost his little son, the light of his eyes, in a cholera epidemic.

At the far end of the veranda his little daughter, the only remaining child, slept in a cot covered over with a mosquito net. We paced up and down, and I tried in my clumsy way to comfort and console him. But he said, 'Well, padre, it is the will of God. That's all there is to it. It is the will of God.' Fortunately, I knew him well enough to be able to reply without being misunderstood, and I said something like this, 'Supposing someone crept up the steps onto the veranda while you slept, and deliberately put a wad of cotton soaked in cholera germ over your little girl's mouth as she lay in that cot on the veranda. What would you think about that?'

'My God,' he said, 'what would I think about that? Nobody would do such a thing. If he attempted it and I caught him, I would kill him with as little compunction as I would a snake and throw him over the veranda. What do you mean by suggesting such a thing?'

'But John,' I said quietly, 'isn't that just what you accused God of doing when you said it was his will? Call your little boy's death the result of mass ignorance, call it mass sin, if you like, call it bad drains or communal carelessness, but don't call it the will of God.'"[88]

How often we want to blame God for suffering and tragedy when it strikes.

Many years ago my cousin, who was only twenty-eight years old, was hit from behind by a truck as she was letting her two children off for school. For six weeks she lay in a hospital bed in a coma and finally she died.

If God is a "good" God, if God truly loves us as we have been taught, why then does God allow people to suffer? Why didn't God intervene when the truck hit my cousin's car? Why didn't God heal her when she was lying in a coma in a hospital bed? Why didn't God prevent Helen from contracting multiple sclerosis? Why didn't God intervene and save the Jews at Auschwitz and other camps? Why didn't God intervene and save His Son from death on a cross?

We might ask, too, why do loved ones die? Why do our bodies age and so many experience the pain of arthritis, the dimness of vision and hearing, and so many develop alzheimer's disease?

When you experience those losses, many want to turn to God in anger.

Road rage, the experience of a driver becoming more and more frustrated until they vent their anger on other drivers, is on the increase. The news headlines tell of those who cut others off in traffic, pull a gun and start shooting at other cars, or vent their anger in other destructive ways.

When the frustrations of life become too much, we may want to take out our frustrations on God. Some may find that sacrilegious, but in the Bible, God does not seem to forbid or condemn an honest expression of anger toward Him, especially during times of great suffering. With God's permission Job has lost his wealth, his children, and his health. Job's anger at God is obvious to Bildad, one of his three visitors, who says to Job: "You who tear yourself to pieces in your anger, is the earth to be abandoned for your sake?" (Job 18:4) God did not condemn Job for expressing how he felt toward God.

In the book of Jonah, God responds to Jonah's anger by teaching him, not punishing him. Jonah had disagreed with God's decision to spare the city of Nineveh. The author says, "When God saw what they did and how they turned from their evil ways, he had compassion and did not bring upon them the destruction he had threatened. But Jonah was greatly displeased and became angry." (Jonah 3:10-4:1)

God understood and accepted Jonah's anger and then used a bush or a vine to teach Jonah. God caused the bush to appear suddenly. It provided Jonah with shade, but the next day God caused it to wither away. Jonah expressed concern for the bush. God was trying to teach Jonah that if Jonah could be concerned about the loss of a bush, why shouldn't God be concerned about the lives of the people of Nineveh?

Job and Jonah did not reject God. It was out of their faith in God that they raised their objections about what was happening. And that should be our goal, as well. It's all right to be angry at God if that anger leads us to attempt to understand God. However, if we use our anger to reject God, then it serves no useful purpose.

We need to remember that anger is an emotion created by God. Angry feelings themselves are not a sin, but it is in the expression of anger in thoughts or behaviors that sin may occur.

Since God already knows our thoughts and feelings, our expression of anger to God helps us more than it does God. Admitting and expressing our anger toward God moves the anger out in the open where it can be dealt with. It can help to put our anger in the context of a larger perspective, God's perspective.

For example, Job did not learn the purpose for his suffering, but he was satisfied after his encounter with God because his outcry was heard. God convinced Job of his love and care for the world, and Job realized that his suffering was understood by God. Job talked angrily with God and came away with a stronger faith in God.

Rejecting God will not change the nature of the world. Suffering and death still await everyone. Anger and hate provide only ineffective shields to these life-shattering events. At some point, all anger, even anger at God needs to be addressed and thought given to how "bad things" that happen to us could exist in God's world.

I don't believe that a loving God would want His children to suffer. That is why God sent Jesus, to show us how much God does care for us as individuals. If Jesus taught that God loves us, then it makes no sense that this same God would seek to cause us suffering and pain.

We might wonder where God was when Jesus was suffering and dying on a cross, but I believe God was there with His Son, feeling the pain of what Jesus was experiencing.

God was willing to suffer so that we would know God cares about our sufferings.

I do not believe that God causes our pains. Some are caused by bad luck, some are caused by bad people, and some are simply an inevitable consequence of our being human and being mortal, living in a world of natural laws.

We may not be angry with God, but as we grow older, we may be angry with growing older. We can be angry with health problems, aches and pains, loss of sight or hearing, loss of independence, as the following letter indicates. It was written by an anonymous writer to the "Senior Forum" section of the newspaper. The author writes: "I could use some advice on dealing with an ornery grandmother. She is in good health and mental condition. Until two years ago, she lived in her own home but worried about her increasing bills. She declined to live with us because of our smaller home. I suggested she sell hers and we sell ours to jointly finance a more suitable home.

While building, she became increasingly agitated about living with us and losing her independence. By the time we moved in, she was running away from home, hitting me, locking herself in her room, going on hunger strikes, etc. She attributed all of this to my lack of understanding about people her age and what it's like to lose your independence."

Of all our emotions, perhaps none is more troublesome to the Christian than anger. Many of us were raised with the idea that it is not Christian to be angry. We picture Jesus so often as meek and mild. Because of our Lord's emphasis on loving one another and turning the other cheek, it can be disturbing to find ourselves becoming angry at times. We are uncertain whether it is right or wrong to feel this way.

There were times, however, when Jesus got angry. In response to criticism by the Pharisees for healing on the Sabbath, Jesus "looked around about them in anger." Jesus was angry when he drove the moneychangers from the Temple. He was upset that they were exploiting the poor by charging them a high rate of interest as they bought their animals for the sacrifices in the Temple.

Jesus was angry at injustice, places where persons were being unfairly treated, exploited or hurt. Jesus was moved to anger by the self-interest that elevated self and tradition above human need.

There are times, then, when we ought to get angry, especially in the fight against injustice, corruption, greed and evil.

Anger is a part of who we are. It is a part of the way God has created us. Anger is normal. The denial of anger or anger misdirected contributes to many of the problems of our lives and our society. Perhaps that is why the Apostle Paul wrote, "If you become angry do not let your anger lead you into sin and do not stay angry all day." (Ephes. 4:26)

Paul recognized that anger is normal. It is not sinful in itself. I grew-up in an atmosphere in which it was regarded as not-Christian to express my anger as well as even be angry. It took me many years before I realized that it is normal to be angry.

Paul assures us that anger is not sinful in itself, but he is also quick to add, "do not let your anger lead you into sin." Anger is sinful when it is used to hurt someone else.

Equally as destructive, however, can be suppressing our anger.

Three hermits inhabited a cave and rarely spoke. One day a horse wandered into their abode. "That was a pretty brown horse," the first hermit said more than a year later.

Another year passed. The second hermit said, "It was white, not brown."

Two years later, the third hermit piped up, "If there's going to be this constant arguing, I'm leaving!"

Anger kept in can result in depression, ulcers, high blood pressure, maybe even a susceptibility to cancer. The analogy to a pressure cooker is perhaps appropriate. You cannot sit on that steam forever without it seeking an outlet.

Perhaps that's why John L. Lewis, the labor leader, who expressed his anger for President Franklin Roosevelt in no uncertain terms, lived vigorously to the age of eighty-nine, while Roosevelt, who more often smiled than expressed anger, died at age sixty-three of cardiovascular disease. Likewise, Harry Truman, known for his colorful outbursts, lived to the ripe old age of eighty-eight.

It can be dangerous to express our anger, but it is also dangerous to suppress it.

I read one time of a woman who was afflicted with arthritis in her hands and wrists. It was so painful that she gave up playing the piano at her church. Medication helped some, but the pain persisted and even seemed to grow worse. One day her doctor asked her if she had some deep resentments or hatred in her life. At first, the woman denied that she had any such feelings. Then her eyes filled with tears. She had a sister whom she felt had cheated her in a business venture. The two women had not spoken to each other in years. The doctor told her that her physical problem could be related. He suggested she talk with her sister.

The woman took the doctor's advice, went to her sister, forgave her and their relationship healed. To her surprise, her arthritis improved remarkably. It didn't go away entirely, but she began playing the piano at church again. Some say better than ever.

There are healthy, constructive ways of coping with our anger. Paul's reference to not staying angry all day, or as another translation has it, "before the sun goes down," offers a sense of urgency to deal with our anger before the anger does harm to you as well as other relationships.

When we find ourselves getting angry, one thing we can do is stop to analyze our resentments and the things we're angry about. We might discover that most of them are not worth getting angry about. Stop and ask yourself if it's really that important. Is it really worth staying angry or upset about?

Often when we're angry with someone we live with it can be helpful to get away from the situation for awhile until we can "cool" down and calmly discuss whatever the problem that resulted in our getting angry.

I like the story about the doctor who once took the train from an Eastern city to Chicago and sat near a couple who had recently celebrated their 50th wedding anniversary. The doctor asked them the secret of their living together so happily for so many years. Humorously, but with much truth, the husband replied: "When we were married, we agreed never to argue. If an argument began, I took my hat and went out-doors."

"Did it work that easily?" asked the doctor.

"Yup," the man replied. "I've been outdoors most of my life, and my health is fine!"

If you are angry with someone and express your anger to them, stick to the issue. It's so easy to get into name calling and criticizing the other in a personal way. The problem is not the person, but what the person did or said that got you upset. Castigating the other personally in retaliation only magnifies the situation and anger between you. Think about the issue or the problem and stick to arguing about that.

Use statements beginning with *I* rather than *you*. That way you own the feeling . Starting a sentence using *you* conveys the message that you are blaming the other person.

The tone of a discussion is of equal importance to the words being said. Reply in an even tone rather than responding with loud retorts. When someone yells or shouts at us we're tempted to try to out yell or out shout them. Try not to fall into that trap for it only escalates the anger.

When we or a loved one are in pain it can be easy to let our pain and frustration get the best of us. We can get irritable and lash out at another family member. When we're the target of someone's anger try to listen to what the person is saying . Usually people tend to think about what they will say in return. Instead, focus on what the other person is angry about and try to paraphrase to them what they said. This will help them know you're listening and will help clarify the issue or problem.

Sometimes we become angry at ourselves because we expect too much of ourselves. This can be especially true when we start to lose our physical mobility, our sight or encounter other physical problems. We may expect to still be physically able and capable as we were when we were in our thirties or forties.

If your anger is a result of your own impatience and expectations, ask God for patience.

Our physical aches and pains, and the loss of loved ones and friends, are all part of the aging process, and happen to everyone. Some may think of aging as a punishment, but it is a part of God's creation. We may get angry at times by the changes we experience to ourselves and others, but according to the Bible, it is God's plan to prepare us for an eternal life with God. As Paul wrote, "Though outwardly we are wasting away, yet inwardly we are being renewed day by day. For our light and momentary troubles are achieving for us an eternal glory that far outweighs them all." 2 Cor. 4:16-17

CHAPTER FIFTEEN
THE FAITH THAT OVERCOMES FEAR

We live in a time of fear. Perhaps that has always been true. When I was growing up there was a fear of a nuclear holocaust. I can remember practicing in school what to do in the event of a nuclear attack. We were to hide under our desks. That probably wouldn't have done any good, but that's what we practiced. Some people built fall-out shelters in their basements and stocked them with enough canned food to last for months.

In every generation or decade there probably has been something to fear. Since September 11, 2001, the fear of terrorists has attracted our national attention. And there are always local fears. Living in south Florida there is the fear of a devastating hurricane from June through November of every year.

Some people live in constant fear that something dreadful is going to happen in their life. For example, a man was awakened by his wife. She said she heard something downstairs. He slowly got up, went downstairs and found himself staring into a gun. The burglar ordered him to hand over all the household valuables, then started to leave. The husband stopped him. "Before you go," he said, "I'd like you to come upstairs and meet my wife. She's been expecting you every night for over thirty years."

On the positive side, fear is the elemental alarm system which warns us of danger. Fear can be creative. Many advances in science and technology represent a desire to escape from some dreaded condition. The fear of pain or death, for example, has led to advances in medicine. So fear can be necessary and creative.

But fear can also be paralyzing and crippling. I know a woman who needs cataract surgery, but is terrified to have it done because her mother died while undergoing cataract surgery eighteen years earlier. At that time patients underwent anesthesia and her mother had a heart condition. The procedure has changed a lot in those eighteen years, but the fear is still very real.

Certainly some fear is a part of our everyday lives. Especially as we grow older, many fear illnesses that will leave us incapable of caring for ourselves, such as alzheimer's or macular degeneration, or a stroke. Many fear falling and breaking a hip or a leg. Many fear they will end up in a nursing home. Many fear they will end up in a nursing home without adequate care or financial resources. Many fear they will be embarrassed by incontinence or other problems. Many fear losing a spouse or fear a loss of income. Some may fear the coming of death.

Fear can be such a pervasive and crippling influence on our lives which is why it is perhaps no mere coincidence that the Bible repeats the command "fear not" 365 times, or once for every day of the year.

Since fear is a reality in our lives which will not go away easily, it is important that we find a faith that will help us overcome our fears. The task is not to banish all fear, but fear carried to the point of immobility or fear that keeps us from enjoying life is a fear that needs to be overcome, or at least made manageable.

It might help to realize that most of our fears have been learned! Many psychologists feel that there are only two unlearned and innate fears: the fear of falling and a fear of a sudden loud noise. Every other fear we have picked up somewhere, though we may not be aware of when and how. I have a fear of heights, for example, but I have no remembrance of when and how I have that fear.

So often it is not the fear of outward circumstances so much as it is a fear of our own ability to cope with a situation that is the problem. Like trees, we would not be afraid of the high winds if we knew our roots were deep and would hold. It's the shallowness of our roots and faith in ourselves and God that gives us apprehension most often, not life's gusts and gales.

It is important, then, that we admit our fears. Sometimes we're afraid to even admit that we're afraid. We may see our fear as a weakness or view ourselves as a failure because we're afraid. Neither one is true. Admitting or naming our fear can be the first step in overcoming or living with our fear.

Jesus had gone up a mountain to be by himself and to pray. He had instructed his disciples to take their boat to the other side of the lake. During the night a storm came up. The disciples were struggling against the wind and the waves and making little progress. If you've ever been on a boat during a storm when the waves are splashing over the side you know how frightening that can be. Adding to the fear of the storm was the sight of what appeared to be a ghost, and they were even more terrified. It was Jesus walking on the water.

According to British scholar, William Barclay, the word which is used for "walking" can also mean "to walk about." This passage from the Gospels may describe a miracle in which Jesus actually walked on the water, or it may equally mean that the disciples' boat was driven by the wind to the northern shore of the lake. Jesus came down from the mountain to help them when he saw them struggling, and he came walking through the surf of the shore towards the boat and came so suddenly upon them that they were terrified when they saw him.[89]

Peter was so excited he got out of the boat and started walking on the water to Jesus. But when he noticed the strong wind, he was afraid and started to sink.

Which reminds me of the story of a minister, a priest and a rabbi who went fishing together. After awhile the priest said he'd left some of his tackle on shore and he needed it. So, he proceeded to stand-up, get out of the boat and walk across the water to the shore. The minister couldn't believe his eyes. Especially when a few minutes later the priest said he, too, had left some tackle on shore and he proceeded to also walk across the water. The minister just couldn't believe it. He thought that if they could walk on the water, so could he. His faith was just as strong as theirs. So, he stood up, stepped over the side of the boat and immediately sank to the bottom. The priest and the rabbi were watching from the shore. And one said to the other, "Do you suppose we should tell him where the rocks are?"

There were no lifeguards, rescue boats or rocks nearby when Simon Peter tried to make that famous walk, and giving in to his fear, he sank.

Fear is a powerful force, but faith is more powerful. That is why the Psalmist could exclaim, "I sought the Lord, and he heard me, and delivered me from all my fears."

I am afraid of heights. I don't like to climb ladders, or be up in a balcony near the edge. Once someone told me, don't look down when you're up high, but look up. And that helps. Just as it helps when climbing a ladder, so it helps in life to ease one's fears. Don't look down at the fear, but look up to Jesus.

In the time of need, Jesus came to the disciples. In our times of need, Jesus likewise comes to help us. When life was a struggle, Jesus was there to help with his calm voice of assurance, "Take heart, it is I; have no fear."

When we start concentrating on our fears, like Peter, we sink. But when we trust in Christ to help us we can find the courage we need.

There can come times in our lives when we feel we can go no further. There can come times when we are faced with problems that seem unsolvable, or burdens that are too heavy, or decisions that leave us immobile. We may feel helpless, powerless and afraid. It is at times like these that we must reach out in faith and trust in God to help us. Our faith is the rock to stand on.

Peter started to sink because he took his mind away from Jesus and started to think about the wind and about himself. We give in to fear when we focus on ourselves and not on God. When we put our faith in God then God comes to us and gives us the power we need to stand up to our fears.

Dr. Martin Luther King, Jr. says he had an easy time in life until he became a part of the leadership of the Montgomery, Alabama bus protest. Almost immediately after the protest had been undertaken, he began to receive threatening telephone calls and letters in his home. Sporadic in the beginning, they increased day after day. At first he took them in stride, feeling that they were the work of a few hotheads who would become discouraged after they discovered he would not fight back. But as the weeks passed, he realized that many of the threats were in earnest. He felt himself faltering and growing in fear.

After an especially strenuous day, he settled in bed. It was late. His wife had already fallen asleep and he was about to doze off when he received another threatening call. He hung up, but he could not sleep. It seemed that all of his fears had come down upon him at once.

He got out of bed and began to walk the floor. Finally he went to the kitchen and heated a pot of coffee. He was ready to give up. In this state of exhaustion, when his courage had almost gone, he decided to take his problem to God. His head in his hands, he bowed over the kitchen table and prayed aloud: "I am here taking a stand for what I believe is right. But now I am afraid. The people are looking to me for leadership, and if I stand before them without strength and courage, they too will falter. I am at the end of my powers. I have nothing left. I've come to the point where I can't face it alone."

At that moment he says he experienced the presence of God as he had never before experienced God. It seemed as though he could hear the quiet assurance of an inner voice, saying, "Stand up for righteousness, stand up for truth. God will be at your side forever." Almost at once his fears began to pass from him. His uncertainty disappeared. He was ready to face anything. He says, "The outer situation had remained the same, but God had given me inner calm."

Three nights later their house was bombed. Dr. King says, "Strangely enough, I accepted the word of the bombing calmly. My experience with God had given me a new strength and trust. I knew now that God is able to give us the interior resources to face the storms and problems of life."[90]

The way to deal successfully with our fears is to put our faith in God. When we do we will seek to face our fears. We will find we can relax even as we experience fear because God's power will keep us calm, and we will discover the power that will help us overcome our fears. Jesus told his disciples as he is telling us, "Take heart, it is I; have no fear."

I think of a woman in one of my churches. I'll call her Ruth. She and her husband were in their late 60's, when he was diagnosed with cancer. He went through treatments, but died several months later. Initially, Ruth was lost. Her husband, John, had done everything, from handling finances to driving Ruth everywhere. Ruth had a driver's license, but she had never driven by herself more than a short distance to the grocery store and shopping mall. She had a daughter who lived about an hour away, but Ruth was afraid to drive by herself to visit her daughter.

Ruth had a strong faith. Through her faith she got up the courage to drive to her daughter's. It was not an easy time for her, but she did it! She felt that God was with her!

Ruth had a good friend living in Nova Scotia. Her friend kept encouraging her to take a trip with her. Through much persistence, Ruth finally agreed. The friend came to Ruth's and they flew out of New York for a week's visit to Cancun.

Ruth had never flown before. This was again another example of faith overcoming her fear of flying.

The next year Ruth actually drove to Nova Scotia from New Jersey to visit her friend.

The following year, with the insistence from the friend, Ruth got up enough courage to go on a three-month cruise to Europe. While on the cruise, Ruth met a gentleman from Australia. One thing led to another and they fell in love. Three or four months after she returned, he came to America, proposed, they were married, and she moved to Australia with him! Talk about faith overcoming your fear!

Faith in God gives us the strength we need to face-up to our fears, but faith also calms us to the point where we can think about, evaluate and perhaps change our thoughts about that which we fear. We need to ask ourselves, exactly what is it that I fear? When most people say for example, that they are afraid to speak in public, that's not the real fear. The real fear is that they're afraid of making a mistake and being perceived as a fool.

When we say we're afraid of falling because we might break a hip or a leg, faith can help us begin to ask, what can I do to minimize the chance of falling? It might mean using a walker each time I go out in public.

If your eyesight is not as good as it used to be, you could: use white or reflecting tape to mark changes in floor levels; move chairs and tables away from places where you walk most often; light your home evenly. Light all stairways. Put light switches at both the bottom and the top of the stairs. Use a night light. Get rid of shiny surfaces, to cut down on glare. Use a lot of reds and yellow-oranges in your home. They are easier to see. Use contrasting paint colors where you need to be able to see the difference in surfaces. For example, use a light color for walls and a darker color for doorways. You can do this with stairs, too.

If you have lost some of your hearing, you could: carpet the floors and put curtains in the windows. This will reduce background noises and echoes. Background noises can prevent you from hearing other things. Buy a vibrating alarm clock and an amplified TV if you have trouble hearing them. Get an amplified handset for your telephone. This makes the other person's voice louder. If your hearing loss is severe, you may want to get a teletypewriter for your phone. This machine types out telephone messages.

If you have limited mobility or strength, you could: install large, lever-type controls on faucets, door latches and appliances. Remove doors on the inside of the house. Install handrails on both sides of stairways. Also install them in the tub and perhaps by the toilet. Install a ramp for entering and leaving the house. Tack down loose edges of carpeting. Use nonskid treads. Remove rugs that slide. Or put nonslip pads under them. If you use a wheelchair, put door handles, light switches, tools and dishes at a level where you can easily reach them.

If we're afraid or worried about medical costs, it can be helpful to find out exactly what Medicare will cover. This government health insurance program can give some security to those worried about costs. While Medicare does not cover everything, it can give some feeling of security knowing what it does cover.

It also helps to focus on today, not tomorrow or yesterday. So many of our fears are based on something that happened in the past. We're afraid to go out today because when we went out yesterday we fell. Or, we're afraid of what might happen in the future; we might fall if we venture outside our home.

It also helps to focus on the things you can control rather than those you can't. The things you can't control should be left to God.

In addition to being afraid of accidents around the house, there is also the fear of crime. Many older people feel more vulnerable because of their physical loss of strength, mobility, vision or hearing. There are some things you can do to try to minimize the potential for crime around your house. Are the entrances to your home lighted? Lighting the outside of your house may turn thieves away. Lighting makes it easier to see someone outside. Are any doors or windows hidden by trees or shrubs? Thieves can use trees and shrubs to hide. Make sure trees and shrubs are trimmed so entrances can be seen by neighbors or from the street. Use large, easy-to-read numbers to post your house number. This makes it easier for police and fire fighters to find your home. Plus, keep your house number well lit at night. Do all the entrances to your house have secure locks? Make sure all doors are always closed and locked. In one of the retirement communities here in Florida, thieves were entering open garages and stealing articles. Do you have a peephole on the main door? If you do, use it before opening the door. If you don't have a peephole, always find out who is at the door before opening it. Be leery of strangers wanting to come in to use the phone or bathroom. Many seniors have been victimized by a couple entering a house on the pretext of an emergency. One talks with the occupant, while the other, on the pretext of using the bathroom, actually looks around for valuables. Use window locks as much as possible. Get locks for any windows without locks. Keep a list of emergency numbers near the phone. The number 911 is used in most communities for police, fire or medical emergencies, but if it is not, keep a list of phone numbers handy for emergency situations. Get a dog. Unfortunately, many senior communities don't allow pets, although some allow dogs up to a certain weight or size. A dog's bark will usually deter someone trying to break in to your house. Plus, walking your dog can be good exercise.

While outside your house, stay alert. Avoid walking alone, especially at night and in high-crime areas. Don't dress in a showy manner. Leave good jewelry in a safe place. Don't carry a lot of cash. Park in well-lit areas at night.

People of all ages fall victim to fraud. Stories abound, however, of seniors who have used their retirement savings for investments that sound too good to be true, and usually are. But be wary too of advertisements or salespeople for miracle cures, home repairs and charities. Check them out with the better business bureau first.

Senior abuse can be another source of worry. Sometimes safety is threatened by your own relatives or other caretakers. Some abuse is physical. Some is mental. Some is verbal. And some caretakers plot to take seniors' money or other belongings. To cut down on the chances of being abused, some helpful suggestions might be to: plan weekly contact with a friend outside your home; ask friends to visit you in your home; send and open your own mail; know where all your valuables and important papers are; have Social Security or pension checks sent directly to your bank; do not sign anything unless someone you trust has read it.

The key to coping with fear is to admit it, accept it and deal with it. We can deal with it by finding ways to get around or overcome what we're afraid of and by trusting in God's help and strength.

One of the most prayed prayers in all the world that people have found as a source of strength and courage in coping with fear and worry is the prayer that Reinhold Niebuhr wrote many years ago:

God grant me the serenity
To accept the things I cannot change;
The courage to change the things I can,
And the wisdom to know the difference.

CHAPTER SIXTEEN
LIVING WITH PAIN

"After thirty, a body has a mind of its own." Bette Midler

Pain is an inevitable part of life. Even Jesus did not escape pain and suffering. His death on a cross must have been extremely physically painful. According to Dr. Paul Maier, "the victim's extremities were bound or nailed to the cross, and he was left to hang, sometimes for several days before he died, as a public example and warning to others to avoid his crime…Jesus' hands were nailed to the crossbeam, which was then lowered onto a vertical stake…and his feet were spiked onto it. He was probably made to straddle a wedge placed between his legs, as in other crucifixions, which would have borne his weight sufficiently so that the nailed hands would not, in fact, have torn apart."[91]

Jesus endured the pain from the cross for only a few hours. Many people endure the pain of arthritis or other physical ailments for years, sometimes wishing they could die.

One way to cope with pain is to try to get some relief from it. The most common method is through drugs and medications such as aspirin, bufferin, tylenol and others, some stronger in their effects, such as codeine or morphine, prescribed by a doctor. Other people may try to dull pain through alcohol or other drugs.

Sometimes exercise helps, especially for joints that have become stiff because of arthritis. Water therapy has been especially helpful to some people.

Dr. Miriam Nelson of Tufts University has developed a strengthening routine. She believes that as your muscles grow, your pain should decrease. In a 16-week study conducted by Nelson, arthritis patients who completed an at-home strength-training program reported a 43 percent decrease in pain and a 71 percent increase in muscle strength. The subjects, ages 55 and older, also reported much more ease getting out of chairs, climbing stairs, even putting on socks and shoes. "They were amazed at the difference," says Nelson. "It helped brighten their whole outlook on life." This is another benefit of exercise. Exercise can boost your mood, reduce anxiety, even lift depression.[92]

Dr. Kent Adams, an associate professor of exercise physiology at the University of Louisville in Kentucky, found similar results in his studies on osteoporosis patients. "They tell me, 'My husband and I went out dancing and I felt great' or 'I went on a vacation and for the first time I was able to climb the steps on castles in Europe.'"

"There are studies on people close to 100 years old who have gotten stronger through resistance training," says Adams. In an eight week study, nursing home residents ages 86 to 96 increased their muscle strength by 174 percent and increased their walking speed by 48 percent. Two subjects were even able to discard their walking canes.[93]

Diet is also important in controlling pain. Research shows that three nutrients- vitamin C, beta carotene and folate help reduce pain. Dr. Nelson suggests at least six servings of produce a day, three each of fruits and vegetables, especially the leafy green kind, like spinach. Good beta-carotene sources include sweet potatoes, carrots and mangoes.

Your weight is also important. For every extra pound you put on, according to Dr. Nelson, your knees and hips experience three extra pounds of pressure. Studies show that if the average person dropped about 11 pounds, he or she would reduce osteoarthritis pain by half.

Some people view their pain and suffering as a punishment. Rabbi Harold Kushner, in his book, "When Bad Things Happen to Good People," tells of a time he was called upon to help a family through an unexpected tragedy. The only daughter of a middle-aged couple was a student at an out-of-state college. One morning at breakfast, they received a phone call from the university. Their daughter collapsed while walking to class. A blood vessel burst in her brain. She died before anything could be done to help her.

When he went to see the parents, the first words the rabbi heard were: "You know, Rabbi, we didn't fast last Yom Kippur."

Rabbi Kushner asked why they said that, why did they assume that they were somehow responsible for such a tragedy?[94]

One of the ways in which people have tried to make sense of pain and suffering has been by assuming that somehow our misfortune comes as a result of something we have done, or failed to do.

That is one of the problems in the Old Testament book of Job. Without telling Job what is going on, God allows Satan to destroy Job's house and cattle and his children to be killed. He afflicts Job with boils all over his body so that his every movement becomes physical torture.

Job tries to make sense out of what has happened. Three friends come and try to comfort him, but they seem to say all the wrong things.

One of the friends tells Job, "God never twists justice; he never fails to do what is right. Your children must have sinned against God, and who punished them as they deserved."

But Job takes offense at such logic. He says, "What do you mean He will see to it that the good prosper and the wicked are punished? Are you implying that my children were wicked and that is why they died? Are you saying that I am wicked, and that is why all this is happening to me? Where was I so terrible? What did I do that was so much worse than anything you did?"

Job doesn't claim to be perfect, but says that he has tried, more than most people, to live a good and decent life and we are told at the beginning of the book that Job is good. He questions how God can be a good and just God if the innocent suffer and so many wicked people escape punishment.

Even if our aches and pains are not the result of some sin, as in Job's case, our thoughts, attitudes and beliefs may affect how we cope with pain. Job maintained his innocence. He had a strong, positive belief. We're not told how he coped with his bodily sores, but research has demonstrated that if we think that pain means we'll be disabled, the belief has more to do with disability than the pain itself.

In a 1988 study conducted at Brown University by Dr. John F. Riley and his colleagues, patients diagnosed with symptoms of chronic pain were more likely to be impaired, despite the severity of pain they reported, if they believed that pain implied impairment.

The investigators surveyed fifty-six patients who experienced pain in various parts of their bodies- the mean duration of their pain was 35.1 months- on their attitudes toward pain and disability. They asked the patients to keep diaries of their pain, and they tested the patients' physical strength and mobility. In the end, independent of the pain levels reported, those who believed pain should inhibit their movement were the most inhibited. In other words, the belief that pain implies disability has more to do with disability than the pain itself.

The team also argued that the health care profession may contribute to the downward cycle experienced by chronic pain patients by introducing and reinforcing the belief that being pain-free is the ultimate goal. Medicine, and a society that is bombarded with advertising offers of quick fixes and miracle cures may be cultivating impairment by promoting an undue expectancy of pain relief. In truth, chronic pain is rarely cured completely. [95]

Someone wrote to "Dear Abby" in response to an earlier letter, "Smiling Through the Pain," a reader who has suffered with chronic pain since childhood. I missed that first letter, but the respondent had some good advice on coping with pain:

"Like 'Smiling Through the Pain,' I, too, suffer from chronic pain. When my doctor told me that there were no medications at this time that would make the pain go away, I asked, 'How am I going to endure this?'

She replied, 'Live one day at a time. Live each day to the fullest. Laugh heartily, love deeply, pray daily- and let the rest roll off.'

I then asked, 'How am I going to live with the pain?'

She said, 'Surround yourself with positive things- positive people, sunshine, rainbows, roses, puppies and kittens.'

After reflecting upon what she had said, I realized that this is a great prescription for anyone's life. That doctor probably saved mine. Not only did she give my monstrous disease a name, she helped me to make my life worth living again.

I have good days and bad. I curse the bad ones and praise God for the good ones. The 'good' pain comes when I have accomplished what I wanted to do that day. The 'bad' pain comes when I refrain from doing what I want to do- and hurt anyway.

Every day I get up, get dressed and have something planned to do. And, Abby, I try to perform at least one act of kindness for someone each day. Regardless of my pain, it makes each day seem fuller. I hope you will find this letter appropriate to share with your readers. If it helps someone else who is hurting (for whatever reason), then my effort will not have been in vain."

The Biblical answer is that pain and suffering are a part of life, but God is present to comfort and strengthen us. In some instances, too, it may be sin that has caused our pain. Someone who drives a car well past the speed limit, loses control and ends up with broken bones, has caused their own pain.

Certainly the physical aches and pains due to arthritis, osteoporosis, and other ailments are not, in most cases, due to anything we may have done or not done. They come with growing older. How then do we cope?

Many people in my congregation suffer with physical aches and pains. Mostly the pain is from arthritis. People have difficulty walking or getting up from sitting. My mother experienced pain in her legs and joints for over forty years after she was injured in an automobile accident. She never was able to successfully cope with her pain.

I think then of someone like Washington Roebling. I remember reading about his life. His father, John Roebling, was the engineer with the idea of bridging the East River and connecting Manhattan with Brooklyn. It was a good idea, but all the bridge-building experts and structural engineers of his time said it was impossible. Some agreed that the river might be spanned, but said that a 1,595 foot span would never stand up against the winds and the tides. But John Roebling and his son, Washington, figured out how the problems could be solved.

Then, as construction began, John Roebling was killed, and in the same accident, Washington suffered the bends underneath the water. He survived, but was left with permanent brain damage and could never walk or talk again.

Washington Roebling developed a code of communication by touching one finger to his wife's arm. He communicated the dream through her to the engineers on the project. For thirteen years, Washington Raoebling supervised construction that way. And finally in 1883 traffic streamed across the Brooklyn Bridge. He didn't let his pain keep him from his work.

It's too bad we can't be like the oyster. When a small piece of sand, grit, or some other kind of foreign matter gets in the oyster's body, the irritant signals the oyster to build a layer of mineral material around the irritant. Then, another layer like the first. Then another. If left alone long enough the oyster continues to build and build around the irritation until a large, lustrous, round pearl is created. From the irritation is produced a beautiful pearl.

Like the pearl, sometimes suffering and pain bring benefits to us that are not immediately apparent.

For example, it is said that the best thing that ever happened to boxer Gene Tunney was that he broke both hands in the ring. After this, his manager felt that he could never again punch hard enough to become a heavyweight champion. Instead, Tunney decided that he would become a scientific boxer and win the title as a boxer, not a slugger. Boxing historians will tell you that he developed into one of the best boxers who ever fought. They also will tell you that as a puncher, he would not have had a chance against Jack Dempsey, who was considered by many to be the hardest hitter in heavyweight history. Tunney would never have been champion had he not had the problems of his broken hands.

Do you remember the transformation that came over Lee Atwater, former President George Bush's campaign manager after it was discovered that, at age forty, he was dying of a brain tumor. He said, "My illness helped me to see that what was missing in society is what was missing in me, a little heart, a lot of brotherhood…and to see that we must be made to speak to this spiritual vacuum at the heart of American society, this tumor of the soul."[96]

Suffering can also help people get out of themselves and begin to see others in a different light.

Perhaps the greatest benefit of pain and suffering is that it can remind us or make us aware of our dependence on God.

The Apostle Paul had a physical problem. He had some kind of physical pain that troubled him greatly. In his letter to the Church at Corinth, Paul said, "A thorn was given me in the flesh, a messenger of Satan, to harass me, to keep me from being too elated. Three times I besought the Lord about this, that it should leave me; but he said to me, 'My grace is sufficient for you, for my power is made perfect in weakness"…

Paul found strength through his faith in Christ. The pain was still there, but God's presence enabled him to live with the pain. Because God experienced pain through Jesus, God knows what we go through.

One of the major turning points for Joni Eareckson Tada during her battle with faith after losing the use of her arms and legs in an accident occurred when a friend pointed out to her that Christ knew what it was like to be paralyzed. In his book, "Where Is God When It Hurts?", author Philip Yancey writes: "One night especially, Joni became convinced that God did understand. Pain was streaking through her back in a way that is a unique torment to those paralyzed. Healthy persons can scratch an itch, squeeze an aching muscle, or flex a cramped foot. The paralyzed must lie still, defenseless, and feel the pain. Cindy, one of Joni's closest friends, was beside her bed, searching desperately for some way to encourage her. Finally, she clumsily blurted out, 'Joni, Jesus knows how you feel…you aren't the only one…why, he was paralyzed too.' Joni glared at her. 'What? What are you talking about?' Cindy continued, 'It's true. Remember, he was nailed on a cross. His back was raw from beatings, and he must have yearned for a way to move to change positions, or redistribute his weight. But he couldn't. He was paralyzed by the nails.' The thought intrigued Joni. It had never occurred to her before that God had felt the exact piercing sensations that racked her body. The idea was profoundly comforting."[97]

It is comforting to turn to a Power greater than our own and to discover there is a Friend who understands what we are going through and can help us.

In his book, "Timeless Healing," Dr. Herbert Benson tells the story of a neighbor woman. At six one Sunday morning, a neighbor two houses up the street summoned him for help. They had been neighbors for fifteen years but knew each other only casually. But, a crisis brought them together on this particular day. Marie had been diagnosed with renal cancer months before and treatment had proved unsuccessful. She had come home to be surrounded by the love and attention of her husband and daughters for whatever time she had left. Her husband, Paul, called that morning because Marie had been crying out and in tremendous pain. He had exhausted every method he had been told could help.

Dr. Benson found Marie on a hospital bed in the dining room. The family had removed all the dining room furniture so that their wife and mother could be in the center of the house, wouldn't have to climb stairs, and was near the kitchen and a bathroom. Marie was exhausted and tearful, so tormented by this end-stage cancer and its abdominal pain that she could not sleep. Paul ushered him into the kitchen where the counters were overloaded with pill bottles, all of them designed to bring her relief but none of them effective. "Please help us," Paul said to Dr. Benson.

Knowing that the family was Catholic, Dr. Benson asked Paul to retrieve a crucifix that hung in their bedroom and they placed it in the dining room over Marie's bed. Dr. Benson explained to Marie that perhaps they could lessen her suffering by teaching her how to elicit the relaxation response (see the chapter on prayer). When Dr. Benson explained to her that she needed a word or phrase on which to focus, she decided upon the rosary. Lying there, taking deep breaths, Marie focused her mind on a silent iteration of the rosary. Gradually the furrows that accompanied her clenched mouth and eyes smoothed out, and her breathing slowed and became more regular. Within about ten minutes Marie was asleep.

A few days later Paul called Dr. Benson to say that the improvement had been long-lasting and remarkable. Marie was relying primarily on the prayer, refraining from taking almost all the pain medication. Although Marie was in a great deal of pain, she was free of the terrible distress she had suffered before. Without medication, her mind was clear, her mood brighter. Marie was at peace when she died.

Dr. Benson concluded by saying, "When the mind quiets down, the body follows suit."[98]

Amy Carmichael was a missionary to India for fifty-six years. During the last twenty years, however, she was confined to her room because of injuries suffered in a terrible fall. In site of being daily wracked by pain, she carried on her work for the Lord and composed thirteen books.

In 1948, as she neared the end of her life, Amy wrote this note: "Not relief from pain, not relief from the weariness that follows, not anything of that sort at all, is my chief need. Thou, O Lord my God, are my need- Thy courage, Thy patience, Thy fortitude. And very much I need a quickened gratitude for the countless helps given every day."

When we feel God's presence with us we can withstand almost anything. Byron Janis would agree. For years, Byron Janis, one of the world's great piano virtuosos, has been fighting the effects of crippling psoriatic arthritis. An article in a 1985 edition of Parade Magazine told how he could not make a fist. The right wrist's motion was limited to 40%. The little finger on the left hand was numb, partially paralyzed and scarred from a childhood accident. The joints of the other nine fingers were fused. There was mobility in only one distal joint, that of the middle finger of the left hand.

"Learning to live with pain," he says, "or live with a limitation can give an intensity to life. I thought I had nothing. Now I know I have everything. I'm saying to others, 'If I can do it, so can you!'"

Janus listed the various means he sought to help him, ranging from medical doctors to acupuncturists, but adds, "What helped me most, I can't explain. I developed a very personal relationship with God. I think prayer is important. I think the belief in God is healing."

"No one knows what it's like for other people, but I know that, unless I found a belief in God, I would never have been able to say what I have to say. God works with man and man with God. Not one alone."[99]

"I still have arthritis. But it doesn't have me!" That is the testimony of countless others. I have problems and I have pain, but they don't have me. Why? Because there is One who sees and understands and is able to give me the strength to keep going.

CHAPTER SEVENTEEN
YOU'LL NEVER WALK ALONE

*"And when he had sent the multitudes away, he went up into a
mountain apart to pray; and when the evening was come, he was
there alone." Matthew 14:23*

"He was there alone." So are many older adults. An elderly
widow who lives in a cramped apartment in Los Angeles
wrote a letter to the paper and said: "I see no human beings.
My phone never rings. I feel sure the world has ended. I'm the
only one on earth. How else can I feel? All alone. The people
here won't talk to you. They say, 'Pay your rent and go back to
your room.' I'm so lonely I don't know what to do."

This woman enclosed a dollar and six stamps with her
letter. "Will someone please call me?" she asked. The dollar
was to pay for the call; the stamps were to be used if anyone
would write her.

In my congregation there are many widows and widowers
who have outlived their spouse and find themselves living
alone. For some it can mean making major adjustments. In
some marriages, the husband did everything. He did all the
driving. He took care of all the finances. He managed all the
maintenance and repairs needed around the house. And so,

when he died, his wife was left not just alone, but with great feelings of loneliness because she didn't know what to do. Everything had been done for her by her late husband. She now had to learn how to balance a checkbook. She had to learn how to drive a car. She had to learn what to do to maintain her house.

On the other hand, I've known widowers who are just as lost and lonely when their wife died. Many widowers never learned how to cook or sew a button on a shirt or do the laundry. Some widowers also feel just as lost and lonely.

There are many kinds of loneliness. One common loneliness follows the death of a spouse or a loved one. Sorrow is a personal and individual experience, and often, a very lonely experience.

Loneliness can come as a result of being by yourself. One can feel this type of loneliness living in a house alone, or out on a lake, or even in an automobile driving along the highway.

On the other hand, there can be loneliness in a crowd. This is especially true in a crowded city. One can be walking down a crowded street, with people all around, and yet feel alone. There are those who live in large apartment buildings with people all around them, but they do not feel a part of anyone.

Suffering can bring loneliness. If you have pain in your body or sadness in your spirit, one can feel all alone. Jesus experienced such loneliness on the cross. He cried out, "My God, my God, why have you forsaken me?" (Mt. 27:46) In his suffering, Jesus felt that even God had abandoned him, though such loneliness did not last very long and he felt God's presence was with him.

Many experience what is called cosmic loneliness. We are conscious of living in this enormous universe and yet may feel lost in the bigness of it all. Perhaps that's what the Psalmist meant when he said, "When I look at thy heavens, the work of thy fingers, the moon and the stars which thou hast established; what is man that thou art mindful of him,

and the son of man that thou dost care for him?" (Psalm 8:3,4)
People can feel lost in the vastness of it all.

Many experience loneliness when they try to communicate
with someone and they don't seem to be listening or we can't
get through to them.

A Vermont farmer was the silent type. He and his wife got
to their golden wedding anniversary and finally he broke into
a speech, a long speech for him. He said to his wife: "Sarah, I
have loved you so much that sometimes I could hardly keep
from telling you."

A woman needs to be told. She needs to know that you
think she's important in your life.

There is a tendency to take one another for granted as the
years go by, and we need to be aware of that. Someone once
said: "Before a man gets married, he lies awake in bed all night
thinking about what his beloved said. After they are married,
he falls asleep before she has finished saying it."

There is a constant need for recognition, affection, romance
and affirmation in a relationship, otherwise one or both will
feel lonely even though you're not alone.

There is another kind of loneliness. It is at a time of decision.
We may seek advice and guidance from others, but sooner or
later, each of us must make the decision alone. No one else
can make it for us.

There is loneliness that can come with retirement. When
people move from a life where they have felt essential and
important in their work to a life where they may have time on
their hands they can feel useless. The loss of responsibility can
make one feel unimportant, and in many cases, very lonely.

The key can be to find something to take the place of one's
work, such as a hobby or volunteer work where one can feel
useful once again.

There can be the fear of being alone. Many may fear ending
up in some nursing home alone and forgotten. I have visited
parishioners in nursing homes who have mentioned someone
else in the nursing home and felt sorry for them because no

one ever comes to see them. Many elderly are left alone in nursing homes.

However, there is a difference in being alone and being lonely. For example, Jesus had gone up a mountain to pray and he was alone, but he wasn't lonely. God was with him.

Many people can find happiness and inspiration in moments when they are by themselves. There are times when one needs to be alone in order to think things through, to seek out God's guidance or to meditate. It is necessary at times to get away from others and from distractions. Times of silence and aloneness are conducive to thinking and meditating and relaxation.

Loneliness, however, is never happy. Maybe you have read the classic, *Robinson Crusoe.* It is the story of a man who is marooned on an island by himself. Every day Crusoe comes to his lookout point, where he has rigged up a cloth at the top of a pole. He stands gazing across the sea, hands shading his eyes, searching for white sails against the empty horizon.

Standing there in his tattered clothes, skin bronzed by the sun, hair long and unkempt, he longs for the sound of a human voice.

One day, his solitary vigil once again unrewarded, he turns to go, but stops short in wild surprise, for before him in the sands is an unmistakable human footprint, not his own.

We all need companionship. Even Jesus did. Jesus gathered twelve disciples to teach and to send out to carry on God's work, but also to illustrate the importance of human relationships. God has created us so that we need one another. In Genesis we read: "Then the Lord God said, "It is not good that the man should be alone; I will make him a helper fit for him." (Gen. 2:18)

Many have loved the song:

Me and my shadow,
Not a soul to tell my troubles to;
Just me and my shadow,
All alone and blue.

One way to overcome loneliness is, of course, to get out with other people. In Florida, there are numerous communities just for those over 55 years of age. Within those communities there are usually numerous opportunities to mingle with others. Often there is a community center or clubhouse where one can go to swim, play shuffleboard, horseshoes, cards or just be with other people.

For those who may need some assistance there are assisted living homes, but even there, residents take their meals together and there are often numerous activities designed to bring people together.

Many communities have senior centers where one can go to play cards, games, take trips and just meet others.

Even communities that don't have specific centers or places for seniors have churches or various clubs in which people of all ages can participate.

In this age of computers, those who may live alone and have difficulty physically getting around can meet others over the internet.

It is important for churches to keep in contact with their senior members. Our church has caretakers, members of the Diaconate who have lists of our members and call periodically to check on them and talk. We try to keep our members who have difficulty physically getting around from becoming lonely as well as helping them with any problems, such as driving them to a doctor's appointment or grocery shopping.

If you are lonely, you may need to ask yourself, why? What resources are available for you to get together with other people? If you hesitate in getting out to be with others, what is the reason? Are you lonely because you are making yourself lonely? Are you withdrawn, hypercritical, self-pitying so that you stay away from others or drive people away from you? Or, are you like Jesus, interested in others, who they are, what they think, what they believe? Do you respect the opinions and feelings of others and try to take an interest in them.

Many times it is our own fault that we are lonely. Do we, for example, wait to be asked to do something when we could just as well volunteer our services. Are we waiting to be asked somewhere when there are many places we could go on our own to meet people and make friends, learn new knowledge or acquire a new hobby?

Perhaps one impediment to making friends is the fear of death. Why even begin to be friends with someone when one of us is likely to die soon? Grief is difficult and friendship means grief and sadness.

It is ironic that God has given us a built in need for love and companionship and yet along with love comes the possibility for sadness and sorrow. Most of us learn that irony as we are growing up. When we are teenagers and are attracted to someone, we long to be with that person yet are often afraid to even start a conversation with them for fear we will be rejected. Or, if we've given our love to someone and later they rejected us through divorce or death, people are reluctant to love again for fear of being hurt. And yet we know that someday those we love will be taken from us through death. We cannot prevent that from happening.

It is still true as when Ralph Waldo Emerson said it more than a hundred years ago: "The only way to have a friend is to be a friend."

Everyone needs friends. We need friends for psychological reasons and we need friends for physiological reasons. Studies of aging indicate that having close friends is one of the best things you can do for your body as you grow older.

Everyone needs someone they can count on, someone they can confide in, and someone who will be there for them.

Actress Julie Andrews has had someone like that. According to Glenn Plashin in his book, *Turning Point,* Julie Andrews did not have an easy time of it growing up. Her enormous success on Broadway in *Camelot* and in movies like *The Sound of Music* did not change the fact that there was a void in her life.

Although she was blessed with a soprano voice and toured England singing operatic arias at age twelve, there was a darker side that kept her away from others.

"My parents were both alcoholics," Julie remembers, "and I was a child freak with an adult voice at age eight, forced to grow up much too fast." The result left a void in her life. "I always had wished I'd had more family feeling," she says, "and I needed a good friend."

She found that friend in actress, Carol Burnett.

"We both started performing as kids," says Andrews. "We both came from alcoholic families, and we both had been caretakers, which is a tremendous burden for a kid. Being raised in a chaotic household, we were also both super-neat and super-square."

"Throughout all those years," Andrews says, "the things I first liked about Carol haven't changed a bit. She's ingenuous, she's straight, and she's real. When I was divorced years ago, Carol helped me; when she was divorced, I helped her. Kid problems and romance problems were always easier because we've had each other."

"Also, we regress and both become big kids when we're together- she's the lady and I'm the comedienne. But what comforts me the most in this dizzying world is that I know I can trust Carol completely. She's a sister to me and I love her a lot. I don't think anything could harm that relationship."[100]

Men also need friends. George Burns once said of his friend Jack Benny: "Jack and I had a wonderful friendship for nearly fifty-five years. Jack never walked out on me when I sang a song, and I never walked out on him when he played the violin. We laughed together, we played together, we worked together, we ate together. I suppose that for many of those years we talked every single day."[101]

No matter how successful you and I may be, we need friends. Someone we can confide in. Someone who knows us as we really are and accepts us. Someone who is there for us in good times and bad times.

Sometimes the cause of our loneliness is bitterness, which usually includes a lack of forgiveness toward others. Some people seem to be stuck in feelings of anger towards a spouse who has died. They are bitter that their spouse has left them and have difficulty forgiving them for dying. They are punishing themselves by refusing to forgive their spouse. Their choice of bitterness can leave such people also feeling isolated and lonely.

A very subtle cause of loneliness involves feelings of guilt and a lack of forgiveness toward self. One time there was a particularly sad letter in the Billy Graham newspaper column. Someone wrote: "I'm in my 80s and all alone, and I know it's my own fault. I went through life being disagreeable and demanding that everybody do things my way, and all my relatives turned against me. Maybe someone will learn from my life. I wish I could live it over."

Rev. Graham wrote back, "One of life's hardest lessons is that we cannot change the past."

Regret is a crippling emotion because it leaves us chained to the past and we end up feeling all alone.

The one friend we can all have is God. The hymn, "What a friend we have in Jesus," is so true. God will never let us down and our relationship with God can be one of friendship.

There is a story of two men who were riding together. One of them was busy working a crossword puzzle. He turned to his friend and asked, "What is a word of three letters, with the letter *o* in the middle, meaning man's best friend?" His friend replied, "Dog." The word *dog* did not fit into the puzzle. The man kept working at it, and then turned to his friend and said, "The last letter of that word is *D*." But still they couldn't quite figure out the word. They never did come up with the answer that the first letter of that word is *G*. And in the situations of life there are numerous people who never come to realize that our best friend is GOD.

When we talk about God as our friend it does not mean we are, or may become, God's equal as is true with earthly friends. We need to remember and acknowledge our inequality. God is creator, eternal, almighty, Lord of all, and we are God's finite, sinful creatures. To refer to God as our "friend" means that God desires to have a personal relationship with us. We can go to God with our problems, our concerns, and our happiness, just as we can talk with our friends, but even more so, for there may be some things we withhold from our friends that we need not be afraid to share with God, especially since God knows us better than we know ourselves. As a friend, God desires to help us, to listen to us, to be present for us and with us at all times.

Throughout history, people of faith often were alone in their struggle for justice and righteousness, but they were not alone, for God was with them. Moses called for the pharaoh of Egypt to release the Hebrews from slavery. Elijah had a contest with the prophets of Baal. Daniel fought the lions. Jeremiah was often in danger from political and religious leaders who were angry because of his messages. And in the New Testament, who could have experienced more loneliness than Jesus. He had the disciples as his friends and companions. He accepted and welcomed the outcast of society. He drew crowds wherever he went. And yet he was rejected by those in authority. Even his disciples fled from him in fear for their safety. He was betrayed by Judas. He was denied by Peter. Just when he was most lonely and needed them most.

Jesus had told his disciples, "Look, the hour is coming, has indeed already come, when you are all to be scattered, each to his home, leaving me alone. Yet I am not alone, because the Father is with me. I have told you all this so that in me you may find peace. In the world you will have trouble. But courage! The victory is mine; I have conquered the world." (John 16: 31-33)

How can any of us be as lonely as Jesus was on the cross waiting to die, enduring the jeers and taunts of the crowd, his mission and ministry seemingly defeated and hopeless. How lonely he must have felt. He cried out, not only in doubt, but also in loneliness, "My God, my God, why have you forsaken me?"

Jesus can help us with our loneliness, for he has been through it himself. He knows what it's like to experience loneliness. And so he offers his divine friendship to us as he did to the disciples after they had denied him and he had been crucified. He rose from the grave and that night he appeared in their midst. He had every reason to condemn them for their cowardly behavior, but not one word of criticism came from his mouth. Jesus said to his disciples then, as he is saying to us today, "I am not alone, because the Father is with me."

Admiral Richard Byrd was an explorer of our polar regions. At one point his physical strength was almost gone and he didn't think he was going to live. In his book *Alone,* he wrote these words:

"I solved it by changing my thoughts. When negative thoughts began to come in my mind, I repulsed them and instead filled my mind with thoughts of the presence of God. Suddenly, I had a feeling of confidence and quietness within. The outer situation was just the same, was just as desperate but it didn't look as difficult, for something had happened inside my mind."

As Jesus said, "I am not really alone, because the Father is with me."

CHAPTER EIGHTEEN
HELPLESSNESS

"Life is what we make it, always has been, always will be."
Grandma Moses

In Florida we have hurricane season from June thru November. A few years ago, Florida was hit by four major hurricanes: Charles hit the west coast, Frances hit the east coast, Ivan hit the panhandle, and Jeanne hit the east coast.

The eye of hurricane Frances and Jeanne passed over where I live. My house sustained minor damage. Three or four shingles blew off the roof, a five foot section of a wooden fence blew down and a few shrubs were damaged. Others, however, were not as fortunate. A neighbor lost most of his roof and water flooded the interior.

Those who live here had to put life on hold for several weeks. People felt worn-out and exhausted. There was the anticipation: where would Charles, Frances, Ivan and Jeanne go? We watched for days as the storm tracks changed, bringing a sense of relief as Ivan veered away or fear as Frances came closer. And then there were all the preparations: boarding up our houses or trailers, stocking up on food, water, batteries, candles, and then the worry and fear of what will happen when the storm does come. Will I be safe? What will happen to my house? And then, in the aftermath of the storm, many had to live without power in our Florida heat for days and some, for several weeks.

We feel powerless under such circumstances, and all of us like to feel in control of our lives, no matter what our age.

I think that's why so many elderly are reluctant to give up their driving privileges. It may be a sign that we can't control part of our life. It's also losing some independence.

In 2003, an 87 year-old man plowed through a crowded farmer's market in downtown Santa Monica, California, killing eight people and injuring dozens more.

In the summer of 2000, as a 72 year-old woman exited from a strip mall in Connecticut, her car was struck broadside by a van she had not seen coming. She died three days later of complications related to her injuries.

These stories could be repeated over and over. Certainly there are many drivers, at any age, who should not be driving. Many elderly drivers are very competent and responsible, but there will come a time when each of us must be willing to turn in our car keys because we cannot safely drive. And its not always easy to admit we should no longer be driving a car.

As we age there are physical and mental changes that can affect the ability to drive a car.

Driving experts say that 90 percent of the information needed to drive safely is visual. Yet, as people get older, four crucial visual abilities diminish: visual acuity- the ability to see clearly what is ahead of you, especially at night; peripheral vision- the ability to see what is happening to the left and right while looking straight ahead; accommodation- the speed with which your eyes adjust to changes in light and dark and near and far images, and depth perception- the ability to judge how fast other cars are moving.

Furthermore, older people are more prone to being temporarily blinded by the glare of headlights coming toward them or in their mirrors from vehicles behind them. According to researchers, a 55-year-old person takes, on average, eight times longer than a 16-year-old to recover from glare. Colors, especially red, become harder to see with age. Some older drivers take twice as long as younger drivers to recognize the flash of brake lights.

Other common age-related deficits include eye muscle dysfunction, which impairs the ability to scan the driving environment, and poor contrast sensitivity, which can make it hard to detect curves in the road, see a gray vehicle at an intersection or a pedestrian at a crosswalk.

According to the AAA Foundation for Traffic Safety, the amount of light needed to drive doubles every 13 years. That means a 60-year-old driver needs about ten times as much light as a 19-year-old to see clearly.[102]

With advancing age joints tend to stiffen, making it more difficult to turn one's head when pulling out of a parking area or when backing up. As muscles weaken they can impair a person's ability to steer and brake. Reaction time slows, increasing the response time when faced with any sort of road hazard, especially a vehicle that suddenly stops or turns in front of you.

Hearing problems can affect the ability to detect and respond appropriately to the sirens of emergency vehicles, railroad crossing signals and the warning horns of other drivers.

Your mind may be just as sharp, but it works more slowly as you get older. Thus, in addition to having slower reflexes, older people tend to have greater difficulty doing more than one thing at a time, such as absorbing new information from their surroundings and reacting accordingly.

Then there are a host of health problems that become increasingly common with age that can further limit your ability to handle a car safely.

To the normal effects of aging on the eyes may be added such problems as cataracts, macular degeneration and glaucoma. Other common age-related problems that can impair driving skills include arthritis, diabetes, insomnia, Parkinson's disease, stoke, depression and dementia.

Movements needed to handle a car safely can be limited in someone with arthritis or Parkinson's disease or a person who has suffered a stroke.

Diabetes can cause vision impairing eye damage and, among those with widely fluctuating blood sugar levels, can sometimes result in loss of consciousness. Chronic insomnia can diminish alertness and increase the risk of dozing off at the wheel.

Depression, which may limit a person's ability to pay attention and to obtain restful sleep, can also impair driving skills. And the gradual onset of dementia can cause memory problems and behavioral difficulties that make safe driving problematic, yet dementia and its effects are usually not recognized by the affected person.

There was a woman in my congregation who could get lost just a few blocks from her house. She forgot to renew her auto insurance and was involved in several accidents before one of her daughters came and took her back north with her.

Many of the medications taken to treat health problems can further diminish driving skills. Such drugs as sleep aids, antidepressants, anti-anxiety drugs, painkillers, antihistamines, cough and cold remedies and others can all impair one's ability to drive.

On the other hand, many older people start compensating for slowing reflexes or poorer vision by driving more carefully.

Some of the warning signs for drivers with some forms of dementia, but ones that might be well to keep in mind due to other reasons as well, according to The Hartford Insurance Company are: incorrect signaling, trouble navigating turns, moving into a wrong lane, confusion at exits, parking inappropriately, hitting curbs, failing to notice traffic signs, driving at inappropriate speeds, confusing brake and gas pedals, stopping in traffic for no apparent reason, delayed responses to unexpected situations, increased agitation or irritation when driving, scrapes or dents on the car, garage or mailbox, getting lost in familiar places, and ticketed moving violations or warnings.[103]

When should one give-up driving? Probably when we begin to have accidents and people or police say we shouldn't drive anymore. Before we have accidents would be ideal, but its not always easy to admit when we're having difficulty. Besides, there's that difficulty in giving up our independence. It might be helpful, then, to think about and become familiar with alternate transportation which could still give one a sense of independence knowing we have to decide how and when we're going to use it. Relying on others for transportation can still give a sense of independence, whether it's the use of a bus, a taxi, friends and relatives, or some communities have special buses for the elderly that will come to their house, pick them-up, take them to shop or a medical appointment and bring them back home.

In an AARP 2003 Bulletin article, researchers asked 3,824 drivers over age 50 how and why they limited their driving. About two-thirds reported that they "self-regulated"- restricted their driving in one or more conditions: in bad weather, on freeways and interstates, in heavy traffic or unfamiliar areas, during rush hour, at night, dusk or dawn, or over long distances.[104]

Researchers found that self-regulation was a gradual process, not a sudden shift in behavior. Over time, drivers developed conscious strategies to compensate for failing vision, slower reflexes and stiffer joints.

Some drivers find they are less stressed after hanging up the keys. One gentleman in the research group had been very resistant to stop driving, but once he did, he noticed he was much more relaxed. He realized driving had contributed to his anxiety.

The National Institute on Aging estimates that more than 600,000 people age 70 or older stop driving each year, usually around age 85.

At a nursing home a group of senior citizens were sitting around talking about their ailments. "My arms are so weak

I can hardly lift this cup of coffee," said one. "Yes, I know. My cataracts are so bad I can't even see my coffee," replied another. "I can't turn my head because of the arthritis in my neck," said a third, to which several nodded weakly in agreement.

"My blood pressure pills make me dizzy," another went on.

"I guess that's the price we pay for getting old," winced an old man as he slowly shook his head. Then there was a short moment of silence.

"Well, it's not that bad," said one woman cheerfully. "Thank God we can all still drive!"

In addition to giving up driving, many seniors fear losing their independence and becoming helpless due to failing health. They fear not being able to care for themselves and having to go into a nursing home.

Feelings of helplessness also come from age-related health problems. My wife gets mad when she can't open a jar or the cap on a medicine bottle. Not being able to do things with your hands because of stiffness from arthritis, not being able to read a book because of failing vision, not being able to control one's bladder due to kidney problems can leave one feeling both helpless and frustrated.

People can do some things that will give them some sense of control and independence. There are large-print books available, and if the print still isn't large enough there are machines that magnify the print. There are hearing assisted devices that can magnify sound on the telephone. There are numerous things that can be done around the house to make living easier. Grab bars, for example, can be installed in the bathroom or in other areas of the house. Lighting and color can be used to enable those with visual problems to distinguish objects. Carpeting and furniture can be changed to avoid falls and ease comfort.

Feelings of helplessness can overwhelm us. Sometimes it helps if we can just stop those thoughts and ask ourselves, what can I do?

A good example, is the story of Margaret Boemer, an 84-year-old woman from Delray Beach, Florida, who was lost and alone for nearly three summer days and nights in a swampy South Carolina wilderness full of poisonous snakes and hungry mosquitoes.

Boemer's adventure started in late July, 2003, with a phone call that her 94-year-old brother in St. Stephen, a town about forty miles north of Charleston, was in the hospital with pneumonia.

She got in her car and drove alone to South Carolina. By the time she got there, her brother's health had improved, and he was released to his home. She decided to stay for a while and help him back to health.

After four days, she had the urge to go for a drive. She still owned a couple of acres of vacant land out of town. It was part of the farm she had grown up on as a girl. She wanted to see it again.

However, she got lost. Driving on dirt roads, her car eventually ended up stuck in the mud. She wasn't sure where.

"I heard a train," she said. "So I thought I'd just walk toward the tracks, and from there, I could find my way to St.Stephen."

She walked for much of the afternoon, trudging through the Santee Swamp until she found the tracks, which were on a trestle at the top of a 25-foot embankment.

"I tried climbing up the embankment," she said. "But there was no way I could do it."

She started walking back in the direction of her car, but day turned to night, so she gathered up some grass to make a bed and lay down.

"It was beautiful," she said. "I went to sleep under the stars and the moon."

Meanwhile, one of her daughters had called the house of her recuperating uncle. Learning that her mother had not returned, she and her husband alerted police and drove to South Carolina.

In an unfortunate coincidence, sometime after she had gotten lost, a load of gravel had been dumped at the entrance of the dirt road Boemer had taken. The gravel was there to fix a nearby culvert. When searchers started looking for Margaret, they assumed that nobody would have been able to get on that dirt road because of the gravel roadblock.

And there was another coincidence that day, one that also derailed the search, but may have been a lifesaver for Margaret.

A tropical depression hit the South Carolina coast. The rain, which would continue for much of the weekend, washed away footprints and tire tracks and made searching nearly impossible.

The rain, though, kept Margaret from getting dehydrated and was less punishing than hot, dry, sunny weather.

Margaret drank some of the rainwater as it fell, but she didn't eat anything. And she didn't despair, she said.

"The rain was warm," she said. "I laid down. Then night came and the animals started singing, just making animal noises, but it sounded like singing. I think it was God's way of making me peaceful."

Margaret assumed that people were looking for her. She could see helicopters circling in the distance.

"I put my bra on a stick and waved it over my head," she said. "But the trees were too thick for anybody to see me."

Meanwhile, her adult children had begun spreading fliers about their missing mother. On Saturday night, the third night, searchers found her car.

Later that night, a helicopter pilot using a heat sensor detected Margaret in the swamp and directed 70 searchers toward her. They found her at 1:30 a.m. that Sunday morning.

Margaret was taken to a hospital, where she was determined to be remarkably well, except for being covered in mosquito bites, sunburned and in need of s shower.

When she returned to her home in Florida she was the talk of the community. "She doesn't act as if anything happened to her," said her longtime friend. She asked Margaret how she could sleep when she was out there? Margaret replied, "What else was I going to do?"

Margaret's daughter said she would like to see her mother be less adventurous in the future, but Margaret has her own survival plan when it comes to her adult kids.

"They're not going to boss me too much," she said. "Children do that when you get in your 80s."

Margaret was far from helpless due to her attitude. She didn't allow her surroundings to get the better of her.

Our psychological health as we age can keep us from feeling or being helpless due to age related problems.

This was demonstrated in the Harvard Study, three projects carried out by Harvard Medical School begun in the 1920s, '30s and '40s. These careful scientific studies analyze three very different demographic groups: one of Harvard men, another of inner-city Boston men and the third of gifted California women. In all, 824 men and women were followed from their teens into their 80s. Over the decades, these people were given psychological tests and asked to evaluate their lives and feelings. They responded to questionnaires, interviews by psychiatrists and physical examinations by doctors.

The study divides individuals between 60 and 80 years old into two main groups: (1) the "Happy-Well," those who are physically healthy and find life satisfying; and (2) the "Sad-Sick," those with various ailments who do not seem to enjoy life.

A major finding was that good genes did not account for better aging. Nor did income.

The study's director, Dr. George E. Vaillant concluded that we should try to develop more mature coping styles. The secret to a long and happy life does not lie as much in our genes as in ourselves.

Dr. Vaillant discovered that many people who aged well unconsciously reinterpreted early events in their lives in a more positive light as they grew older. Those who clung to negative events were less happy adults.

Dr. Vaillant points out seven major factors that, at age 50, predict what life's outcome will be at 80:

1. Not smoking, or quitting early. Those who quit smoking before 50 were, at 70, as healthy as those who had never smoked. Heavy smoking was 10 times more prevalent among the Prematurely Dead than among the Happy-Well.
2. The ability to take life's ups and downs in stride. A person will suffer less from life's real problems if he or she has the ability to roll with the punches.
3. Absence of alcohol abuse.
4. Healthy weight. Obesity is a risk factor for poor health in later life.
5. A solid marriage. This is important for both physical and psychological health. According to the study, Happy-Well people were six times more likely to be in good marriages than were the Sad-Sick.
6. Physical Activity. The study showed that the Happy-Well usually did some exercise. The benefits of fitness also extended to mental health.
7. Years of Education. People to whom "self-care and perseverance" are important are also more likely to continue their educations. People seek education because they believe it is possible to control the course of their lives.

People who had five or more of these seven factors at age 50 were one-third less likely to be dead by 80. People who had three or fewer of these factors at age 50, even though they were in good physical shape, were three times as likely to die during the following thirty years.[105]

As you can tell, all these factors are ones that we can control. The study shows that to a great extent we can have some control over our aging.

We all have times when we feel helpless. This can happen at any age. The forces of nature, such as hurricanes, tornadoes, earthquakes and more can leave us feeling helpless against their power. We can have some control over them by the way we construct our homes.

Events in the world can leave us feeling helpless. The economy may be beyond our individual control, but each of us can do something to feel less helpless by the ways we spend, through savings and investments.

We can't control aging and death. Each of us will find our bodies undergoing change. We may find ourselves having difficulty seeing, hearing or walking. To some extent we can gain some control through glasses, hearing aids, artificial joints and other means of assistance.

Many people fear they will become helpless. They're afraid of falling, breaking a hip and being sent to a nursing home for the rest of their life. As a result many are afraid to go out at night. Others may fear losing control of their bowels and become an embarrassment. A doctor may be able to help.

Dying is the final time of helplessness. A dying person grieves the loss of control over life, of normal physical functions, mobility and strength, freedom and independence, the loss of an earthly future, and the loss of normal activity and interests.

You can gain some control, however, over the way you die by designing the care you want. A Living Will details what kind of life-sustaining treatment you want or don't want, in the event of an illness when death is imminent. Another directive, a durable power of attorney, appoints someone to be your decision-maker if you can't speak for yourself. Such a person can find out all the options and make a decision consistent with what you would want in the event you are unable to make decisions for yourself.

Without an advance directive, a hospital staff is legally bound to do everything to keep you alive as long as possible. So advance directives are best written before an emergency situation.

Get your doctor's commitment to support your wishes. If you're asking for something that is against your doctor's conscience, such as prescribing a lethal dose of pain medication or removing life support at a time he considers premature, he may want to transfer you to another doctor. And make sure the person you name as surrogate agrees to act for you and understands your wishes.

Give a copy to your surrogate, your doctor, your hospital, and other family members. Tell them where to find the original in the house, not in a safe deposit box where it might not be found until after death.

Be aware that if you have more than one home and you divide your time between houses, you need to register your wishes with a doctor, hospital and perhaps a surrogate/proxy in each area.

You may also register your Living Will and surrogate/proxy online at uslivingwillregistry.com or call 800-548-9455. The free, privately funded confidential service will fax a copy to a hospital when the hospital requests one. It will also remind you to update it.

We have to realize that we cannot have complete independence in life. We start off as a baby and as a child dependent upon our parents and others to care for us. Around age 18 we tend to want to assert our independence, to be in charge of our own lives. When we graduate from high school, when we get our driver's license, when we get a job and have money to spend, that spirit of independence drives many to want to be on their own.

Yet, we're never completely independent. Throughout our life we depend upon others to help us. We depend upon grocery stores to provide food, shopping centers to provide clothing, furniture and other things, hospitals and doctors to provide medical care, the government to provide for our protection and safety. The list could go on and on.

Perhaps years ago people could be self-sufficient, but those days are long gone. We're dependent and interdependent upon others throughout our life.

As we age we may become more dependent upon others for our care. For some this means care in a nursing home or an assisted living facility.

We can't always control what happens to us, but we can control our reaction to those events. Through the ways we react we can gain some control and feel less helpless. This was illustrated in the story of Margaret Boemer. It is also illustrated in the story of Helynn Hoffa, as told by Sharon Larsen in *Chicken Soup for the Golden Soul*.

Helynn Hoffa was one of the unlucky children who contracted polio. The year was 1928. At first she couldn't even open or close her eyelids, and for two years she was completely paralyzed. She was told she would never walk again.

When she was twelve, she went to Warm Springs, Georgia, to undergo therapy. While there she met the President of the United States, Franklin Delano Roosevelt, who was also there to undergo therapy for polio.

She was sitting on a step of the pool when President Roosevelt came swimming over toward her. They chatted a few minutes and then he asked her what she wanted to be when she grew up?

Helynn remembers shrugging and telling him, "I'm not sure I could 'be' anything. But if I had a choice, I'd like to be an archaeologist."

"Just remember," FDR said softly, "if I can be in a wheelchair and be president of the greatest country in the world, you can be whatever you want."

That encounter with the President has guided Helynn ever since. Helynn eventually became a nun, free-lance writer, artist, bookkeeper, art teacher, sports reporter and even ran her own print shop, publishing company, as well as her own radio show.

At age 64, Helynn contracted post-polio syndrome. This syndrome involves the gradual loss of muscular strength once regained through physical therapy. And so for many years Helynn has spent up to sixteen hours a day in a 1928 model iron lung, which takes up most of her small living room. She adds, "I call it the yellow submarine in honor of my days as an ardent Beatles fan."

She refuses to let long hours in the yellow submarine slow her down. "I spend up to four hours a day dictating my work to an assistant, who then types the text on the computer," she says.

"Simply to live, I have to spend time every day in the iron lung," Helynn says. "But I'm just glad to be alive because life is an adventure and I don't want to miss any of it!"

The only complaint Helynn voices is that she simply doesn't have enough hours in the day to accomplish all that she wants to do.[106]

At age 79, as of the time of the story, Helynn is a remarkable example of the saying, "When life gives you lemons, make lemonade." Helynn has made the best of what life has thrown at her. May you do the same. With God's help, you can, for God can give you the spiritual strength you need to help gain control over all that life may throw your way.

CHAPTER NINETEEN
WHAT DO YOU WANT ON
YOUR TOMBSTONE?

"Be life long or short, its completeness depends
on what it was lived for."
David Starr Jordan

One of the characteristics of human personality has been the desire to be remembered. Most of us like to be recognized while we're alive, and some would like to be remembered after we are gone, at least by the members of our family. Perhaps that's why it has been popular or customary to have tombstones placed beside the graves of the deceased. Some have gone to extremes and built pyramids or temples in order to ensure a kind of immortality on earth.

In his book, *You Are Never Alone,* Dr. Charles Allen recounts a newspaper story about a monument near Lincoln, Kansas. It was built by a man named John Davis, who lived and died near Hiawatha, Kansas. He was a farmer and a self-made man. He managed to amass a considerable fortune in his lifetime. When he was married, his wife's family thought that she had married beneath her. He reciprocated their dislike. He and his

248

wife had no children, and he was determined not to leave any money to his in-laws.

When she died, he decided that he wanted to erect a statue in memory of her. He had an artist design a statue which showed both her and him at opposite ends of a love seat. He liked it so much that he commissioned another statue, this time of himself, kneeling at his wife's grave, and placing a wreath on it. That impressed him enough so that he commissioned still another statue, this time of his wife, kneeling at his future grave site, depositing a wreath. Since she was no longer alive, he had the sculptor add a pair of wings to make an angel out of her. One thing led to another until he had spent some two hundred and fifty thousand dollars on the monument to his wife and himself.

Someone from the town would occasionally suggest that he might be interested in doing something with his money for others. There was a project to build a hospital, and another to build a swimming pool for children. He turned a deaf ear on all such pleas.

He spent all his money on those statues, and eventually he had used up all his resources. He died at the age of ninety-two, a resident of the poorhouse. Very few people attended his funeral, and it was reported that only one person seemed genuinely moved by any sense of personal loss. It was Horace England, who was the tombstone salesman.

The strange thing about this monument is that it is slowly sinking into the ground. Davis left no money to maintain it. The townspeople show no particular concern in perpetuating it. Eventually it will be gone.[107]

The monument represents a monument to spite. Mr. Davis spent all his money on a monument so that none of it would go to his wife's relatives. He loved no one except himself and his wife. He gave no one any reason to love him. He built a monument that would outlast him by a few years, but in the end it turns out to be a sad example of a self-centered life.

Victor Frankl lost his wife, father, mother and brother in Hitler's concentration camps. He was stripped of all his possessions and spent three grim years at Auschwitz and other Nazi prisons.

In such conditions, Frankl faced the question whether life really had any meaning at all. He wrote, "The question which beset me was, 'Has all this suffering, this dying around us a meaning?' For if not, then ultimately there is no meaning to survival; for a life whose meaning depends upon such a happenstance, whether one escapes or not, ultimately would not be worth living at all!"[108]

From his own experience and from observing other prisoners, Frankl came to the conclusion that what matters most in life is the attitude one takes toward his or her life and circumstances. Some people were able to survive conditions that destroyed others. Why? Because they found hope and a sense of meaning and purpose.

Is it possible to find a sense of meaning in life as we age? Men, especially, have found a sense of purpose and meaning through the work they have done throughout their life. As more and more women have entered the workforce during the last decade perhaps studies will begin to show that they have found meaning through work. Historically, women have tended to remain at home and found meaning through their role as mother, wife and homemaker. As men and women retire, can they find meaning and purpose?

A few years ago, the movie *About Schmidt,* starring Jack Nicholson, explored this theme. Jack Nicholson portrayed a newly retired insurance executive. Shortly after his retirement, his wife dies suddenly. He leaves his home in Omaha, Nebraska, in search of himself in a Winnebago. During his adventures he visits his childhood home, chats with a man in a tire store, confuses the attention of a woman while at a campground, then heads to Denver to talk his daughter out of marrying a waterbed salesman.

"He has a sense of irretrievable loss," says Louis Begley, who wrote the book. "He faces the loss of his wife, the loss of the sense that his life had a purpose and a meaning, the loss of friends, bitter loneliness, and the sense that he has botched the relationship with his daughter."[109]

Schmidt eventually finds meaning as he gets involved in helping others, especially

by contributing financially and writing a child in another country through an organization called Childreach.

It's often from being involved in the lives of others that people find a sense of purpose. For example, Leonard Yaffe, of Lake Worth, Florida, writes that his grandchildren gave him a new lease on life. After he retired, Yaffe found he was bored much of the time. He tried volunteering and exercising, but he still felt an emptiness inside. That all changed when his grandchildren were born and he became a part-time caregiver while his daughter worked.

"Truthfully, there were times I was exhausted trying to keep up with two active, growing children," he says. But "the joy they brought me made it all worthwhile, and the void in my life was no longer there. Every time I hear 'Grandpa, I need you,' I say to myself 'I need you, too.'"[110]

Many older adults have found meaning by becoming actively involved in the lives of their grandchildren. My father-in-law was an avid sports fan and found great joy in attending the baseball games of his grandchildren, or playing ball with them at family gatherings.

Grandmothers, too, can find meaning and purpose in spending time with their grandchildren, reading stories to them when they are young, teaching them cooking, sewing, or today, teaching them how to use a computer!

Many older adults today live part or most of the year in warmer climates. Contact can be made easier with children and grandchildren through emails. My six-year-old granddaughter in Ohio loves to receive email from her grandmother in Florida.

Just as men and women found meaning through having and raising children, so too, can meaning be enriched in later years through the continuation of family ties.

Volunteering can be an excellent way to find meaning by older adults as well as contributing to the community and the lives of others.

Dr. Jack McConnell, a pediatrician who later became a pharmaceutical company executive, retired to Hilton Head, South Carolina, where he planned to play golf, dine out and catch up on his reading. But he soon realized that his fulfillment would not occur on the golf course.

One thing led to another, and through his ingenuity, caring, persuasiveness and persistence, McConnell created Volunteers in Medicine, a medical clinic staffed almost entirely by unpaid retirees, to provide free health care for the uninsured working poor and their families.

McConnell's project was so successful that he soon received almost 500 requests for guidance from communities around the country wanting to create similar clinics. His full-time job now is helping these communities follow his example.[111]

Marc Freedman, who runs a nonprofit group called Civic Ventures in San Francisco, related the McConnell story in his book, *Prime Time: How Baby Boomers Will Revolutionize Retirement and Transform America*. In the book, Freedman argues that retired Americans can and should be a powerful social force in programs that are personally fulfilling and socially rewarding.

The appendix of Freedman's book describes 21 groups that provide productive volunteer opportunities for older Americans. There are programs suitable for people in all education and income brackets. For example, there is a group called the Care-a-Vanners, groups of older people who travel in Winnebagos building houses for Habitat for Humanity in projects that involve teenagers whom they mentor.

A study conducted by AARP showed that those aged 30 to 49 are most likely to volunteer. Older adults (ages 50-plus in the study) maintain volunteering levels around 40 percent through age 70. People over age 75 volunteer the least, with more than 70 percent not volunteering at all. This lower rate may be due to changes in health. Unfortunately, most traditional volunteer experiences require mobility on the part of the volunteer and may not take into account that limitations of income or health may restrict access to appropriate transportation.[112]

The fact that older people often have a lot of time available would seem to make them an abundant source of volunteers. However, research has shown that retirees are not as likely to volunteer as those in the work force or homemakers. Those who volunteered before retiring continue to do so as retirees, sometimes for more time and sometimes for less time.

There appears to be a strong relationship between religious behavior (prayer or religious service attendance) and volunteering. Only 29 percent of those who never attend religious services volunteer, compared to over 60 percent of those who attend more than once a week.

Churches and synagogues often depend upon the volunteer help of their members. In my congregation, in which the majority of members are all over age 65, there are many ways for members to volunteer and members are eager to do so. It can be as simple as greeting others on a Sunday morning, to singing in the choir, to helping at our church's thrift shop, to delivering food to the local soup kitchen. There are numerous ways seniors can help.

What motivates older people to volunteer? Dr. Dana Bradley, assistant professor of political science and gerontology at the University of North Carolina, Charlotte, says there are three reasons: enhanced sense of purpose, personal growth and continued productivity.[113]

The reason most cited by the volunteers in the AARP study of civic involvement volunteering was "helping others." Mabel, a 70-year-old former executive secretary, is cited as an example. She volunteers at her senior center several days a week. She makes phone calls to homebound elders as part of a telephone reassurance program. "My phone calls mean so much to them," she says. "I may be the only person they speak to all day. If I couldn't get out, I hope that someone would think to remember me, too." [114]

Having a cause to devote time to helps give meaning to the volunteer.

Others choose to volunteer in order to explore something that has captured their attention, also giving their life meaning and purpose. In this case the volunteer experience becomes a way to achieve personal growth.

A third reason has to do with continued productivity, providing structure to daily life. The routine of daily telephone calls, weekly rehearsals, etc, gives a sense of direction and accomplishment to the volunteer. Consider the retired woman who drives others to doctor appointments or the retired man who once a week volunteers at a science museum, guiding groups of school children on a tour. Their day's schedule is organized around their volunteer experience.

AARP magazine reported that according to research from UCLA, when people look for meaning in their lives, they seem to get a boost in immune function that may keep them healthier.

Many men and women may be afraid to retire. It may be that people don't know what to do with their time. Our society has been so work oriented that many people cannot seem to relax. Even when they have free time, they may feel that they should be doing something. They may feel guilty just doing nothing, or anything that is not connected with work or an achievement kind of activity. It is important that we learn to use our leisure time creatively. There is an importance to using leisure time just to meditate and reflect upon oneself and upon life.

President Jimmy Carter admits he was devastated when he was retired involuntarily at age 56 after a single term as President.

"We went back to our tiny town (Plains, Georgia). I didn't have a job. We were deeply in debt. We thought the best time of our life was over," a feeling that millions of people share upon retiring. "Just because we had lived in the White House didn't make us any different."

"Things looked grim," he says, until "we finally had the courage to do what everybody needs to do: to sit down in a time of quiet contemplation and say, 'OK, what is there that I have? What are my talents? What are my abilities? What have my experiences given me on which I can build for my future? What are some of the things we did when we were young that we really enjoyed and have never had a chance to pursue because we were too busy making a living? What are the talents that I thought I had when I was young that I never was able to develop?'"

He realized that "Our primary purpose in our golden years is not just to stay alive as long as we can, but to savor every opportunity for pleasure, excitement, adventure and fulfillment."[115]

As such, President Carter is a professor at Emory University, a deacon of the Maranatha Baptist Church of Plains and a dedicated and visible volunteer for Habitat for Humanity, an international nonprofit organization that helps the needy build homes for themselves.

He also heads the Carter Center in Atlanta, whose programs worldwide include monitoring democratic elections in developing countries, attempting to eradicate disease, helping African farmers improve crop yields and mediating conflict in countries from Haiti to North Korea.

He is also a prolific author.

From the experience of President Carter, one of the things that keeps him busy is a hobby. He enjoys writing, which can be both a hobby and a way to find meaning, but hobbies can give meaning to life. If one has reached retirement and doesn't have an activity or hobby to occupy one's interest, the prospect of boredom may terrify many individuals into finding another job. Many people do find a part-time job as a meaningful way to spend their retirement time.

If you've never had a hobby, retirement can be a time to pursue an interest or to find a new interest that can become a hobby, as the following poem suggests:

Our New Age Grandma

The old rocking chair is empty today,
For Grandma is no longer in it.
She's off in her car to her office or shop,
And buzzing around every minute.

No one shoves Grandma back on the shelf,
She's versatile, forceful, dynamic.
That isn't a pie in the oven, my dear,
Her baking today is ceramics.

You won't see her trudging early to bed,
From her place in the warm chimney nook,
Her computer clickety-clacks through the night,
For Grandma is writing a book.

Grandmother never takes one backward look,
To slow down her steady advancing.
She won't tend the babies for you anymore
For Grandma has taken up dancing!

She isn't content with the crumbs of old thoughts,
With meager and secondhand knowledge,
Don't bring your mending to Grandma to do,
Grandma has gone back to college.
Author Unknown

But what if you find yourself in a nursing home, or at home, unable to get around, how can one find meaning in such a situation, in which one is unable to pursue a hobby or volunteer? Of course some hobbies can be pursued and some volunteer work done at home, but in extreme cases, in which the mind is still good but the body incapable of the most routine functions, can a meaningful life exist?

Wendy Lustbader argues that "there is a further worth awaiting us in remembering and contemplating, in thinking things over, in letting all that has been said and done assemble itself into something we can grasp."[116]

Even those confined to a nursing home can find meaning, she argues, through the ways we make choices. These are the people who will not let the staff forget what makes them different from the others. "You'd better open Martha's drapes the way she likes them or you'll hear about it." Martha's spirit survives in the ways she makes sure her preferences disturb the routines.

Our choices give us meaning, from the way we like to arrange things on our desk or bureau to the peace we find in looking up at the sky through the branches of a tree.

Illness can also bring about new meaning in relationships. A physical therapist tells how a stroke led to the reconciliation of a father and son who had not spoken in years:

"My patient was a large man, and the dead weight of his stroke made it impossible for his tiny wife to move him at all. His son agreed to come over and learn how to do a wheelchair transfer, but he came in looking so hostile I wanted to call off the whole thing. He didn't even say hello. I explained that he had to grip his father in a bear hug and then use a rocking motion to pivot him from the bed to the wheelchair. The son went over to the bed where his father was sitting and put his arms around him, just like I said. He got the rocking motion going, but then all of a sudden I realized that both of them were crying. It was the most amazing thing. They stayed like that for a long time, rocking and crying."

This son was moved to linger in his father's arms for he first time since boyhood. Frailty can help relationships come together and grow.[117]

Jeanette Reid tells how her mother-in-law found new meaning while a resident of a nursing home. Jeanette says: "My mother-in-law went into the nursing home most reluctantly. She had suffered a small stroke that had left her rather vague and confused. She could not understand why she had to make this move when she was perfectly happy in her own small apartment. For a couple of weeks she was quite disoriented as though she were living in a dream world where the happenings made no sense."

"As familiarity slowly eased this state and she recognized the daily routines, she became depressed. 'What good am I?' she would ask. 'I've worked hard all my life- at home, in the church, helping out my neighbors- and now I'm no use to anyone.' She also felt that she wasn't 'like these people here' and that the other residents didn't like her. But her depression was balanced by a gentle sense of humor she had always expressed about life and about herself and a natural appreciation for people who did their job well..."

"Then my mother-in-law was given a new dinner partner, a delightful, independent woman who was not interested in what she called the 'boring social graces' that seemed so important to the more traditional residents. My mother-in-law and this woman talking and laughing together got the attention of a couple of other residents who were less staid and eager for more liveliness. Soon they were sitting near each other at breakfast, where seats were unassigned- The Breakfast Club they called it- and at musical events and activities planned by the home. I was amazed. For the first time in the thirty-five years that I had known my mother-in-law, I saw this painfully shy, self-conscious, and work-oriented woman was laughing and bantering with friends in a relaxed way."

"Once she got beyond her initial feelings of alienation, she also found work to do. There were older or more infirm residents whom she could visit, read to, tell about recent happenings. She had been a hospital volunteer for a number of years, and she was comfortable in this role and felt she was doing a needed service. I think her years in the home opened up a whole new area of life for her. I know that we became closer than we had ever been. Up until that time, our relationship had been one of polite but distant regard. When she died in 1994, I felt I had known a friend, a woman of courage, humility, and steadiness who became a model for me in her ability to adapt and blossom under unexpected and diminished circumstances."

"In my work with retirement residents, I observed a variety of ways in which individuals found meaning in later life. Some maintained old interests in a new way, others enjoyed the time and freedom to develop latent creativity and new pursuits. Some discovered that the comfortable size of their new community freed them to reach out in friendship and service, others found that removal from the bustle of life offered a welcomed time for meditation and reflection."[118]

It's in giving ourselves to others that people find their greatest sense of meaning and purpose. John Kotre shares a story entitled "The Gift" which illustrates this well.

It is a fairy tale from India for adults, especially older adults. It begins with an old grasscutter named Wali Dad, who comes to the point where he must do something with the pot of pennies he's been accumulating all his life. A simple man, content with his tiny hut, he can think of nothing that he wants for himself, so he goes to a jeweler and buys a golden bracelet. Then he asks a friend who is a merchant, "Who is the most beautiful and virtuous woman in the world?"

"The Princess of the East," says the merchant.

"Then take this bracelet to her. But do not reveal who has sent it."

The land of the East is far away, but the merchant agrees to deliver the bracelet on his next trip there. When he arrives and gives the gift to the princess, she is intrigued. Who is her secret admirer, and what sort of man is he? She decides to send a gift in return, some beautiful and expensive rolls of silk. The merchant brings them back to Wali Dad.

"And what am I to do with these?" the old grasscutter asks, for he has no need of them. He thinks about the matter for awhile, and then he says, "Who is the most handsome and virtuous man in the world?"

"That would be the Prince of the West."

"Then take these silks to him."

So the merchant sets off in the opposite direction, travels a great distance, and eventually comes to the land of the West.

Naturally, the prince is surprised by the gift and curious about its sender. So he reciprocates with something finer.

"A dozen stallions?" asks Wali Dad when the merchant returns. "What am I to do with a dozen stallions? Take them to the Princess of the East!"

When the horses come prancing into her palace, the princess is at a loss for a response. The king suggests that she end the affair by sending back a gift so magnificent that it will put her secret admirer to shame. They send off twenty mules loaded with silver.

But Wali Dad has no desire for wealth. "Take some of the mules for your trouble," he tells his merchant friend, "and deliver the rest to the Prince of the West!"

And the prince refuses to be outdone. Soon a caravan of camels and elephants weighed down with precious gifts is headed back to Wali Dad's hut. No sooner does it arrive than Wali Dad sends it on to the Princess of the East.

At this point, the king and queen can come to only one conclusion. The mysterious admirer wants to marry their daughter. So they set out with the merchant to find him. As they draw near to Wali Dad's village, the merchant grows troubled. What will this procession of royalty think when they are led at last to a little hut and a withered old man within? He rides ahead and warns Wali Dad of what is imminent. Fearing humiliation, unable to accept what may be required of him, Wali Dad heads that night for a cliff; but cannot even bring himself to jump. He collapses on the ground, enveloped in darkness and despair.

Suddenly, there is a great halo of light that grows brighter and brighter. Two angelic beings appear. One touches Wali Dad's clothes, and they turn into elegant robes. The other touches his hut, and it turns into a palace. The next morning Wali Dad receives the king and queen, the princess, and their entire entourage. In the middle of a sumptuous feast, the king gives his enthusiastic consent to his daughter's marriage.

"Alas," says Wali Dad. "As you can see, I am too old to marry. But I know someone who would make a perfect husband for your daughter."

He summons the Prince of the West, and soon the prince and princess fall in love. They marry in Wali Dad's palace, and the families celebrate for days and days. When it's time for everyone to return home, the king and queen, the prince and the princess, and thousands of their flag bearers salute Wali Dad, who salutes them back with a handful of grass he has cut that very morning. It is the sweetest and freshest grass he has ever smelled.[119]

A man does something small and insignificant, the giving of a bracelet, and his tiny gesture multiplies in significance. We never know what something as simple as saying hello to someone we pass on the street may have in affecting that person's life. Someone who is depressed and perhaps thinking about suicide, may see in that smile someone who cares and begin to see life as worth living. You never know.

It is like the mustard seed in one of Jesus' parables: "It is the smallest of all the seeds, but when it has grown it is the biggest of shrubs and becomes a tree, so that the birds of the air can come and shelter in its branches."

Wali Dad's bracelet grows like that mustard seed. Sown in just the right way and place, it becomes rolls of silk, then a dozen horses, then twenty mules loaded with silver, then a caravan of camels and elephants bearing precious gifts. It leads to the marriage of a princess and a prince, from the far ends of the earth.

Wali Dad is near the end of his life and he wonders, what have all his pennies and all his years meant? What difference have they made?

He does not wish to be young again. When offered the chance to marry a young woman, a princess, he is not interested, unlike some men who try to recapture their youth, denying they are growing old, by trying to attract a young woman. Others try to deny growing older by refusing to quit work.

Not Wali Dad. He has accepted that he is no longer young, that he is growing older, and that one day he will die. But before he dies he wants to know if his life has meant anything in this world.

Many people find meaning in their work, or in some sign that shows success, such as an expensive home or car, or in the success of their children. But when we retire, when we age, we can still find meaning through helping others. It could be something as simple as a phone call to inquire about someone's health. Wali Dad didn't care if he was recognized for his actions. He simply wanted to do something to make others happy.

And that is what God calls us to do. God calls us to serve God through our service to helping others. And that is the best way to have a meaningful life at any age!

Brothers David and John Livingstone had very different goals for their lives. John dreamed of being rich and famous. From a young age, David dreamed of following Christ. Both boys achieved their goals.

John Livingstone became rich and famous. David Livingstone became a medical missionary to Africa. He was never rich, although he did become famous as one of the best-known missionaries of the 19th century. In his later years, he was offered the chance to return to England as a hero and live out his last days in comfort. Instead, David chose to remain in Africa, where he lived in poverty. He died of a tropical disease. Both brothers lived out their dreams, yet on John Livingstone's tomb are engraved these words: "Here lies the brother of David Livingstone."[120]

CHAPTER TWENTY
HOW OLD ARE YOU?

"I shall grow old, but never lose life's zest,
Because the road's last turn will be the best." Henry Van Dyke

Age is a quality of mind
If you have left your dreams behind,
If hope is cold,
If you no longer look ahead,
If your ambition's fires are dead,
Then you are OLD.

But if from life you take the best,
And if in life you keep the zest,
If love you hold,
No matter how the years go by,
No matter how the birthdays fly,
You are NOT OLD!

From the above poem it is easy to see that the unknown author views aging as a matter of the mind and spirit. It's not what's on the outside, how we look, that keeps us young, but what's inside, our mind and our spirit. If we're "young at heart," that will go a long way towards what growing older is like for us. And that's what I've been trying to say throughout this book.

Today, the average person in the United States lives nearly 78 years. But there are those who beat the average to live longer and in good health.

For years we've been told that the best way to stay healthy is to eat the right foods, maintain a healthy weight, exercise, and hope you have good genes. All of this is true, though there have been individuals who have reached 100 years and, when asked their secret, will tell how they have smoked all their life or had a daily beer, or done something that doesn't fit standard medical advice. Instead, research has shown that how well we age is tied to our personality traits, the social relationships we have formed and, perhaps most important, our ability to cope with stress.

"We now know that aging is about a body that doesn't deal well with stress anymore," says Robert Sapolsky, a Stanford University neuroendocrinologist.[121]

Scientists estimate that the maximum potential life span of the human body is about 120 years. They came to this conclusion after observing the oldest ages achieved by a variety of organisms, noting that aging, no matter what the species, seemed to follow a consistent mathematical formula. The maximum age achieved by any species appears to equal about six times the number of years from birth to biological maturity. So humans, who take about twenty years to reach maturity, have the potential to live six times as long as that, or about 120 years.

Studies of Swedish twins who were raised apart showed that only about thirty percent of aging can be explained by genes. Successful agers, then, have some control over the aging process.

Increasingly, researchers are viewing stress, how much stress we face in a lifetime, and how well we cope with it, as one of the most significant factors for predicting how well we age.

One reason successful agers may be better at handling stress is that they have a lot of social support. Successful agers are not loners. People who age well tend to be close to family and have a strong network of friends and social relationships. Marriage seems to help men stay healthier according to studies. Married men tend to live longer than single men. Among women, it doesn't seem to matter if they are married or not, as long as they have other close relationships.

The importance of family life and social relationships on physical health has been shown consistently in both animal and human studies.

In primate studies, relationships make a difference in the quality of old age. "One of the crappiest positions you can get late in life is to be an old baboon in a troupe where you were once a young baboon," says Robert Sapolsky of Stanford. Baboons, especially high-ranking ones, spend their lives terrorizing those with lower rankings. But rankings change. When the powerful baboons get older, the young baboons they once terrorized end up in power with the opportunity to get revenge.

But there is one group of male baboons that escapes the stress of old age. These are the baboons that spent their middle age establishing close relationships with the female baboons. Late in life, these baboons get harassed just as much as any other baboon, but they aren't as bothered, because they have a network of nice, female baboons that keep them company, groom them and generally act as a buffer against what would otherwise be a miserable life.

"Connectedness in old age is enormously important," Sapolsky says.[122]

The same thing that helps baboons age successfully also helps humans. Studies have shown that relationships make a great difference in aging.

It isn't the practical support of relationships that seems to make the difference, having somebody to cook for you, for example, or drive you to a doctor's appointment.

The MacArthur Foundation study, which evaluated 4,000 older people from Massachusetts, North Carolina and Connecticut, focused on the one-third of the group that had the highest mental and physical function at the outset. Researchers then followed up with them at three and eight years. Researchers discovered that whether or not the study subjects had a high frequency of emotional support; i.e., they spoke and met often with family and friends, was a strong predictor of who would improve physically over time. In other words, having friends and family in your life increases the likelihood that you will get out more, keep moving and actually improve with age.[123]

The church, then, can be an important extended family and means of support for us as we age. It is very important to help all ages of our members feel a part of the church fellowship. For those unable to drive anymore, it might mean providing transportation for them to and from church services, meetings and events. It might mean periodic phone calls, visits or emails to them, both to check on their well-being, but also to let them know their church cares about the.

Personality traits such as optimism, adaptability and a willingness to try new things also seem to be linked to better aging. This was apparent in the Nun Study, which for three decades has collected data from the School Sisters of Notre Dame living in Mankato, Minnesota, as well as elsewhere in the Midwest, East and South.

The study is important because extensive family, medical and social history from the nuns is available. The goal of the Nun Study is to determine the causes and prevention of Alzheimer's disease and other brain diseases, as well as the mental and physical disability associated with old age.

A study was done of handwritten autobiographies from 180 nuns, who wrote them, on average, at the age of 22. The writings were scored for emotional content and compared with survival rates from the age of 75 to 95. What researchers noticed is that the nuns who wrote with the most positive attitude at a very young age were 2 1/2 times more likely to be alive in late life than the sisters who came across with a more negative point of view at a young age.

The Nun Study is important because so much in these women's lives is the same- the food they eat, the quality of medical care they receive, the life they lead. Consistently, the nuns who age well are those with distinct personality traits such as a sense of humor and adaptability. Many of these nuns still developed illnesses and health problems associated with aging, but those who aged the most successfully were those who adapted to each new challenge, including illness or disability.

"Everyone experiences normal day-to-day stress, and we all have the same physiological response in terms of higher blood pressure and higher stress hormones," says David Snowdon, the University of Kentucky neurology professor who founded the Nun Study. "But because of their positive outlook, our suspicion is that (the sisters who have aged well) can come back down to their baseline level quicker. They didn't grind on their stress. They had their stress response, and they got over it."[124]

Stress takes a significant physical toll on our bodies. Not only does stress appear to accelerate aging, but also the older we get, the longer it takes for our bodies to turn off the stress response.

A team of researchers has found that severe emotional distress, like that caused by divorce, the loss of a job or caring for an ill child or parent, may speed up the aging of the body's cells.

Though doctors have linked chronic psychological stress to weakened immune function and an increased risk of catching colds, among other things, they are still trying to understand how tension damages or weakens tissue. New research suggests a new way such damage may occur and opens the possibility that the process can be reversed.

In the experiment, Dr. Elissa Epel and Dr. Elizabeth Blackburn of the University of California at San Francisco led a team of researchers who analyzed blood samples from 58 young and middle-aged mothers, 39 of them caring for a child with a chronic disorder. Using genetic techniques, the doctors examined the DNA of white blood cells, which are central to the body's immune response to infection.

The scientists focused on a piece of DNA, called the telomere, at the very tip of each cell's chromosomes. Like the head of a split matchstick, the telomere shrinks each time a cell divides and duplicates itself. Cells may reproduce themselves many times throughout life to repair and strengthen their host organs, to grow or to fight disease.

A chemical called telomerase helps restore a portion of the telomere with each division. But after 10 to 50 divisions the number varies by tissue type and health. The telomere gets so short that the cell is effectively retired and no longer replicates.

Change in telomere length over time, is thought to be a rough measure of a cell's age and vitality.

And when the researchers compared the DNA of mothers caring for children with disabilities, they found a striking trend. After correcting for the effects of age, they calculated that the longer the women had taken care of their children, the shorter their telomere length, and the lower their telomerase activity. Some of the mothers were years older than their chronological age.[125]

In the chapter on stress, I mentioned the importance of exercise, eating well, and maintaining your weight, but there is also the importance of a positive attitude, social relationships and faith in God.

Successful agers have faced the same stressors as the rest of us. They just have better coping skills, which any of us can also learn.

The Spanish explorer, Ponce de Leon, set out in 1513 to find the legendary Fountain of Youth. His journey brought him to the part of our country known today as Florida. It was Ponce de Leon who gave it this name.

Ponce de Leon failed to find the Fountain of Youth because he looked in the wrong place. Had he looked in a book, the

Bible, he would have found in its pages reference to the true Fountain of Eternal Youth. He could have read words such as these, "Whoever drinks the water I give will never be thirsty. The water I give will become a spring of water gushing up inside that person, giving eternal life." (John 4:14)

In the adventure film, *Indiana Jones and the Final Quest*, Indiana Jones, played by Harrison Ford, begins a dual search for his father, played by Sean Connery, and the Holy Grail. The Holy Grail was purported to be the cup Jesus used at the Last Supper and later it was given to Joseph of Arimethea, who used it to catch some of Jesus' blood at His crucifixion.

Regardless of the amount of truth in the storyline, it is an entertaining movie. In one scene, the Nazis are trying to secure the cup, but cannot penetrate the passageway. There are three traps that have been set to keep intruders away. Indiana Jones knows the answer to the passageway, but refuses to use that knowledge. One of the Nazis then shoots his father and says, "Now Dr. Jones, the only way to save your father is through the miraculous power of the Grail."

Indiana Jones does get the Grail and it does save his father. But it is not the cup that saves him. It is his father's faith in the God of the cup. Indiana Jones' father asks him, "What do you believe in now, son?"

That's a good question for each of us. What do you believe in now? What is your faith like as you approach the end of life?

My mother-in-law suffered a stroke at age 79 and died after a few days in the hospital. Her father was a Methodist minister, her brother became an Episcopalian priest, and her son-in-law (me) became a minister in the United Church of Christ. For many years she belonged to a Presbyterian church. But going through the deaths of two husbands who each went through a prolonged illness, left her wondering towards the end of her life if God really cares about us or if there really is a God.

What we believe in will, in large measure, determine how well we spend our remaining days on earth whether they be many or few.

There is a fountain of life, of hope and joy. It comes from trusting in God, who offers the fountain of eternal youth to any who would receive it.

It was the Apostle Paul who said, "Therefore we do not lose heart. Though outwardly we are wasting away, yet inwardly we are being renewed day by day. "   (2 Corinthians 4: 16)

Paul wasn't exempt from the aging process, but he found himself inwardly refreshed and restored. He kept young in spirit and that can happen to us as well.

When we hear the word pilgrim, what should come to mind are those brave men and women who traveled across the Atlantic Ocean in their boat, the Mayflower, and landed on Cape Cod.

A number of years ago I visited Plymouth Plantation, the recreated settlement of the Pilgrims. As I viewed the rows of roughly-hewn, clapboard houses on a hill over looking the Atlantic Ocean, I thought to myself, how brave and deeply religious these Pilgrims must have been. What courage and faith it must have taken to stay in this wild and uncivilized country, and in the heart of winter, at that.

As I think of those Pilgrim ancestors, it seems to me that we have something in common with them, for I think of life itself as a pilgrimage.

The word pilgrim originated during the Middle Ages. In the beginning it was not a title, but a description. The root word meant simply a stranger passing by. In the Middle Ages one frequently saw strangers passing by on their way to some sacred shrine. They were not vagabonds. They were not refugees. They were not tourists. They were persons with a purpose and a destination who were on their way somewhere, and they were called pilgrims.

When William Tyndale was looking for a word to translate into English the description of Abraham we find in the letter to the Hebrews, he thought of the word pilgrim.

In 1630, Governor William Bradford, looking for a word to describe the life of the Plymouth separatists, recalled this passage in Hebrews and wrote that the people of Plymouth, like the patriarchs of old, were pilgrims.

If you think about it, we are just passing through this life. We set sail at the beginning of our lives, or at the beginning of each day, not knowing where we will end up. Who knows what lies before us in terms of our health, our prosperity, our family ties.

The New Testament letter to the Hebrews reminds us that Abraham left his home, lived in tents, and became a pilgrim because he believed that God would bring to pass that which was promised.

A pilgrim people understands that life is not a destination, but a journey made in faith. We look toward the future, we look toward every day in hope, faith and joy because we know that God is there to help us. It is a journey that has no end.

As the years pass, as the seasons come and go, as we change outwardly, as many of our friends and loved ones leave us, we need to realize that there is One who never changes, there is One who is everlasting and eternal, and that is God.

Many things change and pass away, but God endures forever. God's love and care is from everlasting to everlasting.

May this assurance of God's continued help and love help us to accept middle age, old age and any age as part of God's plan.

Life can be good at any age when God is a part of our life.

QUESTIONS FOR DISCUSSION

<u>Chapter 1</u>

1. What do you think about growing older?
2. What fears or worries do you have about growing older?
3. What positive aspects are there in growing older? What do you think about those who weren't successful until later on in life?
4. What do you think about some of the Biblical men and women? Do you think the Bible reported their true age?
5. Read Genesis 11. What would it have been like for someone like Abraham and Sarah at their age? What was it like for you to move when you retired, or someone you know?
6. What were your thoughts of the elderly when you were growing up? What are your memories of your grandparents?
7. How are the elderly portrayed on television, in the movies and in advertisements?

<u>Chapter 2</u>

1. What do you consider to be the signs of aging?

2. What fears or worries do you have about the physical, mental, emotional and spiritual aspects of aging? What can you do about those fears?

Chapter 3

1. When is it difficult to be thankful?
2. Can you be thankful in all circumstances?
3. Recall those times in your life when you can see God was at work?
4. How dependent are we upon others? Upon God?

Chapter 4

1. How does attitude affect the way we feel?
2. What makes it difficult to have or maintain a positive attitude?
3. Dr. Burns cites some examples of negative thinking. Do you identify with any?
4. Does your faith affect your outlook? If so, is it positive or negative?

Chapter 5

1. Can you tell when you're under stress? What are some of the signs?
2. How do you react to stress?
3. Are there any things you specifically do to help you cope with stress?
4. Of the different ways of coping with stress, which ones appeal to you?
5. How did Jesus handle stress? Read Matthew 14: 22-34. What were some of the stresses Jesus encountered?

Chapter 6

1. Do you think prayer can have an affect on our health?

2. How are mind, body and spirit connected?
3. Have you tried the "relaxation response"? If so, what phrase did you use?
4. How has God answered your prayers?

Chapter 7

1. Who are we?
2. What do Genesis 1 & 2 and Psalm 8 say about who we are?
3. What are the ways the government, society, advertising, entertainment and others view humankind, as well as the elderly?
4. How is your self-esteem affected by aging?
5. What does Jesus' parable of the landowner in Matthew 20: 1-16 say about our worth?

Chapter 8

1. What do you believe about life after death? What do you think it will be like if you do believe in it?
2. Read 1 Corinthians 15. Paul uses the imagery of nature to refer to the resurrection body. Is the use of nature a helpful way to understand the resurrection?
3. Are you aware of anyone who has had a near-death experience? If so, what was it like for them?
4. Is it meaningful to think of heaven as like a loving home?
5. How do we prepare ourselves for our own death?

Chapter 9

1. What are your favorite holiday memories?
2. What are your worst holiday memories?
3. How do you celebrate holidays today, especially Christmas, Thanksgiving and birthdays?

Chapter 10

1. What physical responses have you experienced in times of grief?
2. What have your emotional responses been in times of grief?
3. What have your spiritual resources been in times of grief?
4. John 11:33-36 describes Jesus' reaction to Mary when she tells him of the death of her brother. How does Jesus' expression of grief compare to your own experiences of grief?
5. How does it help you to know that God grieves?
6. What is your greatest fear about death?

Chapter 11

1. How do you structure your time in retirement?
2. What is your pattern of coping with change?
3. What are some of the losses you have experienced in life?
4. What are some of the changes in the world you remember, like changes in technology, politics, science, religion, health, etc.?
5. What "new beginnings" have you made in your life, especially in retirement?

Chapter 12

1. Do you agree with Morrie that you "learn how to die and you learn how to live?"
2. If this is the day the Lord has made, how can we rejoice and be glad in it?
3. Are you aware of how God might be trying to awaken you to a new and deeper experience of God's love?
4. What opportunities do you have for volunteering in your church and community?

Chapter 13

1. What were the "good old days" for you?
2. What is important to remember?
3. What memories need to be forgotten?

Chapter 14

1. Who or what do you blame when things go wrong and tragic events happen?
2. Is suffering a punishment from God?
3. Do you ever get angry at God? Is it ok to get angry at God?
4. Do you feel angry at times about growing older?
5. How do you handle anger?

Chapter 15

1. What are your fears?
2. How has faith in God helped you with your fears?

Chapter 16

1. How do you cope with pain?
2. What kinds of pain do you experience?
3. Do you view pain as a punishment?
4. Do you feel God understands your pain since Jesus knew the physical pain of the cross?

Chapter 17

1. Have you ever felt lonely? What are some of the circumstances?
2. Read Psalm 142. The author asks of God, "Set me free from my prison." In what way can loneliness be like a prison?

3. In spite of experiencing loneliness, the author says he has experienced God's presence. How do your experiences compare with those of the author?
4. The author pours out his complaint and tells his troubles to God. How can prayer be helpful in times of loneliness or isolation?
5. What would you like to say to God when you feel alone?
6. What practical steps could we take to move out of our loneliness?

Chapter 18

1. What form of helplessness worries you the most?
2. What can you do to help you gain some control?
3. What do you think is the proper age to give up driving?
4. What end of life issues would you want?

Chapter 19

1. What words or phrase would best characterize your life?
2. How can you find a meaningful life? What is a meaningful life for you?
3. What volunteer work have you been involved in and was it meaningful to you?

Chapter 20

1. What do you think makes for successful aging?
2. Do you agree/disagree that growing older is not for sissies?
3. How can the church help those who are elderly?
4. How important is a youthful spirit as we age? What is a youthful spirit?
5. How important is faith to having a youthful spirit?

FOOTNOTES

1. Paul Aurandt. <u>Paul Harvey's "The Rest of the Story."</u> (Garden City, New York: Doubleday & Co., 1977), p. 159.
2. Richard Corliss and Michael D. Lemonich, "How to Live to Be 100," <u>Time,</u> August 30, 2004, p. 42.
3. Janet K. Belsky, <u>The Psychology of Aging</u>, (Monterey, California: Brooks/Cole Publishing Co., 1984), p. 47.
4. Ibid.
5. Ibid., p.48.
6. Ibid., p. 71-77.
7. Ibid., p.78-83.
8. Ibid., p. 84.
9. Ibid., p.93-96.
10. Ibid., p.85-90.
11. Ibid., p.124.
12. Susan Jacoby, "Great Sex," <u>Modern Maturity</u> Sept.-Oct. 1999, pp. 43-45
13. Belsky, p. 167.
14. Ibid, p. 168
15. Ibid., p. 169.
16. Dr. Amir Soas. <u>The Palm Beach Post,</u>22 September 2004.
17. Ibid.
18. Belsky, p. 228.
19. Ibid., p.253.
20. _____, <u>Mature Years.</u> P.44-46.
21. Ann Landers. <u>The Palm Beach Post.</u> 27 November 1997.

22. Diana Karter Appelbaum. <u>Thanksgiving.</u> (New York, New York: Facts On File Publications, 1984), p. 153.

23. Norman Cousins. <u>Anatomy Of An Illness.</u> (New York, New York: W.W. Norton & Co., Inc., 1981) pp. 27-48.

24. Dr. Shauna S. Roberts, "Need a Boost? Try Humor," <u>Diabetes Forecast</u>, Oct. 2005, pp. 31-32.

25. Lorilyn Rackl, "Humor Can Keep You Healthy," <u>Reader's Digest,</u> Sept. 2003, pp. 63-71.

26. The Nun Study. <u>The Palm Beach Post.</u> 28 July, 2005.

27. Albert Ellis and Michael E. Bernard, <u>Clinical Applications of Rational-Emotive Therapy,</u> (New York, New York: Plenum Press, 1985), pp. 9-14.

28. Mark McGinn

29. Martha Davis, Matthew McKay and Elizabeth Robins Eshelman, <u>Relaxation and Stress Reduction Workbook.</u> (Oakland, California: New Harbinger Publication, 1982) pp. 110-112.

30. David Burns. <u>Feeling Good.</u> (New York, New York: Penguin Books, 1980) pp. 28-47.

31. McGinn, p.

32. Christopher Peterson and Lisa M. Bossio, <u>Health and Optimism.</u> (New York, New York: Macmillan Inc., 1991) pp 37-38.

33. Jane A. McAdams. "The Gift of Hope".<u>Journal of American Medical Association.</u> 1985, Vol. 254. p. 1222.

34. <u>Modern Maturity,</u> July-August 2002.

35. Hans Selye. <u>Stress Without Distress.</u> (New York, New York: The New American Library, 1974). Pp 11-17.

36. Ibid

37. Kenneth Pelletier, pp 108-113.

38. Ibid, pp 124-134.

39. Dr. Paul Rosch, "Stress and Aging," <u>The Newsletter of the American Institute of Stress</u>, No. 11, 1996, p. 3.

40. Ibid

41. <u>AARP</u> January 2005.

42. Mary Susan Miller, <u>Child Stress,</u> (Garden City, New York: Doubleday & Co., Inc., 1982), p. 41.

43. Kenneth Pelletier, pp 252-262.
44. Dr. Brian Bauknight, <u>The Brain-Mind Bulletin</u>, No. 7, March 24, 1986.
45. Herbert Benson. <u>The Relaxation Response.</u> (New York, New York: William Morrow and Co., Inc., 1975) pp 110-111.
46. Herbert Benson. <u>Beyond the Relaxation Response.</u> (New York, New York: The Berkley Publishing Group, 1984), p.
47. William Shakespeare. <u>Hamlet.</u>
48. Carole Fleck, "Pills, Potions and Powders," <u>AARP</u>, Nov. 2001, pp. 18-19.
49. Charles L. Wallis, ed., <u>The Teasure Chest.</u> (New York, New York: Harper & Row, Publishers, Inc., 1965) p. 12.
50. Ibid, p. 14.
51. Christine Russell. "Attitude Puts Spring Back In Step." <u>The Palm Beach Post.</u> 7 March 2000.
52. Jo Foxworth, "8 Ways to Boost Your Self-Esteem," <u>Woman's Day</u>, 11 November 1986, p. 40.
53. Anonymous
54. Raymond A. Moody. <u>Life After Life.</u> (Covington, Georgia: Mockingbird Books, 1975), pp. 19-98.
55. Brendan Koerner, <u>U.S. News & World Report</u>, March 31, 1997.
56. Charles Allen. <u>You Are Never Alone.</u> (Old Tappan, NJ: Fleming H. Revell Co., pp. 77-79.
57. Joanne Smith and Judy Biggs, <u>How to Say Goodbye.</u> (Lynnwood, WA: Aglow Publications, 1990), pp. 43-53.
58. Elizabeth Kubler-Ross. <u>On Death and Dying.</u> (New York, New York: MacMillan Publishing Co., 1969), p. 65.
59. C.S. Lewis. <u>A Grief Observed.</u> (New York, New York: The Seabury Press, 1961), p.67.
60. J. Wm. Worden. <u>Grief Counseling and Grief Therapy.</u> (New York, New York: Springer Publishing Co., 1982), pp. 11-17.
61. Ibid

62. Jimmy Carter. <u>The Virtues of Aging.</u> (New York, New York: The Ballantine Publishing Group, 1998), p. xii.

63. Judith Viorst. <u>Necessary Losses.</u> (New York, New York: Random House, Inc., 1986) pp. 324-325.

64. Leland and Martha Bradford. <u>Retirement.</u> (Chicago, Ill.: Nelson-Hall, Inc., 1979), p. 11.

65. Bob Phillips, <u>Over the Hill and On a Roll</u>, (Eugene, Oregon: Harvest House Publishers, 1998), p. 35.

66. Wall Street Journal

67. 1832

68. 1867

69. Jimmy Carter, pp 1-3.

70. Ibid

71. Judith Viorst, p. 335.

72. William Bridges. <u>Transitions.</u> (Reading, Mass.: Addison-Wesley Publishing Co., Inc., 1980), p 90

73. William Barclay. <u>The Gospel of Matthew Vol. 1</u> (Philadelphia, Pa.: The Westminster Press, 1958), pp. 55-64.

74. William Bridges, pp. 144-145.

75. Mitch Albom. <u>Tuesdays With Morrie.</u> (New York, New York: Doubleday Press, 1997), pp81-85.

76. Jane Brody, "There Are Ways for Seniors to Live an Active Retirement," <u>The News</u> 31 July 2001, D5.

77. Ibid

78. Ibid

79. Jane Brody, "Effects of Aging," <u>The News</u> 27 February 2001, D4

80. Charles Allen. <u>All Things Are Possible Through Prayer.</u> (Old Tappan, NJ: Fleming H. Revell Co., 1958), pp. 16-17.

81. Corrie ten Boom. <u>Don't Wrestle, Just Nestle.</u> (Old Tappan, New Jersey: Fleming H. Revell Co., 1979)

82. Todd Outcalt, "The Best Things in Life Are Free" in <u>Chicken Soup for the Golden Soul.</u> (Deerfield Beach, Florida: Health Communications, Inc., 2000), p 227.

83. Elaine Pondant. Stories for the Family's Heart. (Sisters Publishing, 1998), pp 189-191.
84. John Irving. A Prayer for Owen Meany. (New York: Ballantine Books, 1989), p.44.
85. Charles Allen, Prayer Changes Things, (Old Tappan, New Jersey: Fleming H. Revell Co., 1964), p. 15.
86. Charles Allen, All Things Are Possible Through Prayer, (Old Tappan, New Jersey: Fleming H. Revell Co., 1958), pp. 78-79.
87. Harold Kushner. When Bad Things Happen to Good People. (New York, New York: Avon Books, 19810 pp. 15-16.
88. Leslie Weatherhead. The Will of God. Nashville, Tenn.: Abingdon Press, 1944), p. 10-11.
89. William Barclay.The Gospel Of Matthew, Vol. 2, pp. 115-117.
90. Dr. Martin Luther King, Jr. Strength to Love. (New York, New York: Simon & Schuster, inc., 1968), pp. 131-132.
91. Paul Maier. First Easter. (New York, New York: Harper & Row Publishers, 1973), pp. 77&78.
92. Suzanne Schlosberg, "Pain Busters," AARP Magazine, Jan-Feb. 2004, p.63.
93. Ibid, p. 67.
94. Harold Kushner, p. 11.
95. Herbert Benson, Timeless Healing, (New York, New York: Scribner, 1966), pp 60-61.
96. Thomas H. Naylor, William H. Willimon, Magdalene R. Naylor, The Search for Meaning, (Nashville, Tenn.: Abingdon Press), p. 71.
97. Philip Yancey. Where Is God When It Hurts?(Grand Rapids, MI: Zondervan Publishing C.)
98. Herbert Benson. Timeless Healing. pp. 125-126.
99. Dr. Isadore Rosenfeld. "Live Now, Grow Old Later" in Parade Magazine. (23 May 1999), pp. 14&15.
100. Glenn Plashin, Turning Point, (New York, New York: Carol Publishing Group, 1992)

101. Alan McGinnis, <u>The Friendship Factor,</u> (Minneapolis, Minn.: Augsburg Press, 1979), p. 35.

102. Jane E. Brody, "With Advancing Age Come Limits on the Ability to Drive," <u>The News,</u> 27 February 2001, D4.

103. Ibid

104. Elizabeth Pope, "MIT Study: Older Drivers Know When to Slow Down," <u>AARP Bulletin,</u> July-August 2003, p. 11.

105. Lou Ann Walker, "We Can Control How We Age," <u>Parade Magazine,</u> Sept. 16, 2001, pp. 4-5.

106. Sharon Larsen, "FDR and Me," <u>Chicken Soup for the Golden Soul.</u> (Deerfield Beach, Florida: Health Communications, Inc., 2000). Pp 186-189.

107. Charles Allen.<u>You Are Never Alone.</u> Pp. 145-146.

108. Viktor E. Frankl, <u>Man's Search For Meaning.</u> (Boston, Mass.: Beacon Press, 1939) p. 105.

109. Louis Begley. <u>About Schmidt.</u>(New York, New York: Ballantine Books, 1996).

110. Beth Baker, "Grandparents Speak Out," <u>AARP Bulletin,</u> April 2001, p.32.

111. Jane Brody, <u>The News,</u> 31 July 2001, D5.

112. Dr. Dana Bradley, "A Reason to Rise Each Morning," <u>Generations: Journal of the American Society on Aging,</u> Vol. 23, No. 4, pp. 45-50.

113. Ibid

114. Ibid

115. Jimmy Carter, p. 2.

116. Wendy Lastbader. <u>Generations.</u> P. 21

117. Ibid

118. Jeannette Reid, <u>Generations.,</u> pp. 51-55.

119. John Kotre, <u>Generations,</u> pp. 65-70.

120. Robert Sapolsky, "Stress Can Age Genes" in <u>The Stuart News,</u> 30 November 2004.

121. Ibid

122. Dr. Paul Rosch, p. 9.

123. The Nun Study. <u>The Palm Beach Post.</u> 28 July, 2005.

124. Benedict Carey, "Study: Stress Can Age Genes," <u>Treasure Coast Newspapers,</u> Nov. 30, 2004, A8.

125. Michael P. Green, <u>Illustrations for Biblical Preaching</u>, (Grand Rapids, MI: Baker Book House, 1989). Cited in Tommy Barnett, <u>Adventure Yourself</u>, (Lake Mary, Fl: Creation House, 2000), pp. 131-132.

BIBLIOGRAPHY

<u>BOOKS</u>

Albom, Mitch. Tuesdays With Morrie. New York: Doubleday Press. 1997.

Allen, Charles. All Things Are Possible Through Prayer. Old Tappan, N.J.: Fleming H.

Revell Co. 1958.

Allen, Charles. Prayer Changes Things. Old Tappan, N.J.: Fleming H. Revell Co.

1964.

Allen, Charles. You Are Never Alone. Old Tappan, N.J.: Fleming H. Revell Co.

1978.

Appelbaum, Diana Karter. Thanksgiving. New York: Facts on File Publications.

1984.

Aurandt, Paul. Paul Harvey's "The Rest of the Story." Garden City, New York:

Doubleday & Co. 1977.

Barclay, William. The Gospel of Matthew 2 vols.. Philadelphia: The Westminster

Press. 1958.

Begley, Louis. About Schmidt. New York: Ballantine Books. 1996.

Belsky, Janet. The Psychology of Aging. Monterey, Cal.: Brooks/Cole Publishing
Co. 1984.

Benson, Herbert. The Relaxation Response. New York: William Morrow & Co., Inc.
1975.

Benson, Herbert. Beyond the Relaxation Response. New York: The Berkley Publishing
Group. 1984.

Benson, Herbert. Timeless Healing. New York: Scribner. 1996.

Bradford, Leland and Martha. Retirement. Chicago: Nelson-Hall, Inc. 1979.

Bridges, William. Transitions. Reading, Mass.: Addison-Wesley Pub. Co., Inc.
1980.

Burns, David. Feeling Good. New York: Penguin Books. 1980.

Canfield, Jack; Hansen, Mark Victor; and Meyer, Paul J. Chicken Soup For the Golden
Soul. Deerfield Beach: Health Communications Inc. 2000.

Carl, William J., ed. Graying Gracefully. Louisville: Westminster John Knox Press,
1997.

Carlson, Dosia. Engaging in Ministry with Older Adults. The Alban Institute. 1997.

Carter, Jimmy. The Virtues of Aging. New York: The Ballantine Publishing Group,
1998.

Clements, William M. Care and Counseling of the Aging. Philadelphia: Fortress Press.
1979.

Cousins, Norman. Anatomy Of An Illness. New York: W.W. Norton & Co., Inc. 1981.

Davis, Martha; McKay, Matthew; and Eshelman, Elizabeth Robins. Relaxation and Stress

Reduction Workbook. Oakland: New Harbinger Publication. 1982.

Ellis, Albert and Bernard, Michael E. Clinical Applications of Rational-Emotive Therapy.

New York: Plenum Press. 1985.

Finley, Anita & Bill. Live To Be 100 Plus. Boca Raton: Senior Life Press. 1992.

Frankl, Viktor E. Man's Search for Meaning. Boston: Beacon Press. 1939.

Green, Michael. Illustrations for Biblical Preaching. Grand Rapids: Baker Book House.

1989.

Hansen, Mark Victor and Linkletter, Art. How to Make the Rest of Your Life the Best

Of Your Life. Thomas Nelson Pub. 2006.

Haverwas, Stanley; Stoneking, Carole Bailey; Meador, Keith G. and Cloutier, David.

Growing Old In Christ. Grand Rapids: Wm. Eerdmans Publishing Co. 203.

Irving, John. A Prayer for Owen Meany. New York: Ballantine Books. 1989.

Kimble, Melvin A.; McFadden, Susan H., ed. Aging, Spirituality and Religion. Vol. 2.

Minneapolis: Fortress Press. 2003.

King, Martin Luther Jr. Strength To Love. New York: Simon & Schuster. 1968.

Knutson, Lois D. Understanding the Senior Adult. Alban Institute. 1999.

Koenig, Harold and Weaver, Andrew J. Counseling Troubled Older Adults. Nashville:

Abingdon Press. 1997.

Kubler-Ross, Elisabeth. On Death and Dying. New York: MacMillan Publishing Co., Inc.

1969.

Kushner, Harold. When Bad Things Happen to Good People. New York: Avon Books.

1981.

Lewis, C.S. A Grief Observed. New York: The Seabury Press. 1961.

Loughhead, Elizabeth J. Eldercare. Nashville: Abingdon Press. 1987.

Maier, Paul L. First Easter. New York: Harper & Row Publishers. 1973.

McGinnis, Alan. The Friendship Factor. Minneapolis: Augsburg Press. 1979.

Miller, Mary Susan. Child Stress. Garden City: Doubleday & Co., Inc. 1982.

Moody, Raymond A. Life After Life. Covington, Georgia: Mockingbird Books. 1975.

Naylor, Thomas H.; Willimon, William H. and Naylor, Magdalene R. The Search for

Meaning. Nashville: Abingdon Press. 1994.

Pelletier, Kenneth. Mind as Healer, Mind as Slayer. New York: Dell Publishing Co., Inc.

1977.

Peterson, Christopher and Bossio, Lisa M. Health and Optimism. New York:

Macmillan Inc. 1991.

Phillips, Bob. Over the Hill and On a Roll. Eugene: Harvest House Publishers. 1998.

Pipher, Mary. Another Country. New York: Penguin Press, Inc. 1999.

Plashin, Glenn. Turning Point. New York: Carol Publishing Group. 1992.

Pondant, Elaine. Stories for the Family's Heart. Sisters Publishing. 1998.

Saussy, Caroll. The Art of Growing Old. Minneapolis: Augsburg Fortress Publishers.

1998.

Selye, Hans. Stress Without Distress. New York: The New American Library. 1974.

Selye, Hans. The Stress of Life. New York: McGraw-Hill Book Co. 1976.

Settin, Joan. Gerontologic Human Resources. New York: Human Science Press, Inc.
1982.
Skala, Kenneth. American Guidance for Seniors. Falls Church, Virginia: G&S.
1996.
Smith, Joanne and Biggs, Judy. How to Say Goodbye. Lynnwood, WA: Aglow
Publications. 1990.
Srode, Molly. Creating a Spiritual Retirement. Woodstock, Vt.: Skylight Paths
Publishing. 2003.
Taylor, Blaine. The Church's Ministry With Older Adults. Nashville: Abingdon Press.
1984.
TenBoom, Corrie. Don't Wrestle, Just Nestle. Old Tappan, NJ: Fleming H. Revell Co.
1979.
Tournier, Paul. Learn to Grow Old. New York: Harper and Row Publishers, Inc. 1972.
Viorst, Judith. Necessary Losses. New York: Random House, Inc. 1986.
Wallis, Charles, ed. The Treasure Chest New York: Harper & Row. 1965.
Weatherhead, Leslie. The Will of God. Nashville: Abingdon Press. 1944.
Weaver, Andrew J.; Koenig, Harold G. and Roe, Phyllis C. Reflections On Aging and
Spiritual Growth. Nashville: Abingdon Press. 1998.
Wershow, Harold J., ed. Controversial Issues in Gerontology. New York: Springer
Publishing Co. 1981.
Worden, J. Wm. Grief Counseling and Grief Therapy. New York: Springer Publishing
Co. 1982.
Yancey, Philip. Where Is God When It Hurts? Grand Rapids, MI: Zondervan Pub. Co.

Journals, Magazines and Newspapers

Baker, Beth. "Grandparents Speak Out." AARP Bulletin. April 2001.
Bauknight, Brian. The Brain-Mind Bulletin. March 24, 1986.
Bradley, Dana. "A Reason to Rise Each Morning." Generations: Journal of the American
Society on Aging. Vol. 23, No. 4.
Brody, Jane. "With Advancing Age Come Limits On the Ability to Drive." The News.
27 February 2001.
Brody, Jane. "There Are Ways for Seniors to Live an Active Retirement." The News.
31 July 2001.
Brody, Jane. "Effects of Aging." The News. 27 February 2001.
Carey, Benedict. "Study: Stress Can Age Genes" Treasure Coast Newspapers
30 November 2004.
Corliss, Richard and Lemonich, "How to Live to Be 100." Time. 30 August 2004.
Fleck, Carole. "Pills, Potions and Powders." AARP November 2001.
Foxworth, Jo. "8 Ways to Boost Your Self-Esteem." Woman's Day. 11 November 1986.
Jacoby, Susan. "Great Sex" Modern Maturity Sept-Oct. 1999.
Koerner, Brendan. U.S. News & World Report. 31 March 1997.
Landers, Ann. The Palm Beach Post. 27 November 1997.
McAdams, Jane. "The Gift of Hope" Journal of American Medical Association
Vol. 254. 1985.
_____ "The Nun Study" The Palm Beach Post 28 July 2005.
Pope, Elizabeth. "MIT Study: Older Drivers Know When to Slow Down."
AARP Bulletin July-August 2003.

Rackl, Lorilyn. "Humor Can Keep You Healthy" <u>Reader's Digest</u> Sept. 2003.

Roberts, Shauna S. "Need a Boost? Try Humor." <u>Diabetes Forecast</u> Oct. 2005.

Rosch, Paul. "Stress and Aging." <u>The Newsletter of the American Institute of Stress</u>

No. 11. 1996.

Rosenfeld, Isadore. "Live Now, Grow Old Later." <u>Parade Magazine</u> 23 May 1999.

Russell, Christine. "Attitude Puts Spring Back in Step." <u>The Palm Beach Post</u> Mar. 2000

Soas, Amir. <u>The Palm Beach Post</u> 22 Sept. 2004.

Sapolsky, Robert. "Stress Can Age Genes." <u>The Stuart News</u> 30 Nov. 2004

Schlosberg, Suzanne. "Pain Busters" <u>AARP Magazine</u> Jan-Feb 2004.

Walker, Lou Ann. "We Can Control How We Age." <u>Parade Magazine</u> 16 Sept. 2001.